## PRAISE FOR THE FIRST EDITION

"What happened to the country I grew up in?" As a journalist I hear that question all over America, especially from older white people. Blacks and all but the most recent immigrants say it too. Let Bill Frey expertly explain the change and why it is good for everyone. A great read!

—**JUAN WILLIAMS,** Fox News political analyst and author, *Eyes on the Prize: America's Civil Rights Years, 1954–65*

William Frey is a numbers guy. *Diversity Explosion* is a smart but not daunting exposition of the demographic revolution already under way. Frey breaks down the intriguing ways we'll watch America change: at work, at school, in the voting booth, and in the culture at large. He shows us the next America and then tells us all the reasons he's concluded we can handle it.

—**RAY SUAREZ,** visiting professor, Amherst College, and author, *Latino Americans: The 500-Year Legacy That Shaped a Nation*

William Frey . . . explores the future in his newly published book, *Diversity Explosion*. He is one of the nation's most astute demographers and has long been a reliable guide to the population shifts remaking America and to the longer-term cultural and political implications of those changes.

—**DAN BALZ,** *The Washington Post*

Growing demographic diversity is one of the key trends shaping the next century in the United States and elsewhere. A new book from the Brookings Institution, *Diversity Explosion: How New Racial Demographics Are Remaking America*, captures the extent of this revolution in ample spatial detail. Demographer William H. Frey, widely known for his public research offerings from the Metropolitan Policy Program at Brookings, makes a career statement in this masterful work.

—**DOWELL MYERS,** *Journal of the American Planning Association*

Any forward thinker is bound to ask the question—what will the world be like in ten years? Twenty? What about fifty years? In his new book, *Diversity Explosion*, demographer and Brookings Institution Senior Fellow William Frey attempts to answer these questions with regard to America's rapidly changing demographics.

—**ZACK WILKS,** Urban Democracy Lab

*Diversity Explosion* is written for a large audience. Specialists will nevertheless appreciate the remarkable effort made at synthesis. . . . Frey's goal is to communicate the magnitude of the new racial demographic shift and its potential to the common layman. This goal is successfully achieved, thanks to the effective prose of the author and the abundance of tables, figures, and maps that richly illustrate the book.

—**ALAIN BÉLANGER,** *Canadian Studies in Population*

# DIVERSITY EXPLOSION

## HOW NEW RACIAL DEMOGRAPHICS
## ARE REMAKING AMERICA

WILLIAM H. FREY

BROOKINGS INSTITUTION PRESS
WASHINGTON, D.C.

Copyright © 2015, 2018
THE BROOKINGS INSTITUTION
1775 Massachusetts Avenue, N.W., Washington, D.C. 20036
www.brookings.edu

The Brookings Institution is a private nonprofit organization devoted to research, education, and publication on important issues of domestic and foreign policy. Its principal purpose is to bring the highest quality independent research and analysis to bear on current and emerging policy problems. Interpretations or conclusions in Brookings publications should be understood to be solely those of the authors.

*Library of Congress Cataloging-in-Publication data*

Frey, William H.
  Diversity explosion : how new racial demographics are remaking America / William H. Frey.
      pages            cm
  Includes bibliographical references and index.
  ISBN 978-0-8157-2398-1 (hardcover : acid-free paper) 1. United States—Race relations. 2. Minorities—United States. 3. United States—Race relations—Statistics. 4. Minorities—United States—Statistics. 5. United States—Population. I. Title.
  E184.A1F739 2014
  305.800973—dc23                                                        2014017118

9 8 7 6 5 4 3 2 1

Printed on acid-free paper
Typeset in Mercury and Avenir
Design and Composition by Naylor Design, Inc., Washington, DC

Dedicated to the memory of my father,
Elwood H. Frey

# Contents

# Preface

More than fifty years after the peak of the civil rights movement, race in America is again on the front burner in political discourse, popular culture, and youthful activism. Especially since the 2016 presidential election, debates about immigration, the value of political correctness, and race itself seem to be more common than discussions about the national economy or foreign policy. Diversity commissions and initiatives are being instituted by scores of industry associations, now including Major League Baseball and the Academy of Motion Picture Arts and Sciences. Young adults on college campuses today seek comfortable safe spaces and are joining movements such as Black Lives Matter. These are signs that both fresh and long-standing racial issues are being recognized by new generations of Americans.

Yet this is a far different time demographically than the 1960s. Racial diversity today is more central to the fabric of America. By 2020, the U.S. census is expected to show that two-fifths of the nation's population identifies with a racial group other than white. This will especially be the case for about half of the population of children under 18, among whom whites are declining in number as a result of the aging of the nation's white population.

These facts and others presented in this book underscore why the phrase "demography is destiny" is increasingly relevant for understanding the nation's future. While America's rapidly changing racial demography may not fully determine this destiny, these powerful demographic forces will shape it to a greater degree than ever before. Racial minorities will power all of the growth in the U.S. labor force as older white baby boomers continue to retire. They will make the difference between growth and decline in small towns, suburbs, and exurbs. And they will alter the nation's electorate such that neither major political party will be able to afford to ignore the interests of all racial groups.

Despite recent political volatility regarding race, signs point to an America open to these changes. Multiracial marriages have soared. More minorities now live in suburbs than in cities. Neighborhood segregation, although still high in many areas, is declining. And though younger generations are sensitive to issues around the nation's new diversity, they are embracing it.

Since the first edition of this book was published, I have given talks to dozens of audiences, including college students, industry associations, political consultants, military groups, government agencies, chambers of commerce, and nonprofit organizations. What I have learned from these experiences is that when presented with the facts, those who are initially startled to see the rapidity of these demographic changes seem genuinely curious and prepared to adapt to them.

In this updated edition, the "Race and Politics" chapter contrasts the racial and demographic underpinnings of the elections of Barack Obama with that of Donald Trump and speculates on how these dynamics might play out in future presidential elections. The chapter "Old versus Young: The Cultural Generation Gap" incorporates new information from the U.S. Census Bureau and other surveys, and throughout the book, national statistics are updated. The 2010 census, the most recent authoritative basis of local demographic information, remains the source of population statistics for geographic areas.

The goal of this updated edition remains the same as that of the first: to provide accessible information about the nation's changing racial demographics to a broad audience of readers. It is my belief that these changes are a good-news story for America because they hold the potential for continually reinvigorating the country's demography and economy. It is my hope that, as readers learn the facts about these changes, they will better understand the need for and value of preparing for them.

William H. Frey
*Washington, D.C.*
*April 2018*

# A Pivotal Period for Race in America

# 1

America reached an important milestone in 2011. That occurred when, for the first time in the history of the country, more minority babies than white babies were born in a year.[1] Soon, most children will be racial minorities: Hispanics, blacks, Asians, and other nonwhite races. And, in about three decades, whites will constitute a minority of all Americans (see figure 1-1). This milestone signals the beginning of a transformation from the mostly white baby boom culture that dominated the nation during the last half of the twentieth century to the more globalized, multiracial country that the United States is becoming.

Certainly in the past, the specter of a "minority white" nation instilled fear among some Americans, and to some extent it continues to do so today—fear of change, fear of losing privileged status, or fear of unwanted groups in their communities. These fears were especially evident during the decades following World War II, when immigration was low and phrases such as "invasion," "blockbusting," and "white flight" were

FIGURE 1-1

**U.S. White and Minority Populations, 1970–2050**

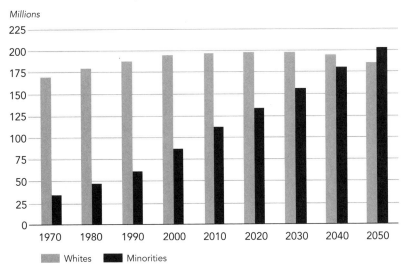

Source: U.S. censuses and Census Bureau projections, released March 2018.

commonly used in the context of black-white segregation. Such fears are evident today as other racial minority groups have become more numerous. These fears were especially visible during and since the 2016 presidential election with public backlashes against immigration, claims of political correctness, and other reactions to the nation's growing racial diversity.

Yet if demography is truly destiny, then these fears of a more racially diverse nation will almost certainly dissipate. In many communities, a broad spectrum of racial groups already is accepted by all, particularly among the highly diverse youth population. Moreover, as this book illustrates, a growing diverse, globally connected minority population will be absolutely necessary to infuse the aging American labor force with vitality and to sustain populations in many parts of the country that are facing population declines. Rather than being feared, America's new diversity—poised to reinvigorate the country at a time when other developed nations are facing advanced aging and population loss—can be celebrated.

The sweep of diversity that has just begun to affect the nation is the theme of this book, which draws from my examination of the most recent U.S. census, census surveys, projections, and related sources. As a demographer who has followed U.S. population trends for decades, even I was surprised by the sheer scope of racial change that came to light with the 2010 census—a change that is continuing. The story that the data tell is not just more of the same. I am convinced that the United States is in the midst of a pivotal period ushering in extraordinary shifts in the nation's racial demographic makeup. If planned for properly, these demographic changes will allow the country to face the future with growth and vitality as it reinvents the classic American melting pot for a new era. In my experiences speaking publicly and answering press inquiries, I have seen the intensity of Americans' questions and thoughts about issues surrounding race. After having absorbed these startling demographic trends and their implications, I wanted to interpret and expound on the dramatic shifts that they illustrate so that a general audience of readers can appreciate their force, promise, and challenges. Key among these changes are

—*the rapid growth of "new minorities": Hispanics, Asians, and increasingly multiracial populations.* Between 2015 and 2060, Hispanics and Asians will roughly double in size, and the multiracial population will triple (see figure 1-2). New minorities have already become the major contributors to U.S. population gains. These new minorities—the products of recent immigration waves as well as the growing U.S.-born generations—contributed to more than four-fifths of the nation's population growth since 2000. That trend will accelerate in the future.

—*the sharply diminished growth and rapid aging of America's white population.* Due to white low immigration, reduced fertility, and aging, the white population grew a tepid 1.2 percent in 2000–15. In less than 5 years, the white population will begin a decline that will continue into the future. This decline will be most prominent among the younger populations. At the same time, the existing white population will age rapidly, as the large baby boom generation advances into seniorhood.

FIGURE 1-2
**U.S. Race Groups and Projected Growth**

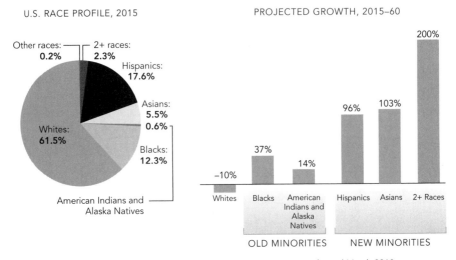

Source: American Community Survey, 2015, and Census Bureau projections, released March 2018.

—*black economic advances and migration reversals.* Now, more than a half-century after the civil rights movement began, a recognizable segment of blacks has entered the middle class while simultaneously reversing historic population shifts. The long-standing Great Migration of blacks out of the South has now turned into a wholesale evacuation from the North—to largely prosperous southern locales. Blacks are abandoning cities for the suburbs, and black neighborhood segregation continues to decline. Although many blacks still suffer the effects of inequality, along with uneven treatment by the criminal justice system, and segregation is far from gone, the economic and residential environments for blacks have improved well beyond the highly discriminatory, ghettoized life that most experienced for much of the twentieth century.

—*the shift toward a nation in which no racial group is the majority.* The shift toward "no majority" communities is already taking place as the constellation of racial minorities expands. In 2015, 24 of the nation's 100 largest metropolitan areas were minority white, up from just 14 in

2000 and 5 in 1990. Sometime after 2040, there will be no racial majority in the country. This is hardly the America that large numbers of today's older and middle-aged adults grew up with in their neighborhoods, workplaces, and civic lives. One implication of these shifts will be larger multiracial populations as multiracial marriages become far more commonplace.

The "diversity explosion" the country is now experiencing will bring significant changes in the attitudes of individuals, the practices of institutions, and the nature of American politics. Racial change has never been easy, and more often than not it has been fraught with fear and conflict. Yet for most of the nation's history, nonwhite racial groups have been a small minority. Partly because of that, blacks and other racial minorities were historically subjected to blatant discrimination, whether through Jim Crow laws, the Chinese Exclusion Act, or any of the many other measures that denied racial minorities access to jobs, education, housing, financial resources, and basic rights of civic participation.

What will be different going forward is the sheer size of the minority population in the United States. It is arriving "just in time" as the aging white population begins to decline, bringing with it needed manpower and brain power and taking up residence in otherwise stagnating city and suburban housing markets. Although whites are still considered the mainstream in the United States, that perception should eventually shift as more minority members assume positions of responsibility, exert more political clout, exercise their strength as consumers, and demonstrate their value in the labor force. As they become integral to the nation's success, their concerns will be taken seriously.

## GENERATIONS AND GEOGRAPHY ON THE FRONT LINES OF CHANGE

Change will not come without challenges. In fact, a big part of the impending clashes related to race will have demographic roots because of how diversity spreads across the country—both generationally and geographically.

**Diversity by Generation, "From the Bottom Up"**

If nothing else, the diversity explosion is generational in character. New minority growth is bubbling up the age structure, from young to old. Today, this growth is most visible among America's children—the post-millennial generation. This has to do, in part, with the more youthful population of Hispanics, the nation's largest minority group. Due to recent waves of Hispanic immigrants who were younger than the total population and to their somewhat higher fertility, Hispanics are decidedly younger than the population at large. This relative youthfulness, with many adults in peak childbearing ages, ensures continued sizable contributions to births, irrespective of future immigration. Asians, the second-largest new minority, also contribute to population gains among youth. In addition, the still tiny multiracial population, with a median age of just around 20 years, has the greatest potential for growth.

Nonetheless, the aging of the white population is a primary reason why racial churning is beginning at younger ages. Since 2000, the number of white youth in the United States already has declined as more white individuals passed the age of 18 than were born or immigrated. The white decline is projected to continue not only among children but eventually among younger adults and then middle-aged adults, as smaller white generations follow larger ones.[2] Barring unanticipated increases in white immigration, the long-term scenario for whites is one of lower fertility and increased aging. This means that the younger population will lead the way toward the nation's diversity surge. This diversity is already ubiquitous in schools, on playgrounds, and in other civic arenas that young people inhabit. Diversity means that new minorities, including Hispanic and Asian children whose parents or grandparents came from different nations and speak different languages, will become classmates, dating partners, and lifelong friends with younger generations of established minorities and whites.

Yet this youth-driven diversity surge is creating a "cultural generation gap" between the diverse youth population and the growing, older, still predominantly white population. This gap is reflected in negative attitudes among many older whites toward immigration, new minority growth, and big government programs that cater to the real economic and educational needs of America's younger, more diverse population. It has shown up in politics, among other places, as was evident in the demographic voting patterns in the 2008 and 2012 presidential elections won by Barack Obama, as well as the 2016 election won by Donald Trump. The gap is not a result of racist attitudes per se. It reflects the social distance between minority youth and an older population that does not feel a personal connection with young adults and children who are not "their" children and grandchildren.

Yet the future well-being of seniors and the nation as a whole depends on the ability of today's youth to succeed in tomorrow's labor force. Youth will play a central role in contributing to the nation's economy and to the retirement and medical care programs that directly benefit the older population. The financial solvency of those programs will be particularly challenging because the mostly white senior population will continue to swell as it absorbs the large baby boom generation (see figure 1-3). Attitudinal changes will occur but may take some

FIGURE 1-3
**Children and Seniors, 2010–40**
Size and Race Make-up of Populations under Age 18 and Age 65+

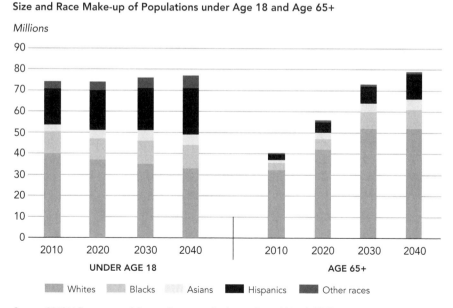

Source: 2010 U.S. census and Census Bureau projections, released March 2018.

time, as the long-held views of the baby boomers, who grew up in a highly segregated, low immigration, post–World War II America, slowly adapt to these inevitable generational shifts.

### Diversity Dispersal "From the Melting Pot Out"

As the diversity surge spreads from younger to older generations, a parallel geographic spread of new minorities is occurring from traditional Melting Pot regions to the rest of the country. This trend is distinct from those of the 1980s and early 1990s, when Hispanic and Asian growth was heavily concentrated in large immigrant gateways like New York, Los Angeles, San Francisco, Chicago, Miami, and Houston. Those largely immigrant minorities were content to cluster inside the traditional gateways within communities of the same race and language, where they could rely on friendship and family connections for social and economic support. At the same time, most mainstream domestic migrants, primarily whites, were moving to the economically ascendant interior West and Southeast—portions of the country that might be termed the New Sun Belt (shown in figure 1-4). Being more footloose than the new minorities, these migrants followed growing employment opportunities in places such as Atlanta and Phoenix.

Those separate migration flows—to Melting Pot areas by new immigrant minorities and to New Sun Belt areas by mostly white domestic migrants—seemed to portend a regional demographic balkanization.[3] The scenario painted was one in which the Melting Pot regions would remain racially distinct from other growing parts of the country in much the same way that cities once were racially distinct from their growing suburbs. Such a division would have extremely adverse implications for racial integration nationally, not to mention for politics. Adding further support to that prediction was the fact that whites were moving away from the major immigrant magnets, suggesting a flight from diversity, even though the move had more to do with the availability of jobs in the New Sun Belt and high housing costs in large coastal areas.[4]

Fortunately, the predicted balkanization proved temporary. By the late 1990s and early 2000s, new minorities began to follow the broad-based migration flows to the New Sun Belt for many of the same reasons as white domestic migrants. Hispanics and Asians dispersed not only to

FIGURE 1-4
**New Minorities in the Melting Pot, New Sun Belt, and Heartland Regions**

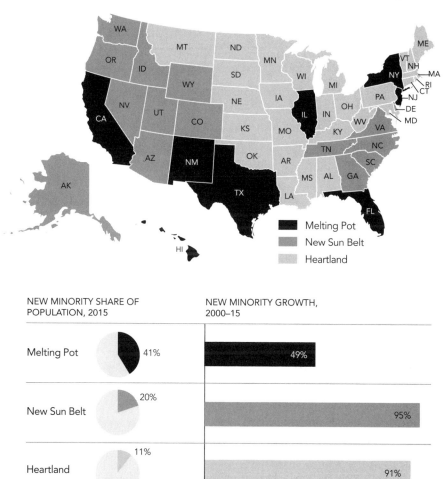

New Sun Belt states but also to the Heartland region of the country—defined here as slow-growing portions of the nation's interior and New England—in response to jobs in low- and high-skilled industries. Like whites and blacks, they wished to escape higher costs of living in many immigrant gateways, and in the process, they began to form new same-race communities away from the Melting Pot areas.[5]

Yet as they disperse to new destinations, Hispanics, Asians, and other new minorities are not always welcomed with open arms. Although they are filling important niches in the economy by taking jobs in construction, services, and software engineering and are, especially in the Heartland, providing a much-needed increase in population, they also are standing on the front lines of racial integration. White backlash is common in places where the cultural generation gap is most evident and where the growth of young new minorities is most rapid. Still, this ongoing dispersal of new minorities can lead to a softening of the rigid racial and political divisions that I feared would develop as separated migration patterns were taking shape in the 1980s. The integration and assimilation of new minorities across the country will occur unevenly, but the pattern is showing no sign of letting up.

## RACIAL CATEGORIES IN THE UNITED STATES

It is probably fair to say that there is no definitive classification of race in the United States. Racial categories are neither completely biologically nor scientifically determined. They have a history of being constructed in ways that play into national politics and stereotypes, and they are constantly in need of revision.[6] That said, the categories used in the recent U.S. census and by other government agencies maintain important social and legal distinctions and have more recently come to characterize a renewed pride in the cultural identity of the groups represented. For this reason, this book uses a racial classification that is broadly, though not completely, consistent with that used in the 2010 U.S. census, in which Americans self-reported their race.

The racial classification used here differs from census and federal guidelines that treat Hispanic origin as an item separate from race—that is, that ask census respondents separate questions about their Hispanic origin and their race.[7] Instead, this book treats Hispanic origin as a racial category. As a result, other racial categories—including whites, blacks, Asians, and American Indians or Alaska Natives—pertain to non-Hispanic members of those groups. This approach permits establishing a set of mutually exclusive racial categories in which Hispanic origin is one of the categories.[8] It also is broadly consistent with common use of race labels in national surveys, media reporting, and everyday parlance, wherein, in standard usage, "whites" or "Anglos" refers to non-Hispanic whites.

In focusing on Hispanics in chapter 4 and Asians in chapter 5, I discuss the origins of these groups in more detail (distinguishing, for example, between Mexicans and Cubans or Asian Indians and Chinese). In some parts of the book, due to data restrictions, alterations to these definitions are made and noted.[9] In response to the growth of the multiracial population in the United States, an important innovation was introduced in the 2000 and 2010 censuses that permits respondents to identify with two or more races.[10] However, because the official census definition does not consider Hispanic origin as a race, the "two or more race" population is probably considerably larger than the one reported in the censuses. I discuss the latter undercount more fully in chapter 10.

There will, no doubt, be other alterations as well. Although the country is far from having achieved "postracial" status as a society, it is safe to predict that racial classifications will be modified in the future as multiracial marriages and populations proliferate and the nation's diversity surge continues. For the present, I believe that the classification used here, consistent with common everyday usage, is appropriate for the task at hand.

## A ROADMAP OF THE CHAPTERS THAT FOLLOW

The precedent-setting racial changes now under way in the United States are affecting the demographics of racial groups themselves and the places where their members choose to live. Together, these changes will impact many aspects of the nation's demographic fabric, ranging from the future of neighborhood segregation to presidential politics. Yet these shifts are occurring in the context of a varied national landscape, moving at different speeds in different places. Furthermore, the shifts are emanating from starting points that are different for new minorities, blacks, and whites.

This book provides a nuanced view of these shifts by highlighting new trends that stood out based on my examination of the 2010 census, later surveys, and related sources. They support the view that the nation is in the midst of a pivotal period in its racial demographic makeup. The story begins in chapter 2 and continues in chapter 3, which outline the broad parameters of change—generational and spatial—that the nation will experience as new minority growth spreads across the country.

## Shifting Upward and Outward

The spread of diversity from the bottom to the top of the nation's age structure, discussed in chapter 2, focuses first on the nation's youth. One might say that the experience with children in the early twenty-first century is the tip of the iceberg, foreshadowing what is in store for the rest of the population as these children age. In light of the absolute decline in the nation's white child population, the growth of the nation's child population was entirely due to Hispanics, Asians, and multiracials. In fact, since 2000 the entire youth population has declined in 25 U.S. states— mostly in those that did not attract enough new minorities to counter declines in the white population. In other states, child populations grew substantially—largely because of new minorities. Texas, for example, gained 1.3 million children from 2000 to 2015, with Hispanics accounting for nearly 90 percent of that gain.

These shifts underscore the importance that new minorities will play in future U.S. growth. But they also call attention to the need to improve access to formal education and job training for minority children and, for some, to English language training. This is especially needed among Hispanic children, who will contribute mightily to workforce gains as white baby boomers retire and who continue to lag behind other groups in high school completion and higher education.

Yet improving educational opportunities may be politically difficult given the cultural generation gap between the increasingly diverse child population and a largely white older population. Far into the future, Hispanic working-age adults will have a much higher "youth dependency burden" than working-age whites, for whom senior dependency will rise markedly. Therefore government spending on education and other youth-related programs will be more popular among Hispanic and other minority voters than among whites, who will be more concerned with government programs for seniors. Elaborating on this tension, chapter 2 outlines the ways in which differences between these generations in attributes and attitudes may affect their views of change and their choices of political candidates. At least for now, the generation gaps are widest on the West Coast and in the Southwest.

Chapter 3 discusses the nation's evolving racial geography, highlighting key aspects of new minority dispersal in the context of other racial settlements across the country. This dispersal is largely directed from the Melting Pot states to rapidly growing New Sun Belt states, a phenomenon that did not come into its own until the late 1990s. Along with the dispersal, there will continue to be a softening of the divide that formerly existed between the more diverse and less diverse regions of the country.

The New Sun Belt region is becoming transformed by Hispanic, Asian, and multiracial populations that are turning southern and interior western communities into evolving melting pots. Many of these areas are gaining new minorities and blacks more rapidly than whites. In Las Vegas, for example, the white portion of the population decreased from 75 percent in 1990 to 45 percent in 2015. The rapid growth of Hispanic and Asian populations is changing state and metropolitan consumer markets and politics and, in some cases, bringing confrontation with longtime residents. At the same time, new minorities are also dispersing to slowly growing areas in the Heartland—areas that are losing whites and blacks at the same time. Overall, the vast majority of the nation's 3,100 counties and its more than 350 metropolitan areas became less white between 2000 and 2015, as minority white areas continued to spread across the New Sun Belt and beyond.

### Hispanics, Asians, Blacks, and Whites

Chapters 4 through 7 focus on specific racial groups: Hispanics and Asians, which are the nation's largest new minorities, as well as blacks and whites. The current demographic profiles of each of the groups arise from their distinct histories and settlements. Yet those historical patterns are changing—more dramatically for Hispanics and Asians, but also for blacks and whites—in ways that are setting the stage for their future integration, especially in the New Sun Belt.

Chapter 4 examines the rapid dispersal of the nation's Hispanic population. Although classed here as a new minority, Hispanics (before they were given that name) have a long history in the United States, given its extensive border and involvement with Mexico. The newness of this group stems from the rapid growth in recent decades of not just the Mexican American population but all residents of Hispanic origin, including immigrants and their descendants from many other Latin American countries. Each of these groups begins from somewhat different "starting point" settlements in the United States, and their latest dispersal patterns have shifted each group to new destinations of all sizes—located largely in New Sun Belt states but also in most other parts of the country. This broad spread was noticeable from 2000 to 2010, when Hispanic populations more than doubled in the 145 areas considered to be new Hispanic destinations.

Overall, Hispanics are younger, more family oriented, and less educated than the total population. That raises the question of how well recently arrived residents in new Hispanic destinations will fit in with a largely white or white-black resident population. In fact, many new migrants to these areas are "tag-along migrants," lured to low-skilled jobs created by large mainstream migration surges. Even among Hispanics, these migrants tend to rank lower on education, English language usage, and several other measures, making it challenging for them to assimilate. Yet the continued broad outward spread of a mix of several Hispanic groups will infuse the younger populations in these and other areas with a new energy and vitality that will repay investments in their futures.

Often considered the "model minority," the U.S. Asian population is the topic of chapter 5. The population of Asians—the second-largest new minority group—will continue to grow, especially if future immigration policy places greater emphasis on attracting highly skilled individuals. Although some Asian groups, such as the Chinese, Japanese, and Filipinos, have a long-standing presence in the United States, the very rapid growth of Asian Americans—spurred by the provisions of the 1965 Immigration and Nationality Act—is quite recent and involves people from a broad array of Asian origin countries. These Asian immigrants and their children tend to have a better education and more favorable economic attributes than other minorities or whites due, in part, to selective immigration from their countries of origin.

Each Asian American group began from a distinct settlement area, generally on the East or West Coast and in large metropolitan areas, and no one group dominates the Asian American population. Now, almost all Asian American immigrants are beginning to spread to new Asian destinations, with Asian Indians, the most highly educated group, leading the way. "Fitting in" for Asian Americans will not be immediate, given their relatively recent immigrant status and their continued flow into the country. They will, nonetheless, be a needed presence in the U.S. labor force and communities, facilitating links to an increasingly globalized economy.

Chapter 6 discusses the changing demography of blacks in America. Hardly a new minority, blacks were the largest racial minority until 2000, and for most of the nation's history, it was the black population that people most associated with "minority" status. Yet, after centuries of blatant discrimination, the 1960s civil rights legislation planted the seeds for a growing black middle class, which has now developed, even as another segment of the black population continues to be weighed down by poverty. The chapter focuses on an important sign of the black population's changing status—a reversal of its decades-long Great Migration out of the South to a nearly wholesale evacuation of former destinations in the North and West. The newest southward shift of the black population encompasses all blacks, but it is most prominent among the young, the well-educated, and retirees. The greatest growth surges are occurring in economically prosperous areas of the South, especially in Atlanta, and all signs point to a continuation of the trend. Therefore, although there has been a surge of new minorities to the South, blacks are reinforcing the South's traditional image as a largely black-white region—but a more prosperous region than it was in the distant past.

Emerging changes in the majority white population is the topic of chapter 7. Whites, who are still considered the nation's mainstream and who fare better on economic measures than most minorities, will become a declining presence as their slow growth turns to population loss and accelerated aging. That means that regional shifts in the white population across the country amount to what is essentially a zero-sum game. For some areas to gain white migrants, others have to lose them—with little natural increase or white foreign immigration to make up the difference.

Among the 3,100 U.S. counties, more than half showed declines in the white population in 2000–10. Many of these are small, aging, mostly white counties in the Heartland. There also are declines in the white population in industrial Heartland metropolitan areas such as Detroit, Pittsburgh, and Cleveland. Yet some of the largest declines in the white population are in Melting Pot metropolitan areas such as New York and Los Angeles, whose gains are coming entirely from minorities.

White migrants are going mostly to the same New Sun Belt states that are also attracting Hispanics, Asians, and (in the South) blacks. Better employment opportunities and lower costs of living are drawing whites to the interior West and Southeast. The difference for white migration is in the destinations within those states—mostly smaller and exurban areas rather than large cities and suburbs. This "new white flight" is not racially motivated, but it does create a soft separation between whites and minorities, which will eventually be diffused as minority groups continue to disperse.

**Race and the Remaking of America**

The diversity explosion that has begun to take place is transforming the United States in fundamental ways—changing long-held stereotypes about who can live where, who can marry whom, and who can be elected to public office. Chapters 8 through 11 show how several previous "truths" were already being remade during the first decade of the 2000s and in recent presidential elections.

The shorthand description of urban America as "chocolate cities and vanilla suburbs" still remains in the consciousness of many people, at least those of a certain age. Chapter 8 emphatically puts that stereotype to rest by showing that white-only flight to the suburbs is a thing of the past. In fact, nearly one-third of large metropolitan suburbs showed a loss of whites in this century's first decade, and Hispanics are now the biggest drivers of growth of the nation's metropolitan population in both cities and suburbs. Today, it is racial minorities, in their quest for the suburban dream, who are generating new growth and vitality in the suburbs, just as immigrant groups did in the cities in an earlier era. The newest and most notable trend is the accelerated "black flight" to the suburbs. In 2010, for the first time, more blacks lived in the suburbs than in the cities of the biggest U.S. metropolitan regions—joining Hispanics and Asians as well as whites in having that distinction. Although there are vestiges of the old minority city–white suburb residential division, they are largely confined to the slowly growing Heartland. Going forward, suburbs will continue to become a microcosm of a more diverse America, as new generations of suburbanites grow up in communities that bear scant resemblance to suburbia's long-standing white middle-class image.

If there is one word that conjures up the extreme discrimination and isolation that blacks in particular have endured for decades, it is the word "segregation." Yet as chapter 9 reveals, the trends are pointing decidedly away from the highly ghettoized existence that separated blacks from whites for much of the twentieth century. A number of forces—the emergence of a black middle class, black migration to the suburbs and to growing New Sun Belt areas, and integration with new minorities who serve as buffers between racially segregated areas—are leading to pervasive reductions in black-white segregation. Black segregation is still high in many places, particularly in slowly growing northern cities, but the trend toward greater black-white integration seems poised to continue.

The levels of Hispanic and Asian segregation remain decidedly lower than that of black segregation. Both groups are more likely than blacks to live among whites and other minorities, and both are more likely to reside closer to whites in new destination areas as they disperse across the country. In short, a new racial segregation paradigm appears to be at work that suggests greater residential *integration* of the races.

Just as long-held stereotypes about where racial groups can live are disappearing, so are those about whom they can marry. Chapter 10 examines the continued rise in multiracial marriages and their likely impact on populations classed as multiracial. Marriages between racial groups were nearly nonexistent as recently as 1970, and multiracial populations were not recorded in federal statistics until 2000. The rise of new minorities has changed that fact dramatically. Today nearly one in six new marriages is multiracial, including almost half of those involving Hispanics or Asians. Although most prevalent in Melting Pot states, they are growing rapidly in the New Sun Belt and even in some Heartland states.

Perhaps more noteworthy is the increase in marriages between blacks and whites—marriages that would have been illegal in 16 states as late as 1967. Today black-white marriages are not only accepted but common—composing more than one-eighth of all marriages involving blacks. Just as important is the rising number, increasingly evident in the South, of persons who identify as both black and white, a group that now includes about one-seventh of all black toddlers. Together, these trends foreshadow a continued blurring of racial divisions at the household and personal levels that would have been unimaginable even a decade ago.

The political impacts of the nation's new diversity surge were made most vivid during the 2008 election of the first black president of the United States and his 2012 reelection. As chapter 11 points out, the political heft of minorities—both new and old—was responsible for the election and reelection of Democrat Barack Obama. The minority vote was especially crucial for Democrats in 2012, when the Republican candidate, Mitt Romney, lost despite garnering a historically high voting margin among whites. Obama also benefited from the dispersion of Hispanics and Asians to all parts of the Sun Belt, as well as a renewed black migration to the South—together helping to turn former Republican-voting states to the Democrats and ensuring his Electoral College wins.

Yet a cultural generation gap has emerged in voting interests between the increasingly diverse younger generation, that tends to vote Democratic, and the mostly white senior generation, that tends to vote Republican. This was on display in the 2016 election when older Republican baby boomer Donald Trump defeated Democrat Hillary Clinton in the Electoral College, if not in the popular vote. Just as Obama was successful in amplifying the enthusiasm of younger more diverse voters in his victories, Trump drew strength from the support of older, white, blue-collar voters who felt disconnected from a changing America. It was these voters, in particular, that helped him win several northern industrial states that have previously voted Democratic—leading to a *geographic* cultural generation gap between these states, with older populations, and several Sun Belt battleground states that voted for Clinton.

The cultural generation gap, which was evident among voters in each of the Obama and Trump elections, will likely continue—though long-term demographic trends seem to side with Democrats, if current voting proclivities continue. The greatest challenge both parties face will be to meet the often-conflicting needs of voters on both sides of this gap. To do so, they will have to persuade seniors that the key needs among striving young minorities—education, affordable housing, and steady employment—will work to benefit the Social Security and medical care programs that seniors will need in retirement.

Chapter 12, the final chapter of the book, reflects on both the short- and long-term impacts of the new racial demographic tides, pointing to areas where the nation might be proactive in shaping their effects to its advantage. This is not the first time that the United States has had to incorporate new peoples into society. Almost always, doing so has made the country richer, more vibrant, and more economically successful. In many ways, the recent growth of new minorities is a gift to a nation that would otherwise be facing the specter of an aging, slowly growing, and eventually declining population.

# Old versus Young

## The Cultural Generation Gap

**2**

The sweeping racial changes transforming much of the American landscape are segmented by an important demographic dimension: age. The infusion of new waves of Hispanics and Asians and multiracial Americans is most evident among the younger age groups. It was punctuated by the arrival in 2011 of the first "majority-minority" birth cohort: the first cohort in which the majority of U.S. babies were nonwhite minorities, of which Hispanics constituted the biggest minority group—more than one-quarter of all births.[1] Consequently, the racial makeup of the nation's younger population is beginning to contrast sharply with that of the older populations—baby boomers and seniors—which are composed mostly of whites and of which blacks constitute the largest minority group.

As the younger, more diverse part of the population reaches adulthood, clear gaps will develop between its economic interests and politics and those of the whiter older generations. This divide will result in contests over local expenditures—for example, over whether to spend money on schools or senior health facilities—and those kinds of contests seem to be evolving into culture clashes that are now evident in national politics. This chapter examines age-related racial shifts, both current and projected, along with differences between the views of the younger and older generations on a number of issues related to race relations and national priorities.

## AMERICA'S YOUNG NEW MINORITIES

For some time, Americans have been aware that "new minorities"—particularly Hispanics and Asians—are becoming a more important part of the social fabric of the United States. But the most recent information from the census and elsewhere shows how quickly these minorities are transforming the character of the nation's youth. That fact is illuminated most vividly by the change in the U.S. population under age 18 (figure 2-1). From 2000 to 2015, the population of white children *declined* by 6.2 million while the child population in each of the newer minority groups—Hispanics, Asians, and people of two or more races—increased. Hispanics

FIGURE 2-1
**Change in Under 18 Population, 2000–15**

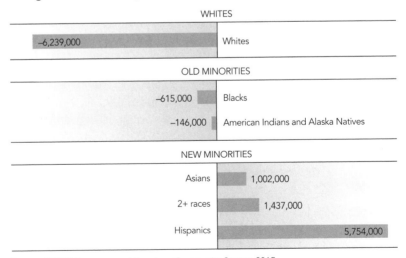

| | WHITES | |
|---|---|---|
| −6,239,000 | Whites | |

| | OLD MINORITIES | |
|---|---|---|
| −615,000 | Blacks | |
| −146,000 | American Indians and Alaska Natives | |

| | NEW MINORITIES | |
|---|---|---|
| Asians | 1,002,000 | |
| 2+ races | 1,437,000 | |
| Hispanics | 5,754,000 | |

Source: 2000 U.S. census and American Community Survey, 2015.

registered the largest absolute increase in children, 5.7 million. Were it not for new minorities, the nation's child population would have declined.

The remarkable decline in the population of white children in America correlates with the fact that whites have become an aging, slowly growing population. During the period 2000–15 there were fewer white births and immigrant children than there were white children passing into adulthood. The small number of births can be explained by two complementary factors. First, white fertility is relatively low. In fact, it is below replacement level, meaning that in the long run there will not be enough births to replace the total white population.[2] Second, the percentage of white women who are in their childbearing years is declining and is smaller than the percentage of such women in other, "younger" minority groups.[3] Both of these trends are likely to continue and should translate into smaller numbers of white births over time.

The population of whites, in fact, is aging more rapidly than that of other racial groups. In 2015 the median age was 43.3 years for whites, 28.7 for Hispanics, 36.5 for Asians, and a staggering 19.9 for the population of more than one race (see figure 2-2). Further underscoring age differences by race, less than one fifth of U.S. whites but nearly one-third of all U.S. Hispanics are under the age of 18. Moreover, all signs point to a slowly growing and a rapidly aging white population in the future. Census projections show the white child population continuing to decline for several decades to come.[4] However, the percentage of the child population composed of minorities, especially new minorities—Hispanics, Asians, and multiracial children—will continue to rise without regard to future immigration scenarios.[5] That is because there is a growing presence of new minorities among women who are in their childbearing years, a result of the immigration of relatively young adult populations from Latin America and Asia in previous decades. Hence, although minority fertility rates are gradually declining, the crude birth rate (births per 1,000 persons) among most minority groups remains higher than that for whites.[6]

A large portion of America's children now comes from a kaleidoscope of backgrounds, as varied as their parents' or grandparents' place of birth. Countries of origin include Mexico, China, the Philippines, India, Vietnam, El Salvador, Korea, the Dominican Republic, Guatemala,

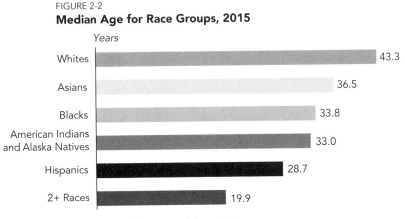

FIGURE 2-2
**Median Age for Race Groups, 2015**

*Years*

Source: U.S. Census Bureau population estimates.

Jamaica, Colombia, Haiti, Honduras, Ecuador, Peru, Taiwan, Brazil, and others. First- and second-generation immigrants from these countries add diversity to the languages spoken in U.S. homes.[7] The growth of the population of new minority children has occurred at just the right time to save the total child population from shrinking in the United States. The impact of new minority children is evident in the changing demographic profile of U.S. children. In 2015 Hispanics constituted 25 percent of children, up from just 12 percent in 1990. Whites constituted just 51.5 percent of youth in 2015, down from nearly 70 percent in 1990, and white children will become a minority of children in 2020. Because the share of white children is on the decline, the shift toward diversity is happening more swiftly among the young than the old.

**Geography of Growth and Decline among Child Populations**
The decline in the white child population dramatically reduced the growth rate of the overall U.S. child population. After 13.7 percent growth in the 1990s, the U.S. population under age 18 grew by only 1.9 percent between 2000 and 2015. In states in which Hispanic and other minority populations were either small or not growing, child populations shrank. There was considerable variation in child growth rates across states, ranging from a 31 percent gain in Nevada to a 19 percent loss in Vermont between 2000 and 2015. Child populations rose in 25 states and the Dis-

MAP 2-1
**Growth of Child Population, 2000–15**

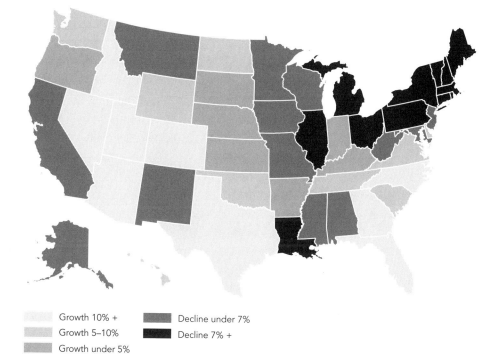

Growth 10% +          Decline under 7%
Growth 5–10%          Decline 7% +
Growth under 5%

Source: 2000 U.S. census and U.S. Census Bureau population estimates.

trict of Columbia in 2000–15, with the most prominent child population gains occurring in the Intermountain West, Texas, and the Southeast (see map 2-1). At the same time, 25 states showed declines in their child populations, most prominently in New England, New York, Michigan, Ohio, Illinois, Pennsylvania, and Louisiana. All of those areas witnessed out-migration of younger groups (and potential parents) for one or more decades, and relatively small infusions of younger minorities could not fully compensate for those losses.

Declines in white child populations were much more widespread. Like the nation as a whole, 47 states registered declines in their white child populations. Amid pervasive losses in the white child population, Hispanics contributed most to the child population gains that did occur.

The states that gained the most children in 2000–15 reveal the outsized influence of Hispanics on child population growth. Texas led all other states, gaining nearly 1.3 million children—with Hispanics accounting for almost 90 percent of the gain. Among the next-biggest gainers—Florida, Georgia, North Carolina, and Arizona—Hispanics were the single biggest contributors to the gains. Utah was the only state in which whites added the most to child population gains, although the number of white children increased only slightly more than the number of Hispanic children. Overall, however, Hispanics were largely responsible for most state and regional child population gains that occurred in 2000–15.

### Minority-White Child Populations

The swift racial transformations among youth in almost all parts of the country are yielding a rising number of majority-minority state populations of children under the age of 18 (map 2-2). Although only four states (Hawaii, New Mexico, California, and Texas) and Washington, D.C., had minority-white populations overall, thirteen states (including those four states and Alaska, Arizona, Florida, Georgia, Maryland, Mississippi, Nevada, New Jersey, and New York) and D.C. had minority-white child populations in 2015. Furthermore, in 24 states, minorities represented more than 40 percent of the child population. During the period 2000–15, many of the states with growing child populations exhibited the greatest declines in the portion of white children. In Nevada, for example, whites declined from 54 percent of children in 2000 to just 37 percent in 2015. In the same period, Florida's child population changed from 56 percent white to 44 percent white.

The dramatic remaking of the nation's child population is well under way, especially in growing parts of the country, where the growth of the child population is synonymous with the growth of the population of minority children. States such as California, Texas, and New Mexico are used to accommodating large numbers of young children from dozens of foreign countries. Yet the new growth of the population of first-generation immigrant children in large sections of the Southeast, Mountain West, and scattered parts of "middle America" represents the front lines of the country's new diversity explosion.

MAP 2-2
**Minority Percent of Child Population, 2015**

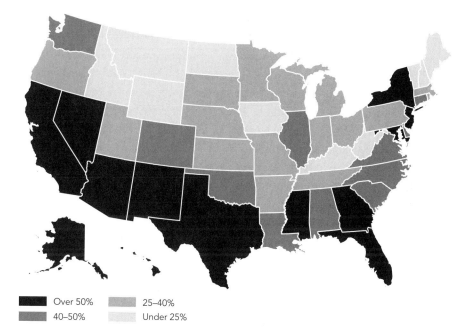

| | Over 50% | | 25–40% |
| --- | --- | --- | --- |
| | 40–50% | | Under 25% |

Source: U.S. Census Bureau population estimates.

## THE DIVERSE FUTURE U.S. LABOR FORCE

Just as the growing new minorities bolstered the size of the nation's otherwise shrinking child population, they will make important contributions to the size of the U.S. labor force in decades to come and the
workforce will continue to become more racially diverse. The contributions of the new minorities are especially vital due to the impending
retirement of white baby boomers. The first baby boomer turned age 65
in January 2011, leading a parade of retiring baby boomers (those born
between 1946 and 1964) that will not end until 2030. The continual loss
of boomers from the labor force will slow its growth considerably. Census projections show that the labor force–age population will grow by
only 4 percent in the second decade of the 2000s and by 1.8 percent in
the 2020s. In contrast, its growth rate was 13 percent in the 1990s and 11

percent in 2000–10.[8] Minorities, particularly Hispanics, will play a key role in future positive labor force growth. Because of its older age structure, the white labor force–age population will decline by 15 million from 2010 to 2030.[9] At the same time, the following minority groups will contribute to gains: Hispanics (16 million), Asians (5.4 million), and blacks (3 million) (figure 2-3).

Although the white share of the overall labor force–age population will show declines—from 64 percent in 2010 to 53 percent in 2030—the change will be especially large in the younger segment of the workforce. From 2010 to 2030, the 18- to 29-year-old Hispanic labor force–age population will grow by 55 percent, increasing its share of that population from 20 percent to 30 percent. This youthful Hispanic spurt raises questions about the preparation of younger Hispanics to fill jobs that require postsecondary education. The immigration of large numbers of Mexicans and other Latin Americans who came to the United States eager to find jobs and a better life has led to the rise of first- and second-generation Hispanics, who now constitute nearly three-fifths of Hispanic youth.[10] That is significant because their foreign-born parents are typically less educated and more likely to be poor than those in most other groups, including native-born Hispanics (see table 2-1). Overall, Hispanic children, especially the children of immigrants, are raised in lower-income communities, have higher high school dropout rates,

FIGURE 2-3
**Projected Change in Labor Force–Age Population by Race, 2010–30**

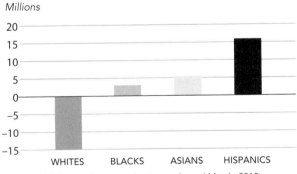

Source: U.S. Census Bureau projections, released March, 2018.

TABLE 2-1
**Education and Poverty Measures, by Race, 2015**

| | RATES | | |
|---|---|---|---|
| | **High school dropouts**<br>(per 100 persons<br>age 16–19) | **Adult college grads**<br>(per 100 persons<br>age 25 and over) | **Children in poverty**<br>(per 100 persons under<br>age 18 in households) |
| Hispanics | 5.6 | 15.0 | 30.5 |
| Foreign-born | 9.9 | 11.3 | 35.2 |
| Native-born | 4.7 | 19.3 | 31.7 |
| Asians | 1.5 | 52.6 | 11.9 |
| Blacks | 4.7 | 20.2 | 36.5 |
| Whites | 3.4 | 34.2 | 12.6 |
| Total | 4.0 | 30.7 | 20.7 |

Source: American Community Survey, 2015; Pew Research Center.

and are less likely to advance to postsecondary education.[11] Moreover, Hispanic children, as has been the case for black children, are more likely to attend underfunded, segregated schools.[12]

Although the children of recent immigrants have paved the way for the U.S. labor force to grow, the future contributions of younger Hispanic workers and blacks will depend on their receiving the opportunities and developing the skills needed to complete high school and pursue postsecondary education. That fact is well recognized by a number of scholars and policymakers, who point to the need for expanding preschool programs, providing more effective instruction for English language learners, and removing barriers—financial and others—to postsecondary education.[13]

Also entering the labor force in larger numbers are Asian children who, even more so than Hispanics, have foreign-born parents—about 85 percent. Because more of their foreign-born parents arrived here because they qualified for employment-based preferential status under immigration law, often after studying at American universities, their overall level of skills and education is higher than that of the population as a whole.[14]

The black labor force–age population will grow more modestly than the former two groups because, as with whites, its sizable baby boom population will be turning 65 through the year 2030. Yet although black educational attainment has risen from much lower levels in earlier decades, high school dropout and college graduation rates for blacks are more on par with those of native-born Hispanics than with those of whites or Asians. School segregation levels are still high for blacks, many of whom reside in financially strapped city school districts.

Overall, immigration in recent decades from Latin America and Asia, along with the higher rates of natural increase (births minus deaths) among Hispanics and Asians, has put the United States in a position to maintain a growing labor force despite the aging of the large baby boom generation. That stands in contrast to the status of many industrialized nations—such as Japan and Italy and other countries in Europe—that are facing declines in their labor force at a time when they could use productivity gains.[15] Another advantage for the United States is that the international heritage and languages of these new labor force entrants help connect the nation to an ever-expanding globalized economy. Nonetheless, to realize the benefits of a growing productive workforce, the diverse child population of today and tomorrow needs to be provided the skills and opportunities to succeed at jobs in an increasingly knowledge-based economy.

## EMERGING CULTURAL GENERATION GAPS

The diversification of the U.S. population from the bottom up of the age distribution holds more than just demographic significance. It reflects an emerging cultural divide between the young and the old as they adapt to change in different ways. Different age groups represent different generations, which were raised and became adults in specific eras and may be more or less receptive to the cultural changes brought about by new racial groups. Figure 2-4 shows U.S. race differences by age group in 2015. One-half of children under age five were white in 2015; in contrast, the oldest age group was 82 percent white.

When viewed more broadly, there is a sharp racial distinction between the baby boomers—who are older than the age of 50—and their elders, on one hand, and, on the other, the younger generations: the millennial generation and their children, who constitute the population under the age of 35.[16] Baby boomers and seniors are more than 70 per-

FIGURE 2-4

**Cultural Generation Gap: Population Composition, by Age and Race, 2015**

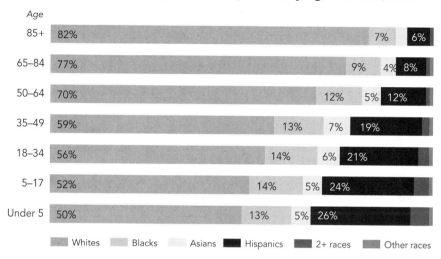

Source: American Community Survey, 2015.

cent white, with blacks representing the largest racial minority. In contrast, millennials and their children are more than 46 percent minority, with Hispanics constituting the largest share of their minority population. Because of the different experiences of these groups, a cultural generation gap is emerging between the younger groups and baby boomers and seniors, who are voicing sharp resistance to America's new racial change. A 2011 Pew Research Center poll shows that only 23 percent of baby boomers and seniors regard the country's growing population of immigrants as a change for the better and that 42 percent see it as a change for the worse. More than one-half of white baby boomers and seniors said that the growing number of newcomers from other countries represents a threat to traditional U.S. values and customs.[17]

The millennial generation, in particular, is known for its racial inclusiveness.[18] The Pew survey found marked differences between baby boomers and millennials with regard to agreement that the following are changes for the better: that more people of different races are marrying each other (36 percent versus 60 percent), that the population of Hispanics is growing (21 percent versus 33 percent), and that the population of Asians is growing (24 percent versus 43 percent). The resistance of baby boomers to demographic change may seem surprising. This much-celebrated generation came to embody the image of Middle America during the second half of the last century. Conceived during the prosperous post–World War II period, they brought a rebellious, progressive sensibility to the country in the 1960s, 1970s, and beyond. With the help of the programs of the Great Society, they became the most well-schooled generation to date and the epitome of America's largely white, suburban middle class, with which most of today's adults now identify.

Yet the baby boomers also came of age at a moment when the United States was becoming more insular than it had been before. Growing up in mostly white, segregated suburbs, white baby boomers had less exposure to immigrants and foreign wars than their parents. Between 1946 and 1964, the years of the baby boom, the immigrant share of the U.S. population shrank to an all-time low (under 5 percent), and the immigrants who did arrive were largely white Europeans. Although baby boomers were interested in righting domestic wrongs, such as racial discrimination, and bursting glass ceilings, they did not have much interaction with people from other countries. The cultural generation gap continues to appear when baby boomers and seniors are compared with the younger segment of the U.S. population. That segment shows sharp racial distinctions, and members are more likely to be first- or second-generation Americans of non-European ancestry and to be bilingual (see table 2-2).

TABLE 2-2
**Differences between Young and Old, 2015**
*Percent*

| Attribute | Under Age 30 | Age 50+ |
|---|---|---|
| European ancestry | 38 | 58 |
| First or second generation in U.S. | 28 | 22 |
| English spoken at home[a] | | |
|   No | 23 | 16 |
|   No, but speaks English very well | 18 | 7 |

Source: American Community Survey, 2015; 2015 Current Population Survey, Annual Social and Economic Supplement.

[a]Persons age 5 and over.

It should not be that surprising, then, that baby boomers are resistant to the new demographic changes among the country's younger population, with whom, for the most part, they do not share close personal or family relationships. This is resulting in a generational divide in a number of areas, such as immigration, affirmative action, and government spending—in particular, over whether funds should go to programs for youth or for seniors. Yet because of the relative size of the baby boom generation and its effect on the voting population, it will have a strong voice in future elections. Younger, more multiracial generations of adults are smaller in size, are less likely to vote, and, at least in the near term, include more nonvoting noncitizens—although, as discussed in chapter 11, their electoral clout is on the rise.

## Youth and Old-Age Dependency

Underpinning the generational divide are shifts in what demographers call old-age dependency and child dependency, which now have a distinct racial dimension. Both historically and internationally, the number of children dependent on the labor force–age population has been larger than the number of dependent retirees. However, in quickly aging countries where fertility is declining and life expectancy is rising, seniors are increasing the numbers of the "dependent" population.[19] That is of concern in the United States, given that government programs aiding the elderly, including those for medical care, cost substantially more than those aiding children. The cultural generation gap between the young and the old can exacerbate the competition for resources because the rise in the number of senior dependents is occurring more rapidly among whites than among minorities, for whom dependent children is a larger issue.

To illustrate, a look at the total U.S. population is in order. The growth of the senior population is affected by both increased life expectancy and, more important, the aging of the baby boomers. From 2010 to 2030, the senior population is projected to grow by 82 percent. In contrast, the labor force–age population (ages 18 to 64) will grow by only 6 percent and the population under age 18 will grow by just 1.6 percent. Therefore, although new minorities and immigrants are driving the increases in the younger and labor force–age populations, the growth of the senior pop-

FIGURE 2-5
**Youth and Old-Age Dependency Ratios, 2010–40**

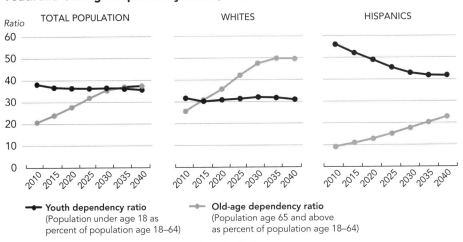

Source: U.S. Census Bureau projections, released March, 2018.

ulation is driven by the mostly white baby boomers. The associated dependency shifts are shown in the left panel of figure 2-5, which contrasts two measures: the old-age dependency ratio (the population age 65 and over as a percent of the labor force–age population) and the youth dependency ratio (the population under age 18 as a percent of the labor force–age population). Although youth dependency was almost twice the level of old-age dependency in 2010 (38 versus 21), youth dependency decreases modestly during the following three decades while old-age dependency nearly doubles—making seniors a substantial portion of the nonworking-age population.[20]

Yet these dependency patterns are distinctly different for whites compared with minorities. The comparison of dependency ratios for whites and Hispanics shows their likely relative priorities with regard to the children-versus-seniors spending issue. For whites, youth dependency is lower than the U.S. total and is not much larger than white old-age dependency in 2010 (32 versus 26). In fact, by 2020, the old-age dependency ratio for whites will exceed the child dependency ratio, and for the two decades that follow, white seniors will outnumber white children. That stands in marked contrast to the position of Hispanics, whose 2010 youth dependency ratio was 56 and whose old-age dependency ratio was only 9. Moreover, Hispanic youth dependency will remain well above 40 through 2040, even as the old-age dependency ratio inches up to 23. In other words, for at least the next two decades, Hispanic children will sharply outnumber Hispanic seniors. Although black and Asian youth dependency is not as marked as it is for Hispanics, it remains higher than senior dependency through at least 2040.[21] Therefore there is no question that the primary concern of working-age Hispanics—and to a lesser extent Asians and blacks—will be their children rather than the older dependent population. For working-age whites, elderly dependents will be a primary concern as well as their own future well-being as they enter their retirement years. This demographic framework provides a concrete basis for considering the cultural generation gap and competition for government resources allocated to children and the elderly.

In discussing the long-term political ramifications of the generation gap, political writer Ronald Brownstein has framed it as a divide between "the gray and the brown," wherein older whites, including aging baby boomers, favor smaller government investment in social support programs except for those, such as Social Security, that directly affect them. For these older voters, big government is associated with higher taxes, which primarily benefit younger demographic groups whose needs they do not fully appreciate.[22] In contrast, more diverse youth, particularly millennials, tend to support greater government spending on education, health, and social welfare programs that strongly affect young families and children. A 2011 Pew Research Center poll showed that when given a choice between a larger government that offers more services and a smaller government that offers fewer, seven in ten millennial minorities but only four in ten white baby boomers favored larger government.[23]

It is important for retiring baby boomers to understand that the solvency of government-supported retirement and medical care programs is directly dependent on the future productivity and payroll tax contributions of a workforce in which minorities, especially Hispanics, will dominate future growth. As indicated above, there is a well-recognized challenge in providing these future workforce participants with the skills needed to make these contributions, and meeting that challenge requires public investment in education and related services. The dilemma, however, is that the largest government programs that directly benefit the elderly, such as Social Security and Medicare, are mostly financed by the federal government and are considered politically sacred by many. In contrast, programs for youth, such as education, are largely funded at the state and local levels and are far more vulnerable to economic downturns and budget cuts given that states, unlike the federal government, are required to balance their budgets annually. Therefore efforts to muster support for child-oriented programs require grassroots support across an often fragmented political terrain. At present, political views divide largely along Republican and Democratic lines. Older whites back Republican candidates for national and many statewide offices, while minorities and younger whites tend to back Democrats, who generally favor more federal spending on programs for families and children. In the future, as discussed in chapter 11, more young minorities will enter their prime voting years and both parties will need to balance the needs and concerns of new and old voters, particularly in regions of the country where the cultural generation gap is emerging.

**Where the Gap Is Widest**

Although the cultural generation gap is forming throughout the nation, the growth of the young new minority population and the steadier gains of the aging white population are occurring at different speeds in different regions. The most racially diverse and youthful populations are in states and metropolitan areas in the Southwest, Southeast, and major urban immigration centers where new minorities have had an established presence. A shorthand measure for the cultural generation gap in a state or metropolitan area is the difference between the percentage of seniors who are white and the percentage of children who are white. In 2015, 78 percent of the U.S. senior population and 52 percent of children were white, so the national gap was 26 percent. But among states, Arizona led the way, with a gap of 41 percent (81 percent of seniors and 40 percent of children were white). Nevada, New Mexico, California, Texas, and Florida were not far behind, with gap mea-

TABLE 2-3
**Major Metropolitan Areas with Largest and Smallest Cultural Generation Gaps, 2015**

| Rank | Metropolitan area | Percent white | | Cultural generation gap[a] |
|---|---|---|---|---|
| | | Under age 18 | Age 65+ | |
| | LARGEST GAPS | | | |
| 1 | Tucson | 35 | 78 | 43 |
| 2 | Phoenix | 42 | 83 | 41 |
| 3 | Riverside | 22 | 59 | 37 |
| 4 | Las Vegas | 31 | 66 | 35 |
| 5 | Dallas | 36 | 71 | 35 |
| | SMALLEST GAPS | | | |
| 1 | Pittsburgh | 78 | 92 | 14 |
| 2 | Cincinnati | 73 | 88 | 15 |
| 3 | St. Louis | 66 | 83 | 17 |
| 4 | Detroit | 59 | 76 | 17 |
| 5 | Birmingham | 56 | 74 | 18 |

[a]Gap = white percent of persons age 65 and over, minus white percent of persons under age 18.
Source: Americn Community Survey, 2015, for metropolitan areas with populations more than one million.

sures greater than 30. Among major metropolitan areas, the largest gaps were in Tuscon and Phoenix in Arizona; Riverside, California; Las Vegas; and Dallas (see table 2-3 and map 2-3).

In contrast, large—mostly white—swaths of the country, including the non-coastal Northeast, Midwest, and Appalachia, are observing slow growth or even declines in their youth populations while remaining home to large numbers of white baby boomers and seniors. The demographic profiles of these regions, along with those of metropolitan areas such as Pittsburgh, Cincinnati, and St. Louis, will eventually converge with those of more diverse parts of the country. But in the interim, they will be adapting, often fitfully, to the changes occurring elsewhere.

Still, the places where the cultural generation gap has generated the most contention are those where the gains in new minorities are large and recent. Arizona is emblematic because of its large gap and recent Hispanic growth of 177 percent from 1990 to 2015. Against that demographic backdrop, it is perhaps no coincidence that a great deal of animosity between whites and Hispanics erupted upon the 2010 signing of

MAP 2-3
**States Classed by Cultural Generation Gaps, 2015**

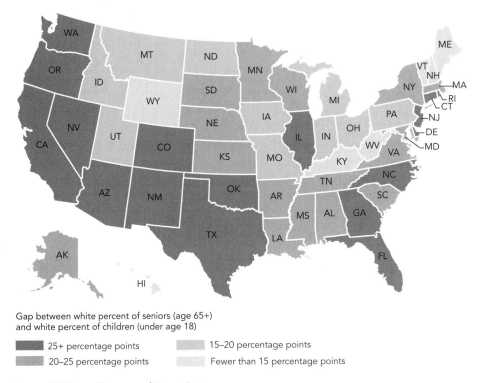

Gap between white percent of seniors (age 65+)
and white percent of children (under age 18)

| | | | |
|---|---|---|---|
| ■ 25+ percentage points | | ■ 15–20 percentage points | |
| ■ 20–25 percentage points | | ■ Fewer than 15 percentage points | |

Source: U.S. Census Bureau population estimates.

the Support Our Law Enforcement and Safe Neighborhoods Act, also known as Arizona State Bill 1070. Although the law was later amended and the Supreme Court struck down key parts, it was one of the strictest anti-immigration laws ever enacted by a state. Provisions included requirements that residents carry papers verifying their citizenship; if they did not, they would be subject to arrest, detention, and potential deportation.[24] Although proponents pointed to increased recent waves of immigration as a source of crime and drug-related incidents at the border, the law was sharply opposed by civil rights groups that believed that it would set the stage for widespread racial profiling of Hispanics in the state. Not surprisingly, a statewide poll taken at the time split along racial lines: 65 percent of whites but only 21 percent of Hispanics were in favor of the new law. Similarly, the law was favored by 62 percent of those 55 years of age and older (across all races) but only 45 percent of those under the age of 35.[25]

Later, other states with recent Hispanic or new immigrant population gains, including Alabama, Georgia, South Carolina, and Utah, proposed similarly strict immigration laws. There is other evidence of broad-based pushback against new minorities among the more established population, including the establishment of strict voter identification laws in several states before the 2012 and 2016 elections, which could disproportionately affect minorities, and concerns, again in Arizona, that public school curriculums were placing too much emphasis on ethnic studies programs.[26]

As young new minorities continue to disperse outward from traditional gateways, the cultural generation gap will likely emerge in both public and private arenas, creating conflict over issues that are important to young minorities (for example, immigration reform, improved public schools, and affordable housing) and those issues important to baby boomers and seniors (for example, medical and retirement benefits). The gap will appear in communities of all sizes, but it will be widest in states where the growth of young minorities is new and the racial demographic profile of the younger generation differs most from that of the older generation.

Perhaps the most pressing and immediate impact of the minority youth surge is being felt in schools, which, among other challenges, must instruct increasing numbers of children who speak a language other than English at home. The availability of effective English language instruction is key to the advancement of new minority children, but it also demands greater resources from school systems. Map 2-4 shows the areas of the country with the highest shares of children who speak a language other than English at home. Nationally, 22 percent of children age 5–17 fell into this group in 2015, up from 18 percent in 2000 and 14 percent in 1990. Four-fifths of the children spoke Spanish.

The population of these children has continued to spread as their parents locate away from regions with traditionally high concentrations of immigrants and Hispanics. These regions are centered in California, Texas, and the Southwest, to the extent that nearly one-half (45 percent)

MAP 2-4

**Percentage of Children Who Speak a Language Other than English at Home, 2015[a]**

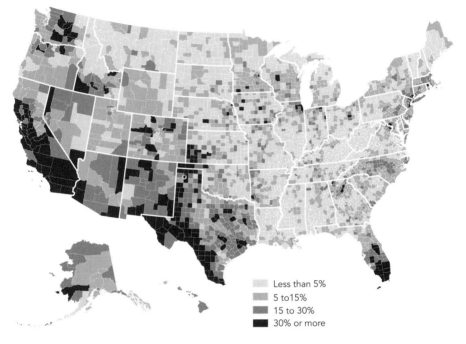

Less than 5%
5 to15%
15 to 30%
30% or more

Source: American Community Survey, 2011–15.
[a]ages 5 to 17

of California's children and more than one-third of children in Texas and Nevada speak a language other than English at home. Although a majority of children who speak a language other than English at home also speak English very well, they still benefit from instruction that recognizes the language transitions that they are making. The need for specialized instruction is especially acute for K–12 public school children classified as being English language learners—or as having limited English proficiency—one of the fastest-growing segments of the student population.[27]

Thus, on a variety of levels, the continuing spread of new minorities from the bottom up of the nation's age distribution creates important opportunities for the growth and productivity of the nation's population and workforce. But that spread also presents challenges in light of the sharp cultural and generational differences that are emerging. The divide will require adaptation on all sides, and policymakers and citizens alike will need to approach these changes with a long view. Rather than seeing the inevitable changes as damaging to the American way of life, it will behoove the nation to consider the future of the country and prepare now for a country that will be majority-minority.

# America's New Racial Map 3

Although the rumblings of America's coming diversity explosion are heard most clearly from the bottom up, from young to old, the explosion is also spreading geographically, from fairly self-contained Melting Pot regions—the traditional immigrant gateways—to other parts of the country. This chapter provides an overview, in light of major immigration and domestic migration shifts, of America's population by contrasting its current racial profile with that of the recent past. It lays the groundwork for the next four chapters by identifying transformations across three different mega-regions of the country: the Melting Pot, the New Sun Belt, and the Heartland.

The long-standing view of America as a melting pot has a geographic dimension that can be traced to the century-old waves of European immigration that brought Irish, Italians, Poles, and other white groups to the country's shores. While most of those groups initially clustered in traditional gateway cities such as New York and Chicago, the ensuing decades led to their gradual dispersal to other parts of the country.[1]

In like manner, America's newest immigrants, from Latin America and Asia, began clustering in distinct gateway regions of the country. The difference is that the country had filled out more broadly before this immigrant-driven, new minority spurt began—a fact that initially created a sharp divide between areas where the new minority growth explosion began and other areas where whites and older minorities resided or dominated population gains. When that divide first appeared, there were fears of a demographic "balkanization" of the population that would separate, culturally and politically, the Melting Pot regions—where new minorities clustered—from the rest of the country. However, at the beginning of the twenty-first century it became clear that those patterns were shifting with the widespread dispersal of the new minorities.

## THREE AMERICAS

To set the stage for understanding new minority geographic shifts, it is useful to lay out three distinct regions of the country that emerged from the migration patterns of the 1980s and early 1990s. At the time, it appeared that the ongoing racial and demographic dynamics underlying these regions could be creating three different Americas.[2]

### The Melting Pot Region

The growth of new minorities, especially Hispanics and Asians, became prominent during this period, a consequence of the Immigration and Nationality Act of 1965, which paved the way for immigration from countries other than Europe.[3] At that time the nation's foreign-born Hispanic and Asian populations were heavily concentrated in just six states—California, New York, Texas, Florida, New Jersey, and Illinois—and in metropolitan areas such as Los Angeles, New York, Miami, Chicago, San Francisco, and Houston. New Mexico and Hawaii can be added to the Melting Pot, given their large Hispanic and Asian populations. Together, those eight states and the urban clusters within them were welcoming environments for new immigrants and their descendants, providing them with communities where they could find social and eco-

MAP 3-1
**Melting Pot, New Sun Belt, and Heartland America**

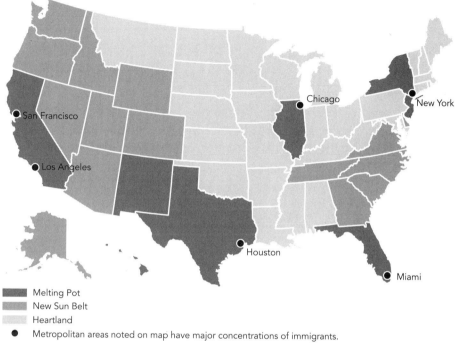

Melting Pot
New Sun Belt
Heartland
● Metropolitan areas noted on map have major concentrations of immigrants.
Source: Author's illustration.

nomic support. Overall, the Melting Pot region represents about two-fifths of the U.S. population (see map 3-1).

The demographic personality of this region was changing rapidly. In addition to becoming more racially diverse with the rapid growth of new Latin American and Asian populations, it was becoming more multilingual, younger, and, with the establishment of distinct racial communities, more culturally vibrant. These changes affected the labor supply, politics, public service needs, schools, music, and local cuisine. America's new Melting Pot region was becoming distinct from the rest of the nation. As the changes started occurring, residents in the rest of the country became aware that heightened immigrant flows were increasing the size of nonblack minorities. However, for most Americans, those changes were taking place elsewhere. For them, images of the new

Americans came largely from television newscasts, movies, and occa-
sional trips to big, diverse cities. Immigration did not affect their everyday life. In other words, they were experiencing the nation's new
diversity "virtually."

### The New Sun Belt Region

 At the same time, the rest of the country was experiencing a different
migration pattern. A good number of Americans who opted to move
were moving not to primary immigrant destinations but to the New Sun
Belt.[4] This region included growing states in the Mountain West and
Southeast, including Idaho, Utah, Colorado, Arizona, and the Southeast
corridor of Georgia and the Carolinas, among others.[5] In this region, the
primary early source of growth was domestic migration of whites and
blacks from other parts of the United States rather than immigration. As
figure 3-1 indicates, in the 1990s the domestic migration rate in the New
Sun Belt was 91 per 1,000 persons while the immigration rate was just
22 per 1,000 persons. In other words, domestic migration accounted for

FIGURE 3-1

**Immigration and Domestic Migration Rates for Three Regions,
1990–2000 and 2000–10**

*Migrants per 1,000 population*

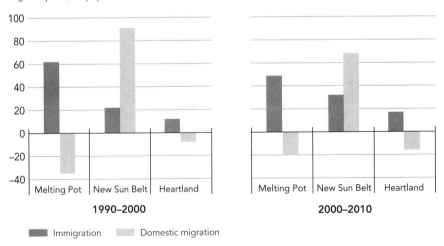

Source: U.S. Census Bureau population estimates.

more than four-fifths of all migration to the New Sun Belt. That stands in contrast to the Melting Pot, which was losing domestic migrants.

Top domestic migrant gainers during this period included Atlanta, Las Vegas, Phoenix, Denver, and Seattle. Although not the largest metropolitan areas in the United States, these places had rapidly growing, diverse economies; warm climates; and living costs that were far less onerous than in the expensive, congested coastal areas that were attracting many immigrants. In fact, those higher costs were among the reasons for the largely white middle-class flight from high-immigration areas to the New Sun Belt (for example, flows from metropolitan Los Angeles to Las Vegas and from metropolitan New York to Atlanta).[6] Blacks also were part of the movement away from large immigrant magnet areas, although they were moving to more rapidly growing areas in the South. The New Sun Belt represented a growth area that extended beyond the older Sun Belt magnets of California, Texas, and Florida, which over time had become more urbanized and dependent on immigrant growth. Although not all parts of the New Sun Belt were consistent gainers, they collectively constituted the nation's new growth frontier.[7] In addition, their metropolitan areas had a more suburban feel, with more recent development, lower density, and, in many cases, more attractions for younger families. They became latter-day regional counterparts to the smaller suburban communities outside big cities in the 1960s and 1970s.[8] The 15 states in this region account for slightly more than one-fifth of the U.S. population.

Meanwhile, most Hispanics and Asians remained clustered in immigrant gateway regions and states, largely because significant numbers of them were immigrants or close relatives of immigrants. These areas were a comfort zone, complete with family, friends, and neighbors and familiar institutions such as churches, community centers, and stores. Family and kinship ties were especially pronounced because family reunification represented a dominant part of post-1965 immigration policy.[9] Therefore shared values, customs, languages, and information about employment opportunities made the Melting Pot region more attractive to new immigrants and their relatives than New Sun Belt areas—where they would truly be pioneers.

**The Heartland Region**

As the Melting Pot region grew rapidly from international migration and the New Sun Belt region grew primarily from domestic migration, the Heartland—including much of the Great Plains, Midwest, Appalachia, interior South, and New England—experienced modest growth because of very little immigration and small or negative domestic migration (see figure 3-1). Much of the Heartland had struggled to overcome downturns in old-line manufacturing industries while other parts were associated with agricultural or resource-based industries. Decades of a strong youth exodus left this region older and more rooted than the rest of the country, and except for concentrations of blacks in urban areas, the region remained far whiter than the rest of the country. Still, the 27 states that along with Washington, D.C., constitute the Heartland represent almost two-fifths of the nation's population.

## FEARS OF DEMOGRAPHIC BALKANIZATION

In the late 1980s and mid-1990s, there was a clear demographic division between those parts of the country that were both receiving and retaining large numbers of new immigrant minorities and other parts of the country where domestic migrants accounted for most of the change in population. The increased demographic disparities that separated the Melting Pot region from the other two regions led to speculation that a new demographic balkanization might be under way.[10] If so, the cultural norms and policies embraced by the older, whiter, and more middle-class populations of the New Sun Belt and Heartland may be pitted against policies that are more attractive to younger, more diverse populations in the Melting Pot, who are middle class or below. In the New Sun Belt and Heartland, that may mean advocating for stronger government support for retirement and medical care, while in the Melting Pot it may mean paying greater attention to affirmative action laws, extending the federal safety net to meet the needs of new first- and second-generation families, and improving access to quality public education. In other words, as the demographic divisions between these mega-regions become sharper, so too may the political divisions.

The white exodus from high-immigration Melting Pot areas was of particular concern because it seemed to reflect a regional version of the racially motivated suburban white flight of decades past.[11] Yet other interpretations suggested that the moves, particularly of low-skilled domestic migrants, stemmed from job displacement by lower-paid immigrant workers, higher taxes to meet the needs of new populations, or a generalized response to the economic restructuring occurring in high-immigration areas.[12] Regardless of its source, this new flight was seen by some as evidence that immigration policy should be curtailed to admit fewer migrants or that the requirements for entry should be tightened. Such policy shifts, it was believed, might ease the pressure on middle-class and low-skilled native-born residents to leave the Melting Pot areas.[13] Another balkanization-related concern was the containment of new minorities largely within the Melting Pot regions. As did the immigrants of a century ago, the new immigrants and their children gravitated to areas with populations of the same race and national origin, for reasons discussed above. Yet, unlike the earlier immigrant waves, the new waves in much of the Melting Pot were dominated by a few large groups, especially Hispanics from Mexico, suggesting that areas with large existing communities would become highly differentiated from the rest of the country.[14]

## THE 2000s: THE NEW SUN BELT AS AN "EMERGING MELTING POT"

Fears about an eventual demographic balkanization began to dissipate during the first decade of the 2000s, when a far wider dispersion of immigrants and minorities occurred than could have been anticipated in the mid-1990s.[15] This trend is illustrated in figure 3-1, which displays relative rates of immigration and domestic migration for each of the three regions. As in the 1990s, the New Sun Belt drew domestic migrants from both the Melting Pot and the Heartland. But from 2000 to 2010, immigration made a markedly bigger contribution to the region's migration growth as the immigration rate increased to 32 per 1,000 persons while the domestic migration rate declined to 68 per 1,000. Therefore, although immigrants accounted for less than one-fifth of New Sun Belt migration gains in the 1990s, they increased their contribution to nearly one-third in the first decade of the 2000s.

The trends are even more dramatic for shifts in the overall Hispanic and Asian populations. The effect of these two new minorities on New Sun Belt growth shows a sharp contrast between the 1990s and the first decade of the 2000s. In the 1990s, Hispanics and Asians accounted for 30 percent of the region's growth; between 2000 and 2010, they accounted for 44 percent. The new minority contributions to 2000–10 growth were especially pronounced in Las Vegas, where Hispanics and Asians accounted for 64 percent of the metropolitan area's growth. Similar patterns were showing up in Phoenix, Salt Lake City, and Denver. As a result of the new minority gains and continued black in-migration, the share of whites in the New Sun Belt region dropped, coming closer to the share in the Melting Pot region. This was the case in 2015. While the minority share of the Heartland's population also increased, it still remained predominantly white (see figure 3-2).

FIGURE 3-2
**Race Profiles of Three Regions, 1990 and 2015**

*Percent*

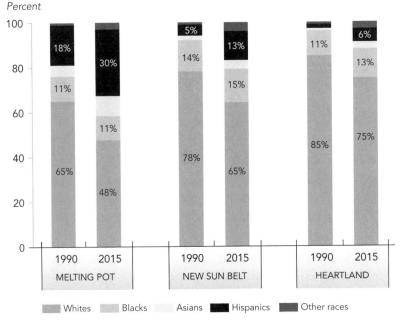

Source: 1990 U.S. census; American Community Survey, 2015.

The spreading of new minorities away from high-concentration areas involves both the dispersal of immigrants and the increased domestic migration of Hispanics and Asians away from the Melting Pot region to other parts of the country.[16] Each of these migration flows is related to the "pushes" and "pulls" of the labor market, which did not operate as well for new minorities in the earlier period. The migration flows that previously led networks of Hispanic and Asian families and friends to traditional gateway areas began to spread outward in the first decade of the 2000s, when low-skilled jobs in manufacturing and meat processing along with low-wage construction, service, and retail jobs sparked by population growth drew Hispanic immigrants and domestic migrants to the New Sun Belt.[17] Many Asian and Hispanic migrants likewise responded to jobs at all skill levels in older metropolitan areas in the Heartland and the New Sun Belt.[18]

An important development since the late 1990s has been the increased domestic migration of Hispanics out of traditional gateways, representing the same middle-class flight that was a largely white phenomenon in the late 1980s.[19] In fact, Hispanics outnumbered whites in domestic migration out of metropolitan Los Angeles in the late 1990s, a stark contrast to the mostly white out-migration in the late 1980s.[20] For Los Angeles and other traditional gateways, Hispanic population gains are increasingly dependent on immigration and fertility as long-term resident Hispanics disperse.

The demographic makeup of the new Melting Pot region is not nearly as distinct from that of the rest of the country today as it was in the early 1990s, given the spread of Hispanics, Asians, and other new minorities to the New Sun Belt and the Heartland. There is now less concern that the country is becoming balkanized. Yet the past demographic profiles of these regions still hold some sway. The Melting Pot, for example, remains distinct on a number of dimensions in 2015 (see table 3-1). Of the three mega-regions, the Melting Pot's population consists of higher shares of those with non-European ancestry, those who are foreign born, and those who speak a language other than English at home. It is also home to the most racially diverse child population.

Yet the rapidly growing New Sun Belt region has now become the "emerging melting pot" in the United States. Not only do new minorities

TABLE 3-1
**Social and Demographic Attributes, Three Regions, 2015**
*Percent*

| Attribute[a] | Melting Pot | New Sun Belt | Heartland |
|---|---|---|---|
| European ancestry | 37 | 46 | 59 |
| Foreign born | 22 | 11 | 7 |
| Language other than English spoken at home[b] | 31 | 21 | 15 |
| Children under 18, by race-ethnicity | | | |
| White | 37 | 55 | 67 |
| Black | 12 | 16 | 15 |
| Asian | 7 | 4 | 3 |
| Hispanic | 40 | 20 | 10 |
| Population growth 2000–15 | 16 | 24 | 7 |

Source: 2000 U.S. census; American Community Survey; 2015, and U.S. Census Bureau population estimates.

[a]All attributes pertain to 2015, except population growth 2000–15.
[b]Persons age 5 and over.

account for a substantial portion of its overall growth, but its population is becoming more like that of the Melting Pot on a number of levels, such as ancestry, nativity, language spoken at home, and racial makeup. The New Sun Belt is clearly being transformed by its new minority populations. In this respect, it serves as a transition region between the Melting Pot and the Heartland. As such, the New Sun Belt is dealing with some of the growing pains that come from incorporating new populations in old communities, which were made up of largely white or "old minority" residents. These include an initial backlash among existing residents who are uncomfortable with the changing population in their school systems, in shopping centers, and at community events. Culture clashes can be exacerbated when new migrant groups, arriving for low-skilled jobs, speak English less than perfectly and have education levels well below the local norm. Often adding to the difficulties are politicians who fan the flames of division by supporting policies that minority residents believe jeopardize their rights and full acceptance. For example, several of the New Sun Belt states have introduced some of the most severe legislation restricting undocumented immigrants' access to jobs, housing, and other services—which critics have argued leads to racial profiling.[21] Clearly, the spillover of new minorities to the New Sun Belt and beyond is softening regional boundaries that were thought to create a racially based demographic balkanization of the country. However, the process of their assimilation and economic incorporation into the New Sun Belt is still very much a work in progress.

## NEW MINORITY AND OLD MINORITY POPULATION SHIFTS

The rapid influx of new minorities associated with recent waves of immigrants and now with their succeeding generations contrasts with the existing settlement patterns of whites and blacks and other older minorities. The United States clearly is a nation in racial demographic flux, but it also is one in which different groups may dominate a local landscape at a particular point in time. That is the case today, in the second decade of the 2000s, when the nation exhibits a kaleidoscope of racial patterns. Map 3-2 displays where different groups are overrepresented across the more than 3,100 counties in the United States.[22] Among the new minorities, Hispanics singly or jointly with other minorities are prevalent in states spanning from California to Texas as well as in parts of the Mountain West, the Southeast, large urbanized portions of the North, and patches of smaller places in the nation's midsection. Asians, with a smaller overall U.S. population, are most prevalent, often along with other groups, in California, Washington, Texas, parts of the Southeast, and major metropolitan areas and smaller towns, including college towns, in all parts of the country.

The current settlement patterns of these two minority groups, although recently expanding, stand in contrast to that of blacks, the largest older minority, whose concentration is clearly in the South—stretching from Texas to Maryland—and many northern and midwestern urban areas. Blacks also combine with other groups to shape "multiple-minority" concentrations, especially in Texas, California, and other parts of the West. For the most part, their concentration is distinctly Southern, a pattern that is reinforced by recent migration among blacks to the South. American Indians and Alaska Natives, who constitute most of the "other" minority category in map 3-2, are heavily concentrated in Oklahoma, Alaska, the Mountain West, and the Upper Great Plains as well as select parts of many other states. About two-thirds of this population lives outside areas designated as American Indian or Alaska Native areas.[23]

The spreading of new minorities coupled with the more established patterns of older minorities leads to a patchwork of racial settlements across the country—one in a continual state of flux. Although it is true that a good part of the territory in the nation's Heartland is still white (that is, not overrepresented by one or more minorities), the population in this part of the country is increasingly smaller, less urban, and likely to grow more modestly than the population in New Sun Belt areas, which are becoming infused with growing minority populations. The following sections expand on the recent dynamics of specific minority groups as well as whites.

### Hispanic Outward Spread

The bulk of the Hispanic population still lives in large gateway regions (Los Angeles, New York, Miami, and Chicago), which together are home to nearly two-fifths of all U.S. Hispanics. However, these areas are losing their grip. Together, they drew 25 percent of national Hispanic population gains in the 1990s but just 16 percent in 2000–10. Houston and Riverside, California, which have larger Hispanic populations, have now displaced Chicago. The metropolitan areas with the fastest-growing Hispanic populations are located predominantly in the nation's Southeast (see map 3-3). Among areas with at least 100,000 Hispanics, those with the fastest growth were located largely in the Southeast, led by Charlotte and Raleigh, North Carolina, and Nashville, Tennessee, each of which experienced a 1,000 percent increase in its Hispanic population in a 20-year period (see table 3-2). Much of that gain was triggered by the attraction of both immigrant and domestic migrant flows of largely low-skilled Hispanic workers, for reasons indicated earlier. However, an increasing share of this growth can be attributed to the natural increase (births minus deaths) of residents as they settle in. Nationally, natural increase accounted for 63 percent of Hispanic population growth between 2000 and 2010.[24]

The spread of Hispanic growth can also be seen when looking at the Hispanic percentages of local populations. Nearly all of the nation's more than 3,100 counties have registered increases in Hispanic populations since 1990. Among the 1,158 counties where Hispanics made up at

MAP 3-2

**America's Racial Kaleidoscope: Counties where minorities are overrepresented, 2010[a]**

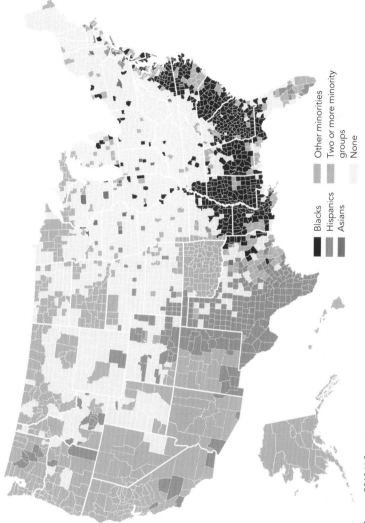

Blacks

Hispanics

Asians

Other minorities

Two or more minority
groups

None

Source: 2010 U.S. census.

[a]Counties where group contains at least the national 2010 share for Hispanics (16.3 percent), blacks (12.2 percent), or Asians (4.7 percent). "Other minorities" pertains to counties where the sum of American Indians and Alaska Natives, persons identifying with two or more races, and persons of some other race constitute at least a 4 percent share of the population. "Two or more minority groups" pertains to counties where two or more of the groups—Hispanics, blacks, Asians, or other minorities—are overrepresented.

MAP 3-3
**Metropolitan Areas with Largest Hispanic Populations, 2010[a]**

HISPANIC POPULATION, 2010

- 2.0 million
- 1.0 million
- 500,000

HISPANIC POPULATION GROWTH, 1990–2010

- 300% or more
- 150–300%
- 100–150%
- Less than 100%

Source: 1990 and 2010 U.S. censuses.

[a]Only metropolitan areas with Hispanic populations exceeding 100,000 are displayed.

MAP 3-4
**Hispanic Concentration Shifts for Counties, 1990–2010**

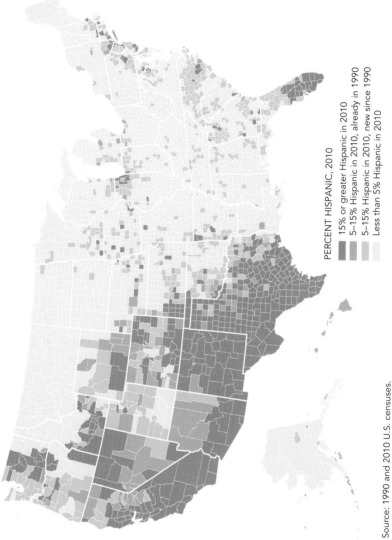

PERCENT HISPANIC, 2010

15% or greater Hispanic in 2010
5–15% Hispanic in 2010, already in 1990
5–15% Hispanic in 2010, new since 1990
Less than 5% Hispanic in 2010

Source: 1990 and 2010 U.S. censuses.

MAP 3-5
**Metropolitan Areas with Largest Asian Populations, 2010[a]**

New York

Washington, DC

Chicago

San Francisco

San Jose

Los Angeles

ASIAN POPULATION, 2010
2.0 million
1.0 million
500,000

ASIAN POPULATION GROWTH, 1990–2010
200% or more
160–200%
100–160%
Less than 100%

Source: 1990 and 2010 U.S. censuses.

[a]Only metropolitan areas with Asian populations exceeding 25,000 are displayed

MAP 3-6
**Asian Concentration Shifts for Counties, 1990–2010**

PERCENT ASIAN, 2010

10% or greater Asian in 2010

2–10% Asian in 2010, already in 1990

2–10% Asian in 2010, new since 1990

Less than 2% Asian in 2010

Source: 1990 and 2010 U.S. censuses.

MAP 3-7
**Metropolitan Areas with Largest Black Populations, 2010ᵃ**

BLACK POPULATION, 2010

- 2.0 million
- 1.0 million
- 500,000

BLACK POPULATION GROWTH, 1990–2010

- 50% or more
- 30–50%
- 10–30%
- Less than 10%

Source: 1990 and 2010 U.S. censuses.

ᵃOnly metropolitan areas with Black populations exceeding 100,000 are displayed.

New York
Philadelphia
Washington, DC
Atlanta
Miami
Detroit
Chicago
Houston
Dallas
Los Angeles

MAP 3-8
**Black Concentration for Counties, 2010**

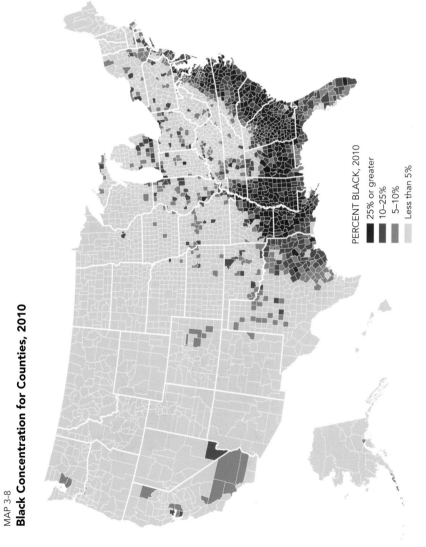

PERCENT BLACK, 2010

25% or greater
10–25%
5–10%
Less than 5%

Source: 2010 U.S. census.

MAP 3-9
**American Indians/Alaska Native Concentration, 2010**

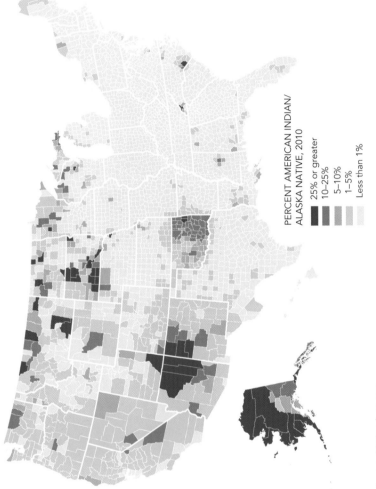

PERCENT AMERICAN INDIAN/
ALASKA NATIVE, 2010

25% or greater
10–25%
5–10%
1–5%
Less than 1%

Source: 2010 U.S. census.

MAP 3-10
**Persons Identifying as Two or More Races: Concentration, 2010**

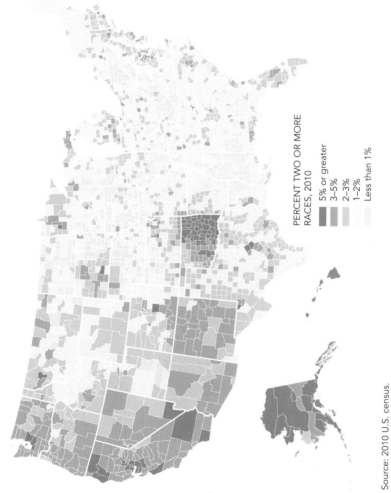

PERCENT TWO OR MORE
RACES, 2010

5% or greater
3–5%
2–3%
1–2%
Less than 1%

Source: 2010 U.S. census.

MAP 3-11
**White Growth by County, 1990–2010**

PERCENT GROWTH, 1990–2010

- 15% or greater
- 10–15%
- 0–10%
- Negative growth

Source: 1990–2010 U.S. censuses.

MAP 3-12
**Percent White, U.S. Counties, 2010[a]**

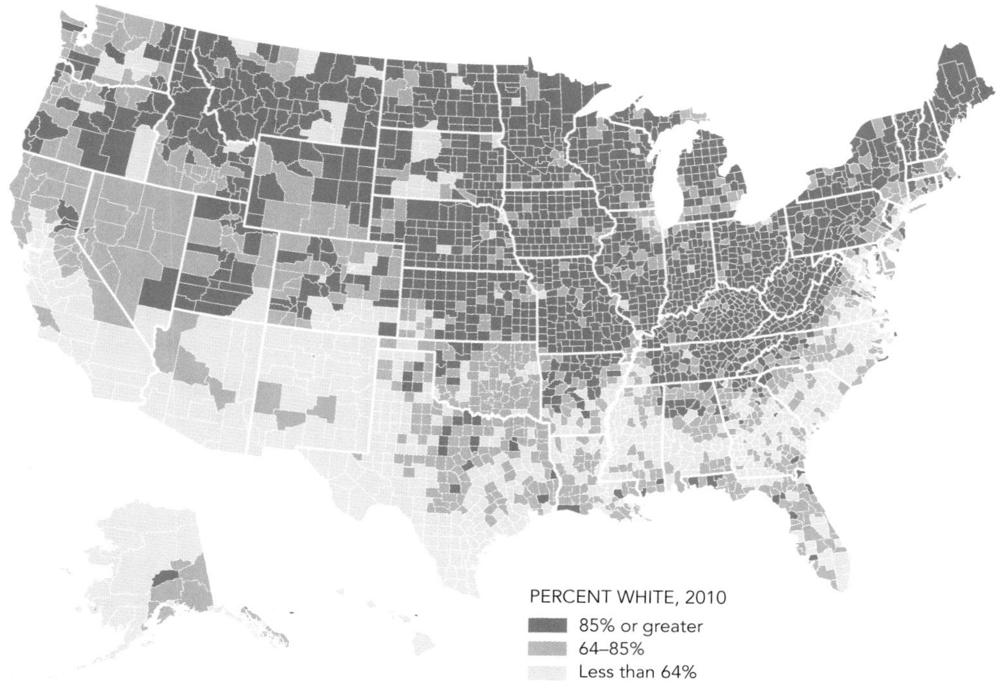

PERCENT WHITE, 2010

85% or greater

64–85%

Less than 64%

Source: 2010 U.S. census.

[a] National white percentage is 64%.

MAP 3-13
**Minority-White Metropolitan Areas, 2010[a]**

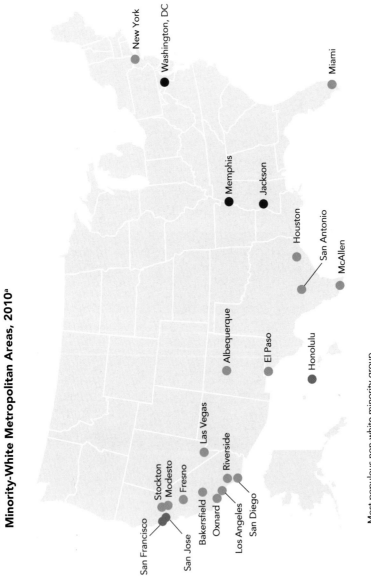

Most populous non-white minority group

● Hispanics
● Blacks
● Asians

Source: 2010 U.S. census.

[a] 22 minority-white areas among the 100 largest metropolitan areas.

least 5 percent of the population, more than one-half reached that threshold between 1990 and 2010 (see map 3-4). As in metropolitan areas, this trend is reflected in a substantial Hispanic spread into counties of the New Sun Belt states as well as a spread inward from the northeastern seaboard into parts of the Midwest, where low-skilled manufacturing, meatpacking, and farming industries attracted new Hispanic workers.[25]

## Dispersal of Asians

Because a greater share of Asians than Hispanics is foreign-born, Asians are concentrated in traditional gateway metropolitan areas.[26] Los Angeles, New York, and San Francisco are home to the largest Asian populations, and they accounted for more than one-third of all U.S. Asians in 2010 (see map 3-5). Yet in the 1990–2010 period, the Asian population more than doubled in areas outside those major gateway areas, largely in areas in the New Sun Belt. Among metropolitan areas with at least 25,000 Asians, Las Vegas witnessed the fastest growth, 625 percent, from 1990 to 2010 (see table 3-2). Other rapid gains occurred in Raleigh,

TABLE 3-2

**Fastest-Growing Metropolitan Areas for Hispanics, Asians, and Blacks, 1990–2010**
*Percent*

| Rank | Area[a] | Growth rate |
|---|---|---|
| Hispanics[b] | | |
| 1 | Charlotte | 1,715 |
| 2 | Raleigh | 1,548 |
| 3 | Nashville | 1,235 |
| 4 | Indianapolis | 853 |
| 5 | Atlanta | 831 |
| 6 | Cape Coral | 651 |
| 7 | Las Vegas | 586 |
| 8 | Lakeland | 542 |
| 9 | Orlando | 435 |
| 10 | Portland | 376 |
| Asians[c] | | |
| 1 | Las Vegas | 625 |
| 2 | Raleigh | 502 |
| 3 | Charlotte | 432 |
| 4 | Atlanta | 399 |
| 5 | Austin | 350 |
| 6 | Orlando | 324 |
| 7 | Phoenix | 314 |
| 8 | Indianapolis | 298 |
| 9 | Nashville | 274 |
| 10 | Tampa | 266 |
| Blacks[d] | | |
| 1 | Las Vegas | 183 |
| 2 | Minneapolis–St. Paul | 170 |
| 3 | Phoenix | 160 |
| 4 | Orlando | 123 |
| 5 | Atlanta | 118 |
| 6 | Raleigh | 95 |
| 7 | Charlotte | 88 |
| 8 | Riverside | 78 |
| 9 | Tampa | 71 |
| 10 | Dallas | 71 |

Source: 1990 and 2010 U.S. censuses.
[a]Metropolitan names are abbreviated.
[b]Areas with at least 100,000 Hispanics.
[c]Areas with at least 25,000 Asians.
[d]Areas with at least 100,000 blacks.

Charlotte, Atlanta, Austin, and Phoenix—areas with significant knowledge-based employment or university clusters. Many Asian migrants, especially those with advanced degrees and specialized skills, have gravitated to those areas.[27] Map 3-6 shows the dispersion of Asians as a percentage of county population. Because Asians represent just 5 percent of the U.S. population, few counties have large shares of Asians, but the number of counties with Asian populations of more than 2 percent grew from 200 in 1990 to more than 400 in 2010. These counties are located in smaller areas of the Southeast, Northeast, and Midwest, including urban, suburban, and rural areas, reflecting a broader residence mix of Asian professionals, farmworkers, and laborers than existed just two decades prior.

**Black Concentration in the South**

The black population grew far more modestly than the two new minorities over the 1990–2010 period, with a rate of 29 percent. In contrast, the growth rate was 108 percent for Asians and 126 percent for Hispanics. Black residential patterns reflect a long-standing southern concentration, the early-twentieth-century "Great Migration" to large cities of the North and West, and the post-1970 reverse migration back to the quickly growing parts of the South.[28] The latter southward shift has been especially pronounced since 1990, as discussed in chapter 6, and continues today.

Although blacks were once directed to well-worn migration channels based on kinship ties, in much the same way that new minorities have been, the post–civil rights generations of younger, more educated blacks have dispersed away from traditional northern and western cities, both to the South and to other parts of the country. Still, the distribution of blacks across metropolitan areas reveals residential settlements, both past and current. The metropolitan area with the largest black population is New York (see map 3-7). New York's sizable black population draws from decades of earlier black migration, new immigration, and natural increase. Yet despite its large size, New York experienced an absolute loss of blacks in 2000–10, due largely to the southward flow of black migrants.

Until 2010, metropolitan Chicago was home to the country's second-largest black population, but Chicago dropped to third place, as large migration flows catapulted Atlanta to second place. Following New York, Atlanta, and Chicago are a mix of earlier black destinations in the North and West (Philadelphia, Detroit, and Los Angeles) and southern areas with large and growing black populations (Washington, D.C., Miami,

Houston, and Dallas). Among large metropolitan areas, rapidly growing black populations are found in southern metropolitan areas like Orlando, Atlanta, Raleigh, Charlotte, and Dallas (see table 3-2). Also growing rapidly (although with smaller black populations overall) are Las Vegas and Phoenix, as a result of populations dispersing from coastal California, and Minneapolis–St. Paul, a nontraditional midwestern destination. The continuing southern concentration of the black population is abundantly clear in map 3-8. However, there are clusters of blacks in smaller-sized urban and suburban areas in much of the Northeast, Midwest, and selected parts of the West, including areas around Los Angeles, San Francisco, Seattle, Las Vegas, and Denver.

### American Indians and Alaska Natives

The American Indian and Alaska Native population is the oldest U.S. racial minority group. With many tribes originating in different parts of the country, this population comprised 2.9 million persons, or 0.9 percent of the U.S. population, in 2010. Its numbers have proliferated over time, a result of not only traditional demographic change components but also the greater likelihood that people with some American Indian heritage will identify themselves as such.[29] In fact, when persons who identified themselves as belonging to multiple races were counted, the 2010 numbers for American Indians and Alaska Natives increased to 5.2 million, or 1.7 percent of the population.[30] This population has a patchy distribution, but it is heavily located west of the Mississippi River. Five states are home to more than 150,000 American Indians and Alaska Natives: California, Oklahoma, Arizona, New Mexico, and Texas. The ten most populous metropolitan areas, except for New York, are located in these states (see table 3-3).

The clustering of American Indians and Alaska Natives reflects both historic and recent settlement patterns. In 2010, less than one-third lived inside reservations or native village areas. The largest area is the Apache reservation, straddling Arizona, New Mexico, and Utah.[31] Other states with large reservation and native village populations are Montana, South Dakota, North Dakota, Oklahoma, Wyoming, and Washington. In addition to Alaska, many of these states, particularly South Dakota, New Mexico, Oklahoma, Montana, and North Dakota, exhibit the highest per-

TABLE 3-3
**American Indian and Alaska Native Populations, Metropolitan Area Rankings, 2010[a]**

| Largest American Indian/Alaska Native populations | | | Highest percent shares: American Indian/Alaska Native of total population | | |
|---|---|---|---|---|---|
| Rank | Metropolitan area | Size | Rank | Metropolitan area | Percent share |
| 1 | Phoenix, AZ | 99,278 | 1 | Farmington, NM | 36.6 |
| 2 | New York, NY | 92,632 | 2 | Flagstaff, AZ | 27.3 |
| 3 | Los Angeles, CA | 90,960 | 3 | Tulsa, OK | 8.3 |
| 4 | Tulsa, OK | 77,388 | 4 | Rapid City, SD | 8.2 |
| 5 | Albuquerque, NM | 51,987 | 5 | Anchorage, AK | 7.4 |
| 6 | Oklahoma City, OK | 51,303 | 6 | Fairbanks, AK | 7.0 |
| 7 | Farmington, NM | 47,640 | 7 | Fort Smith, AR-OK | 6.3 |
| 8 | Riverside, CA | 46,399 | 8 | Albuquerque, NM | 5.9 |
| 9 | Dallas, TX | 43,390 | 9 | Lawton, OK | 5.9 |
| 10 | Houston, TX | 38,236 | 10 | Houma, LA | 4.3 |

Source: 2010 U.S. census.

[a] Pertains to persons who identified American Indian/Alaska Native as their only racial group. Rankings are based on all metropolitan areas (names abbreviated).

centages of Indians and Alaska Natives living both on and off reservations, as is evident when the counties with large Indian and Alaska Native percentages are examined (see map 3-9). Only 700 of the nation's more than 3,100 counties have American Indian populations of greater than 1 percent. Although multiracial persons who identify themselves as partly American Indian are both more numerous and more spread out, their population distribution is still highly concentrated in a small number of areas.[32]

**Multiracial Population**

The rise in racial diversity is apparent in a small but growing minority of the population that identifies itself as multiracial—associated with two or more of the standard racial groups (white, black, Asian, American Indian/Alaska Native, and other races). In the 2010 census, a little more than 9 million people, nearly 3 percent of the population, classified themselves as multiracial, an increase of almost one-third since 2000.[33] The most prominent multiracial combinations are white/black, white/Asian, and white/American Indian and Alaska Native.[34]

TABLE 3-4

**Persons Identifying as Two or More Races, Metropolitan Area Rankings, 2010**[a]

| Rank | Largest two-or-more-race populations | | Rank | Highest percent shares: Two or more races of total population | |
|---|---|---|---|---|---|
| Rank | Metropolitan area | Size | Rank | Metropolitan area | Percent share |
| 1 | New York, NY | 612,704 | 1 | Honolulu, HI | 22.3 |
| 2 | Los Angeles, CA | 566,512 | 2 | Anchorage, AK | 7.7 |
| 3 | San Francisco, CA | 239,784 | 3 | Vallejo-Fairfield, CA | 7.6 |
| 4 | Chicago, IL | 230,168 | 4 | Fairbanks, AK | 6.8 |
| 5 | Honolulu, HI | 213,036 | 5 | Lawton, OK | 6.5 |
| 6 | Riverside, CA | 207,028 | 6 | Stockton, CA | 6.4 |
| 7 | Washington, DC | 205,513 | 7 | Tulsa, OK | 6.4 |
| 8 | Seattle, WA | 183,868 | 8 | Yuba City, CA | 6.2 |
| 9 | Dallas, TX | 179,763 | 9 | Sacramento, CA | 5.9 |
| 10 | Houston, TX | 179,509 | 10 | Bremerton, WA | 5.8 |

Source: 2010 U.S. census.

[a] Rankings are based on all metropolitan areas (names abbreviated).

Metropolitan areas with the largest multiracial populations, led by New York, Los Angeles, and San Francisco, tend to also have large minority populations (see table 3-4). Yet highly concentrated multiracial populations are clustered in large Melting Pot and growing New Sun Belt states, especially in the West, as well as areas with large American Indian/Alaska Native populations and Hawaii (see map 3-10). The population of metropolitan Honolulu has the highest share of multiracial individuals—22 percent. Although most of the country's counties have small multiracial populations constituting 1 to 3 percent of the population, only a tiny number of counties have less. Overall, the multiracial population is growing and becoming more pervasive in New Sun Belt states.

**Pervasive and Declining White Populations**

The most recent census showed that although whites still constitute the majority of the U.S. population, the group grew by a mere 1.2 percent between 2000 and 2010; the total nonwhite population, in contrast, grew by 29 percent. Therefore many parts of the country show faster minority than white growth, including broad stretches where whites are declining. Interestingly, the same areas that are attracting white growth tend to overlap with parts of the New Sun Belt that are increasingly attracting minorities (see map 3-11).

Like domestic migrants in general, whites have left expensive, congested coastal areas in the Melting Pot and small, economically depressed areas of the Great Plains, Midwest, and Northeast for the more rapidly growing parts of the South and West and select suburban and high-amenity counties in other regions. In 2000–10, 53 percent of the nation's more than 3,100 counties suffered white population losses, as did 15 states and 42 of the nation's 100 largest metropolitan areas, including foreign immigrant magnets like New York and Los Angeles. Despite the losses, a large part of the country—with both declining and growing white populations—remains predominantly white. As map 3-12 shows, a broad range of counties in the country's northern interior region are more than 85 percent white. Most of these areas have declining or slowly growing populations whose white losses are not being replenished by new minorities and blacks. In contrast, many counties in the South and West have white population shares below 64 percent, the overall U.S. white share. The seeming contradiction between high growth and low shares of whites reflects the new growing parts of the country—economically healthy areas that are attracting whites, blacks, and new minorities, a description that characterizes much of the New Sun Belt.

## MAJORITY-MINORITY AMERICA

The previous discussion of minority and white population shifts suggests that in much of the Melting Pot and increasingly in the New Sun Belt, the nation's growing diversity is leading to majority-minority areas. This is most likely to be the case in large metropolitan areas, given that both of the major new minority groups and blacks are more likely to gravitate to big urban areas than are whites.[35] Among the nation's 100 largest metropolitan areas, 22 already were minority-white in 2010, as shown in map 3-13—an increase from just five minority-white areas in 1990 and 14 in 2000. Most of these areas are located in the Melting Pot states of California and Texas. The largest of them—New York, Los Angeles, and several others—follow the Melting Pot pattern of white population losses coupled with primarily immigrant-driven gains from new minorities.[36]

So, from a spatial perspective, new minorities are increasingly spreading out from large Melting Pot metropolitan areas to the New Sun Belt. In the latter region, especially in its economically vibrant areas, white and black gains are accompanied by gains among Hispanics and Asians, who take both the low- and the high-skilled jobs that are being created. Every one of the 100 largest metropolitan areas is becoming more diverse, but some of the biggest shifts are occurring in the New Sun Belt, led by Las Vegas, whose white percentage declined from 75 to 48 percent between 1990 and 2010. Some others showing noticeable declines in the share of whites are Atlanta, Phoenix, Seattle, and Charlotte.

Figures 3-3 and 3-4 provide a comparison of racial shifts across four prototypical metropolitan areas: one Melting Pot area (Los Angeles); two New Sun Belt areas (Phoenix and Atlanta); and one Heartland area (Detroit). Los Angeles represents a large immigrant hub that has been

FIGURE 3-3

**Race Components of Population Change in Four Metropolitan Areas, 1990–2010**

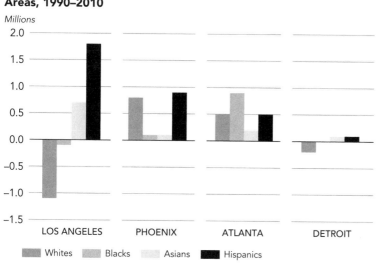

Source: 1990 and 2010 U.S. censuses.

FIGURE 3-4
**Race Profiles of Four Metropolitan Areas, 1990 and 2010**

*Percent*

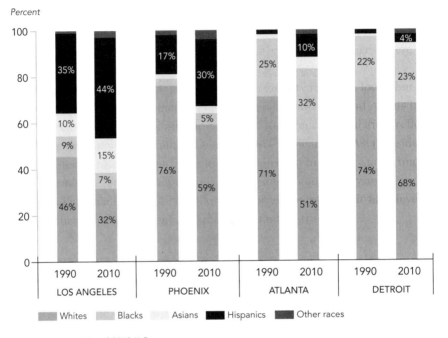

Source: 1990 and 2010 U.S. censuses.

losing middle-income whites and blacks through migration to areas with lower housing costs and better employment opportunities. Some Hispanics and Asians are part of this out-migration, but even larger population gains among these new immigrant groups due to immigration and natural population increase have been the primary sources of the area's population gain for more than 20 years. Consequently, metropolitan Los Angeles, which already was minority-white in 1990, is becoming even more diverse.

Phoenix and Atlanta are New Sun Belt areas that share a pattern of substantial white and black gains as well as new minority gains. Each has drawn whites, both from Melting Pot areas such as Los Angeles and New York and from slow-growth parts of the country that are losing white domestic migrants. In Atlanta, black gains, which come heavily from domestic migration, are overtaking population gains among whites and other minorities. Still, the economic success of both of these areas has lured Hispanics and Asians, thus making each area more diverse than it was in 1990 and on track to become minority-white.

Finally, Detroit represents an example of a Heartland metropolitan area in the industrial Midwest that experienced noticeable white out-migration from 1990 to 2010 that was countered by small gains in the Asian and Hispanic populations. As in other midwestern manufacturing areas, Asian population gains in Detroit are similar to or greater than those for Hispanics.[37] That can be attributed to the fact that many Asians were drawn to these areas by employment opportunities rather than by the family and kinship bonds that drew large numbers of Hispanics to Melting Pot metropolitan areas in the Southwest. The small gains in the black population of Detroit are more a result of natural increase than migration.

Overall, the profiles for Los Angeles, Phoenix, Atlanta, and Detroit paint—in broad strokes—the sweep of new minorities, blacks, and whites across the national landscape toward the New Sun Belt, which functions as a transition area incorporating the growing diversity in the United States. Just as new minorities are bubbling up the age structure, from young to old, across the nation, so too are they moving from large Melting Pot areas to the New Sun Belt and beyond. The four chapters that follow take a closer look at how the new racial dynamics are playing out for Hispanics, Asians, blacks, and whites.

# Hispanics Fan Out
## Who Goes Where?

# 4

Hispanics are poised to make the greatest contribution to the nation's population growth in the foreseeable future. Yet they are hardly a monolithic group. Although public perception often conflates the Hispanic population with Mexican immigrants, U.S. Hispanics increasingly will be native-born Americans from a variety of origins. And as Hispanics spread out beyond the Melting Pot region, their demographic attributes began to vary widely by location. This chapter shows that the concept of the Hispanic community takes on different meanings in different settings and that its greatest potential contribution is likely to occur in those parts of the country where the Hispanic presence is just beginning to emerge.

## NATIONAL PICTURE

As a group, Hispanics have become a formidable presence in the United States and will be a more formidable presence in the future. Although they are classed here as one of the nation's new minorities by virtue of their recent rapid population growth, Hispanics began inhabiting much of today's western U.S. territory well before this region became part of the nation.[1] Yet by virtue of large waves of immigration from Mexico and other parts of Latin America from the 1970s through the 1990s, the Hispanic population more than tripled, from less than 10 million to more than 35 million. Furthermore, despite an immigration slowdown during the period after the 2007–09 recession, the Hispanic population grew by another 15 million in the first decade of the 2000s (see figures 4-1a and 4-1b).[2]

It is important to understand that the most recent Hispanic population growth is due to natural increase (the number of births minus deaths) rather than immigration.[3] Of course, the origins and size of future immigration flows are subject to economic conditions and policy changes. Yet even if immigration from Latin America continues at a similar or slower pace than in the past, the existing Hispanic population is large enough to produce substantial increases in its population through natural increase.[4]

Partly because of the history and the 2,000-mile border that the United States and Mexico share, the largest portion of the U.S. Hispanic population identifies itself as being of Mexican origin. This population includes both U.S.-born and foreign-born residents, some of whom are undocumented.[5] There are more than 30 million residents of Mexican origin in the United States—a number that overwhelms the number of Puerto Ricans and Cubans, who make up the next-largest Hispanic groups. The population of Mexican origin also is growing nearly twice as rapidly as the latter populations. Yet as of 2010, 37 percent of the Hispanic population identified with other Latin American countries or with Hispanic heritage in general.[6] Most of these groups have been growing even faster than Mexicans, Puerto Ricans, or Cubans because of the recent immigration of workers looking for jobs, relatives rejoining families, refugees, and asylum seekers.[7] Between 1990 and 2010, the group of

FIGURE 4-1a
**U.S. Hispanic Population, 1970–2010**

*Millions*

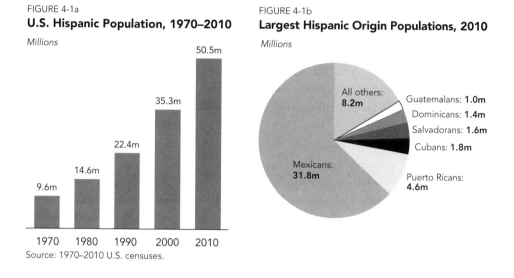

Source: 1970–2010 U.S. censuses.

FIGURE 4-1b
**Largest Hispanic Origin Populations, 2010**

*Millions*

residents identifying themselves as Guatemalans, Salvadorans, and Dominicans grew well over 150 percent, increasing their shares of the Hispanic population (see figure 4-2).

Although the social and economic makeup of the Hispanic population is in a state of flux, it differs markedly from that of the total population, particularly the white population. Hispanic differences with whites stem from the fact that the Hispanic population is younger and grew from immigrants who were heavily attracted by low-skilled jobs. Almost one-third of Hispanics are under 18 years of age, three out of ten Hispanic households are "traditional" families composed of a married couple and their children, and one-half of all Hispanic households include children. In contrast, fewer than one in five white households is a traditional family and only 27 percent of white households of any type includes children (see table 4-1.)

Education attainment among Hispanics also stands in stark contrast to attainment among whites. As of 2015, 34 percent of Hispanic adults but only 8 percent of whites had not graduated from high school. That statistic reflects, to some degree, the arrival of both legal and undocumented Hispanic immigrant workers responding to the

FIGURE 4-2
**Growth of Largest Hispanic Origin Populations, 1990–2010**

*Growth rates*

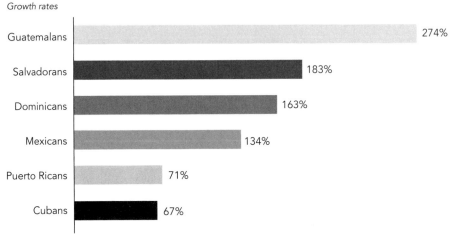

Source: 1990 and 2010 U.S. censuses.

considerable demand for low-skilled workers.[8] Similarly, only 15 percent of Hispanics but more than one-third of whites and 31 percent of the total population held college degrees. Native-born Hispanics are better educated than those born abroad, and U.S.-born Hispanic children have been making strides in educational attainment.[9] Yet the educational gap is still very wide and remains an important obstacle to Hispanic economic and social mobility. This gap mirrors similar gaps between Hispanics and whites with respect to levels of poverty and homeownership. Another change that Hispanics have brought to the U.S. population is the use of the Spanish language, which is especially pronounced among foreign-born Hispanics.[10] Although that adds to the multicultural character of communities across the country and aids in the adaptation of Hispanic immigrants to life in the United States, it also creates a barrier to some employment and educational opportunities. In 2015, 27 percent of Hispanic residents spoke only English at home, and more than three in ten did not speak English very well. Both statistics differ markedly from those of the total U.S. and white populations.

TABLE 4-1

**Social and Demographic Profiles, Hispanics, Whites, and Total U.S. Population, 2015**
*Percent*

| Profile | Hispanics | Whites | Total U.S. |
|---|---|---|---|
| *Nativity* | | | |
| Percent foreign born | 34 | 4 | 13 |
| *English proficiency (ages 5+)* | | | |
| Speaks only English at home | 27 | 95 | 79 |
| Does not speak English very well | 31 | 2 | 9 |
| *Age* | | | |
| Under 18 | 32 | 19 | 23 |
| 18–29 | 20 | 15 | 17 |
| 30–44 | 22 | 18 | 19 |
| 45–64 | 19 | 29 | 26 |
| 65+ | 7 | 19 | 15 |
| *Household type* | | | |
| Married couples with children | 30 | 19 | 20 |
| Married couples without children | 18 | 32 | 28 |
| Other families with children | 20 | 8 | 11 |
| Other households without children[a] | 32 | 41 | 41 |
| *Education (ages 25+)* | | | |
| Not high school graduate | 34 | 8 | 13 |
| High school only | 27 | 28 | 27 |
| Some college | 24 | 30 | 29 |
| College graduate | 15 | 34 | 31 |
| *Poverty status* | | | |
| Percent persons below poverty | 23 | 10 | 15 |
| *Homeownership* | | | |
| Percent owners | 45 | 71 | 63 |

Source: American Community Survey, 2015.

[a]Includes "other families without children" and "nonfamily households" (persons living alone or with nonrelatives).

The sharp contrast between relatively younger Hispanic and older white populations on dimensions such as language, nativity, family type, economic status, and education attainment tends to reinforce the cultural generation gap between the two groups. Yet this gap may abate given that the growing, younger Hispanic population is in a constant state of flux as new immigrants infuse its ranks and future generations take different paths. Second- and third-generation Hispanics and longer-term resident immigrants tend to move toward the mainstream in positive ways, showing greater English proficiency, modest improvements in education attainment, and ascension up the economic ladder (as measured by higher rates of homeownership).[11] They also tend to become "Americanized" with regard to family and household relationships as their fertility rates decline and traditional families become less prominent.[12] These shifts toward the mainstream are occurring slowly. They also differ across types of Hispanic communities and across Hispanics of different national origins.

## OLD COMMUNITIES, NEW COMMUNITIES

The continued Hispanic population spillover from original settlement areas such as Los Angeles, New York, and Miami is now affecting all parts of the country. Many of these moves have been spurred by jobs in construction, retail trade, personal and repair services, meatpacking, and manufacturing.[13] A large number of Hispanic destinations were already economically thriving New Sun Belt areas such as Atlanta and Charlotte. The growth of these areas led to demand for workers in construction and other low-skilled, consumer-driven industries, which in turn drew new waves of Hispanic workers who might be thought of as "tag-along" migrants within the broader migration trend.[14] Atlanta and Charlotte are bigger versions of many smaller metropolitan areas whose recent overall growth has attracted greater numbers of Hispanics. These new destinations—located in much of the New Sun Belt portions of the South and West and increasingly in parts of the North and Midwest— typically had small Hispanic populations as late as 1990, but they have shown dramatic increases since then.

Still another set of Hispanic magnet areas had sizable Hispanic populations to begin with, but because of their robust economies, they became magnets for even greater growth by attracting both Hispanic and non-Hispanic populations. Examples include Dallas and Orlando— the former a New Sun Belt aviation hub and high-tech center that has expanded in many sectors and the latter a tourism and entertainment center that includes more diversified high-tech sectors. These areas, along with others like them, also have attracted tag-along Hispanic migrants. Map 4-1 portrays metropolitan areas whose Hispanic

MAP 4-1
**Hispanic Concentration Areas and New Hispanic Destinations**

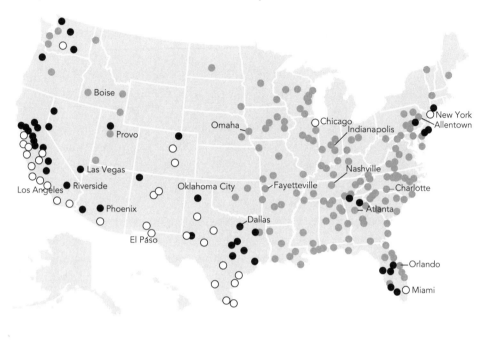

This map displays 222 metropolitan areas classed as:

○ **Hispanic concentration/**
**modest growth** (33 areas)
*Hispanics at least 16 percent*
*of 2010 population and less than*
*43 percent 2000–10 growth*

● **Hispanic concentration/**
**fast growth** (44 areas)
*Hispanics at least 16 percent*
*of 2010 population and at least*
*43 percent 2000–10 growth*

● **New Hispanic destinations**
(145 areas) *Hispanics less than*
*16 percent of 2010 population*
*and at least 86 percent*
*2000–10 growth*

Source: 2010 U.S. census.

growth patterns are of three different types: Hispanic concentration/
modest-growth areas; Hispanic concentration/fast-growth areas; and
new Hispanic destinations.[15]

*Hispanic concentration/modest-growth areas.* These are the more
traditional Hispanic settlement areas, where the Hispanic share of the
population equals or exceeds the national Hispanic share (16 percent).
However, the 2000–10 Hispanic population growth rate in these areas
is less than the national Hispanic growth rate (43 percent). There are

33 of these areas, which include large settlement areas such Los Angeles and New York but also smaller areas such as El Paso and Laredo, Texas; Albuquerque, New Mexico; Tucson, Arizona; and Fresno and Santa Ana, California.

*Hispanic concentration/fast-growth areas.* These are areas, such as Dallas and Orlando, that have sizable Hispanic populations and also have shown rapid growth in recent years. There are 44 such areas, in which Hispanics are at least 16 percent of the population and the 2000–10 Hispanic population growth rate is at least 43 percent. Among these areas are Las Vegas; Phoenix; Riverside, California; Salt Lake City; Houston; and Tampa.

*New Hispanic destinations.* These are areas, such as Atlanta and Charlotte, that have smaller Hispanic populations but an extremely fast Hispanic population growth rate, reflecting recent gains from migration. In these locales, less than 16 percent of the total population is Hispanic but the 2000–10 Hispanic growth rate is at least 86 percent—twice the national growth rate for Hispanics. Among these 145 areas are a slew of areas in the South, including Fayetteville, Arkansas, and Nashville; Mountain West areas such as Provo, Utah, and Boise, Idaho; selected areas in the middle of the country such as Oklahoma City, Omaha, and Indianapolis; and some in close proximity to New York City, such as Allentown, Pennsylvania.

The 145 new Hispanic destinations contain a mere 7.4 percent of U.S. Hispanics; however, these areas are on the cutting edge of growth, having increased their Hispanic populations by 119 percent over the decade. In contrast, the Hispanic growth rate was 61 percent for the fast-growth areas and just 24 percent for the modest-growth areas. The new destinations are of the most interest because they reflect the expanding periphery of the Hispanic growth surge. Among the metropolitan areas with the fastest Hispanic growth rates are Scranton, Pennsylvania; Winchester, Virginia; Knoxville, Tennessee; Wilmington, North Carolina; Louisville, Kentucky; St. George, Utah; and Bend, Oregon.

As indicated above, quite a few of these areas are experiencing faster overall growth than the nation as a whole. In many, Hispanics contributed only a portion to that growth. For example, even though the Hispanic population in Charlotte grew by 153 percent in 2000–10, it contributed less than one-quarter to Charlotte's overall population gain. In St. George, Utah, where the Hispanic growth rate was 185 percent, Hispanics contributed less than one-fifth to the total population gain. Yet in other new Hispanic destination areas, especially in the Northeast, Hispanics were essential to population growth. Both Scranton, Pennsylvania, and Pittsfield, Massachusetts, would have lost population were it not for the rapid Hispanic increases in recent years. In both kinds of new destination areas, Hispanics face the issue of fitting in—with a largely white population in much of the country outside the South and a mostly white and black mixed population in the South. As a group, Hispanics constituted just 6 percent of the total population in these new destinations.

This contrasts with the scenario in Hispanic concentration/fast-growth areas, where assimilation prospects are somewhat better because the new gains add to large, already established Hispanic populations. In Houston, for example, the 2000 Hispanic population of 1.3 million had increased to more than 2 million by 2010. Yet even in these areas there are assimilation difficulties. A significant portion of the recent Hispanic gains have tended to occur in new areas of the city—or often the suburbs—creating challenges to integration with the established community, not to mention access to government services such as social services and language-appropriate schooling.

## HISPANICS IN NEW DESTINATIONS ARE DIFFERENT

Any influx of new people into an established area has the potential to result in cultural clashes and difficulties for the new residents in fitting in. In locales without any history of Hispanic settlement, the changes can be abrupt. The question is this: How different are Hispanic newcomers in quickly growing areas from those in more traditional Hispanic settlements? Or more specifically, are Hispanic residents in new communities less well-equipped to fit in than those in established Hispanic areas? Table 4-2, which contrasts the 2010 social and demographic profiles of Hispanic residents in the three types of metropolitan areas discussed above, reveals clear distinctions between Hispanics residing in new destinations and those in established areas, beginning with the higher share of the Hispanic population residing in new destinations that is foreign born and young. Nearly one-half (46 percent) of Hispanics in new destinations are foreign born. They are also somewhat younger than Hispanics in other area types, reflecting the new movement of foreign-born and young workers with families to these areas. Hispanics in southeastern new destinations are especially likely to be foreign born—

TABLE 4-2

**Profiles of Hispanics in Concentration Areas and New Destinations, 2010**

*Percent*

| Profile[a] | Hispanic concentration/ modest growth | Hispanic concentration/ fast growth | New Hispanic destinations |
|---|---|---|---|
| *Nativity* | | | |
| Percent foreign-born | 41 | 37 | 46 |
| *English proficiency (ages 5+)* | | | |
| Does not speak English very well | 38 | 37 | 42 |
| *Age* | | | |
| Under 18 | 31 | 36 | 37 |
| 18–29 | 20 | 21 | 23 |
| 30–44 | 23 | 23 | 24 |
| 45–64 | 19 | 16 | 13 |
| 65+ | 7 | 4 | 3 |
| *Household Type* | | | |
| Married couple with children | 29 | 36 | 35 |
| Married couple without children | 20 | 18 | 15 |
| Other family with children | 16 | 17 | 17 |
| Other household without children[b] | 35 | 29 | 33 |
| *Education (males, ages 25+)* | | | |
| Less than high school | 38 | 44 | 41 |
| Beyond high school | 35 | 35 | 27 |
| *Poverty status* | | | |
| Percent below poverty | 21 | 21 | 25 |
| *Homeownership* | | | |
| Percent owners | 47 | 55 | 45 |

Source: 2010 U.S. census; American Community Survey, 2006–10.

[a]Average annual values for 2006–10 based on American Community Survey 2006–10 multiyear estimates, except for age, household type, and homeownership values, which are based on the 2010 U.S. census.

[b]Includes "other family without children" and "nonfamily household" (persons living alone or with nonrelatives).

in Atlanta, Charlotte, Nashville, Raleigh, and Memphis, more than one-half of Hispanic residents are foreign born.

Other aspects of new destination demographics follow from those attributes. Hispanics in these areas are less likely to speak English very well and are more likely than Hispanics overall to form households consisting of a married couple with children. The latter household type is especially prevalent in a wide array of areas, including Provo, Greensboro, Atlanta, Tulsa, Omaha, and Boise, where well over one-third of Hispanic households are traditional families. And because new destinations tend to attract low-skilled male workers, especially immigrants, low education attainment is pronounced in new destinations.[16] In traditional settlement areas, there are almost as many Hispanics who have received some post–high school education as there are high school dropouts, but dropouts are more prevalent in new destinations. Hispanics in these areas are also more likely to fall into poverty and less likely to own homes than Hispanics in other types of areas—all attributes that make their assimilation a more daunting challenge.

The Hispanic concentration/fast-growth areas share two attributes with new destinations: their Hispanic populations are relatively young and they have large numbers of males who have not graduated from high school. Many of these areas, such as Houston, Las Vegas, and Bakersfield and Modesto, California, are magnets for low-skilled workers. Yet others, such as Austin and Orlando, have large numbers of Hispanic college graduates. Still, the education challenge among Hispanics is especially pronounced in many rapidly growing metropolitan areas, where the education deficit is largest. This pattern is emphasized in map 4-2, which displays 90 metropolitan areas in which more than 45 percent of all Hispanic adult males do not have a high school diploma. Among the areas with the greatest shares of low-skilled workers are Winchester, Virginia; Rome, Georgia; and Tyler, Texas, where more than 60 percent of adult Hispanic males did not complete high school. The list is dominated by both new destination areas and Hispanic concentration/fast-growth areas, although some traditional concentration areas, such as Los Angeles and Yakima, Washington, also are included.

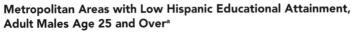

MAP 4-2
**Metropolitan Areas with Low Hispanic Educational Attainment,
Adult Males Age 25 and Over**[a]

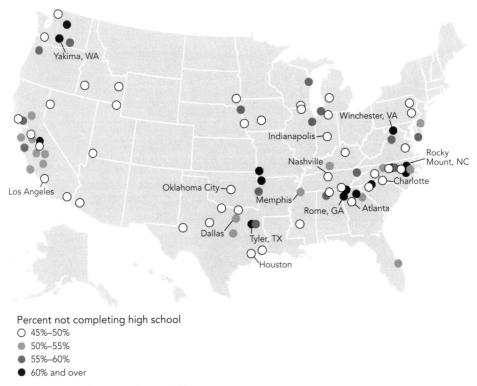

Percent not completing high school
○ 45%–50%
◔ 50%–55%
◕ 55%–60%
● 60% and over

Source: American Community Survey, 2010.

[a]Map displays 90 metropolitan areas with Hispanic populations greater than 5,000 and where at least 45 percent of Hispanic adult males have not completed high school.

The Hispanic educational deficit illustrates the especially great challenge in improving education attainment among current and future generations. Hispanic residents of new destinations are less poised to assimilate than Hispanics in traditional settlements. In general, such residents are more likely to be foreign born, less proficient in English, less educated, and poorer than the Hispanic population as a whole. Yet as youthful, family-oriented members of their new communities, they represent a growing segment of the populations of those areas. These communities will thrive best if extra efforts are made to accommodate their new Hispanic residents.

## MULTIPLE ORIGINS

Although many people conflate all U.S. Hispanics with Mexicans, nearly two-fifths of U.S. Hispanics do not claim Mexican heritage. Hispanic groups stemming from original settlers from Spain arrived in North America centuries ago, giving rise to Spanish-speaking populations. In the twentieth century, Latin Americans arrived because of U.S. demand for labor and changes in immigration laws, which now include refugee and asylum programs.[17] Those programs in turn led to the immigration of Cubans, Salvadorans, Guatemalans, and Nicaraguans, among others, to U.S. shores. In addition are the Puerto Ricans who live in the United States, most of whom already are deemed citizens. Because Hispanic origin groups differ from each other, there is no "typical" U.S. Hispanic.

Table 4-3 presents 2015 social and demographic profiles of the largest groups of Hispanic origin in the United States. One area of divergence is found for foreign-born immigrants. Apart from Puerto Ricans, who for the most part are U.S. citizens, and Mexicans, most other Hispanics are likely to be primarily foreign born. More of the other Hispanic groups either immigrated recently—or, in the case of Cubans, came decades ago as foreign-born refugees.

Majorities of the nation's quickly growing Salvadoran, Dominican, and Guatemalan populations are foreign born. Among these individuals, just a few speak only English at home and more than two-fifths do not speak English very well. In contrast, among Cubans and Mexicans, less than four in ten residents are not proficient English speakers, and less than two in ten Puerto Ricans are not proficient. The groups also differ with regard to age structure and family type. The group with the oldest population is Cubans, among whom there are almost as many seniors as children. Because of their age, two-thirds of Cuban households are childless. At the other end of the spectrum are Mexicans, among whom children constitute 35 percent of the population. Among all Hispanic origin groups, Mexicans have one of the highest shares of households

TABLE 4-3
**Profiles of Hispanic Origin Populations, 2015**
Percent

| Profile[a] | Mexicans | Puerto Ricans | Cubans | Salvadorans | Dominicans | Guatemalans |
|---|---|---|---|---|---|---|
| *Nativity* | | | | | | |
| Percent foreign-born | 32 | 2 | 56 | 59 | 54 | 61 |
| *English proficiency (Ages 5+)* | | | | | | |
| Speaks only English at home | 27 | 40 | 21 | 9 | 12 | 12 |
| Does not speak English very well | 31 | 17 | 39 | 49 | 42 | 54 |
| *Age* | | | | | | |
| Under 18 | 35 | 31 | 20 | 29 | 28 | 31 |
| 18–29 | 20 | 20 | 16 | 20 | 21 | 22 |
| 30–44 | 22 | 21 | 20 | 27 | 21 | 27 |
| 45–64 | 18 | 20 | 27 | 20 | 22 | 16 |
| 65+ | 5 | 8 | 17 | 4 | 8 | 4 |
| *Household type* | | | | | | |
| Married couples with children | 34 | 19 | 20 | 35 | 20 | 35 |
| Married couples without children | 17 | 18 | 26 | 16 | 15 | 13 |
| Other families with children | 21 | 22 | 12 | 24 | 28 | 23 |
| Other households without children[b] | 28 | 41 | 42 | 25 | 37 | 29 |
| *Education (Ages 25+)* | | | | | | |
| Not high school graduate | 39 | 21 | 21 | 48 | 32 | 52 |
| High school only | 28 | 29 | 29 | 25 | 26 | 23 |
| Some college | 22 | 31 | 24 | 18 | 25 | 16 |
| College graduate | 11 | 19 | 26 | 9 | 17 | 9 |
| *Poverty Status* | | | | | | |
| Percent below poverty | 24 | 25 | 18 | 21 | 28 | 27 |
| *Homeownership* | | | | | | |
| Percent owners | 48 | 36 | 52 | 42 | 24 | 31 |

Source: American Community Survey, 2011–15.

[a] Average annual values for 2011–2015 based on American Community Survey, 2011–2015, multiyear estimates.
[b] Includes "other family without children" and "nonfamily household" (persons living alone or with nonrelatives).

made up of a married couple with children. Salvadorans and Guatemalans both have large populations of working-age individuals, a result of their recent migration to take jobs in the United States. They also have a household profile similar to that of Mexicans, in that more than one-third are married couples with children. Puerto Ricans and Dominicans are similar in their age and household structures. Both are relatively young populations. But unlike Mexicans, Salvadorans, and Guatemalans, these two groups have more single-parent families than two-parent families, and they have more childless households than all other groups except Cubans. The family structures of both these groups are more similar to those of U.S. blacks than other Hispanic groups.

Differences on measures of education, poverty, and homeownership also are apparent. Cubans fare the best on all three measures. More than one-quarter of Cuban adults hold a college degree, over one-half own their home, and the Cuban poverty rate is the lowest of any of the groups. The rankings are less consistent among the other groups. On the "skill" dimension of education, Guatemalans, Salvadorans, and Mexicans show the lowest level of skills, as 39 to 52 percent of adults are not high school graduates. Nearly one-third of Dominicans also are low-skilled, but more than two in five have at least some post–high school education. After Cubans, Puerto Ricans fare best, with 19 percent of adults having graduated from college and only 21 percent occupying the lowest skill category. Poverty levels exceed 20 percent for all groups except Cubans. Homeownership rates vary widely. While approximately one-half of Cubans and Mexicans own homes, far fewer Dominicans and Guatemalans do. The homeownership rates for Puerto Ricans and Salvadorans lie between the rates for the other groups.

The largest Hispanic groups hail from Mexico and Caribbean and Central American countries. However, smaller groups from South America, such as Colombians and Peruvians, tend to rank high on several social and economic measures. With regard to education attainment, for example, one-third of Colombians and Peruvians are college graduates, outdistancing the attainment of Cubans. Nearly one-half of the households in these two groups own a home, and a smaller share of these groups than of the others lives in poverty.[18]

## MULTIPLE GEOGRAPHIES

As shown, the common one-dimensional stereotype of U.S. Hispanics is unwarranted. Another reason that it is inaccurate to paint all Hispanics with a broad brush is that they reflect multiple geographies. Each Hispanic group has a different spatial geography based, to a large degree, on its initial settlement in the United States. Although there is increasing convergence—especially toward the newest destinations—it is important to understand who lives where at this moment in time.

Residents of Mexican origin have the greatest presence in the Southwest of the United States. Much of this territory was part of Mexico before the end of the Mexican-American War in 1848, and the area has attracted large Mexican immigrant populations since immigration law was reformed in 1965.[19] Despite recent dispersion to other parts of the country, the three states of California, Texas, and Arizona are still home to 61 percent of the population of Mexican origin; when New Mexico and Colorado are added to the group, the share rises to 67 percent. Among large metropolitan areas, Chicago and New York, ranked fourth and eleventh, are the only non-Southwest areas among the top twenty areas for Mexican populations. Still, among the largest Hispanic groups, residents of Mexican origin are the least clustered in a few metropolitan areas. Only about one-third of Mexican Americans reside in the five biggest metropolitan areas—led by Los Angeles and Riverside, California (see table 4-4).

Three of the most regionally concentrated Hispanic groups are located primarily outside of the Southwest. Nearly six in ten Dominicans live in metropolitan New York, for example, and 77 percent live in just five metropolitan areas. In fact, nine in ten U.S. Dominicans reside in New England, New York, New Jersey, Pennsylvania, or Florida. This population arrived in large numbers beginning in the 1960s, originally in response to political instability; in recent decades, however, economic issues have been a motivation.[20]

Cubans have immigrated to the United States for much of its history, especially in the post-Castro waves of refugees.[21] U.S. Cubans, who are growing more slowly than other Hispanic groups, remain heavily concentrated in metropolitan Miami, which is home to 55 percent of their

TABLE 4-4
**Metropolitan Areas with Largest Hispanic Origin Populations, 2010**

| Hispanic origin population | Group population size | Hispanic origin population | Group population size |
|---|---|---|---|
| **Mexicans** | | **Salvadorans** | |
| Los Angeles | 4,368,745 | Los Angeles | 381,519 |
| Riverside | 1,713,658 | Washington, DC | 228,045 |
| Houston | 1,579,983 | New York | 199,510 |
| Chicago | 1,546,171 | Houston | 140,928 |
| Dallas | 1,458,178 | San Francisco | 77,149 |
| *Percent in top 5 areas* | 34% | *Percent in top 5 areas* | 62% |
| **Puerto Ricans** | | **Dominicans** | |
| New York | 1,177,430 | New York | 835,402 |
| Orlando | 269,781 | Miami | 95,966 |
| Philadelphia | 238,866 | Boston | 91,252 |
| Miami | 207,727 | Providence | 36,931 |
| Chicago | 188,502 | Orlando | 35,486 |
| *Percent in top 5 areas* | 45% | *Percent in top 5 areas* | 77% |
| **Cubans** | | **Guatemalans** | |
| Miami | 982,758 | Los Angeles | 231,304 |
| New York | 135,391 | New York | 101,257 |
| Tampa | 81,542 | Washington, DC | 52,421 |
| Los Angeles | 49,702 | Miami | 47,699 |
| Orlando | 36,724 | Houston | 38,147 |
| *Percent in top 5 areas* | 72% | *Percent in top 5 areas* | 45% |

Source: 2010 U.S. census.

population. Puerto Ricans, like Dominicans, are highly concentrated in metropolitan New York, which has been their primary destination since before Puerto Rico became a U.S. territory in 1898 and particularly in the post–World War II period.[22] Later movement to other parts of the eastern United States, most notably Florida, is evidenced by the concentration of Puerto Ricans in four other top areas—Orlando, Philadelphia, Miami, and Chicago. Although they have some presence in California and Texas, three-quarters of U.S. Puerto Ricans still reside in New York, New Jersey, Florida, Pennsylvania, and New England.

The settlement patterns of the Salvadoran and Guatemalan populations, which have been growing more rapidly in recent years, are more balanced between the East and West. Salvadoran immigration to the United States has picked up substantially since 1990 because of natural disasters at home and employment opportunities and family ties in the United States.[23] Nearly one-half of all Salvadorans reside in metropolitan Los Angeles, Washington, D.C., and New York; beyond those locations, they are heavily concentrated in the rest of California, Texas, and a number of Eastern Seaboard states. Guatemalans also are more evenly distributed across the country than larger groups, such as Cubans and Dominicans. With political instability and natural disasters at home and work opportunities in the United States, they immigrated for various reasons over time, creating their greatest immigration flows in the years since 1990.[24] They are found in the greatest concentrations in Los Angeles and New York and in smaller concentrations in Washington, D.C., Miami, and Houston. They are somewhat more widely scattered than Salvadorans in other parts of the Eastern Seaboard, in the West, and in major metropolitan areas such as Chicago.

## SETTLING IN NEW DESTINATIONS

Although it is true that each Hispanic group has a very strong presence in its initial settlement areas, most groups—not just Mexicans—are contributing to the broad dispersal to new destinations. This is illustrated in figure 4-3, which compares the growth rates for different Hispanic groups in new destination metropolitan areas with rates in other types of areas. Growth rates are faster in new Hispanic destination areas than in other area types for each of the Hispanic groups. Collectively, Mexican, Puerto Rican, and Cuban populations more than doubled in these areas in the first decade of the 2000s. The populations of Dominicans and other Central American groups, including Salvadorans and Guatemalans, more than quadrupled, and the populations of South American groups, including Colombians and Peruvians, more than tripled.

Although Mexicans have driven Hispanic growth in many new destination areas, their population gains often are accompanied or overtaken by those of other Hispanic groups. These gains are usually based on an area's general proximity to a group's major settlement regions, reflecting dispersion from those regions. For example, in Charlotte, where the Hispanic population grew by 153 percent during 2000–10, Mexicans

FIGURE 4-3
**2000–10 Growth Rates for Hispanic Origin Populations**
Concentrated and New Destination Metropolitan Areas, 2000–10

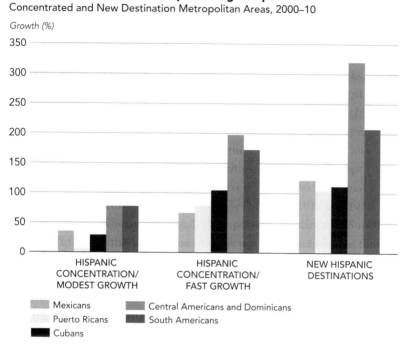

Source: 2000 and 2010 U.S. censuses.

accounted for less than half of that growth, while other groups—Puerto Ricans and other Central Americans, including Salvadorans, Hondurans, and Guatemalans—contributed substantially.[25] Many areas in the Southeast, such as Atlanta, Raleigh, and Chattanooga, had similar profiles. In Jacksonville, Florida, there was also a noticeable Cuban contribution to recent Hispanic growth.

In several new destination areas in the vicinity of New York City, Puerto Ricans contributed greatly to recent population growth. In Allentown, Pennsylvania, for example, where the Hispanic population grew by 96 percent, Puerto Ricans accounted for nearly one-half of that growth, Dominicans and Central Americans accounted for 43 percent, and Mexicans accounted for just 8 percent. Even so, there are many new destination areas, like Oklahoma City, where Mexicans accounted for

FIGURE 4-4
**Hispanic Origin Populations for Selected Metropolitan Areas, 2010**

*Percent*

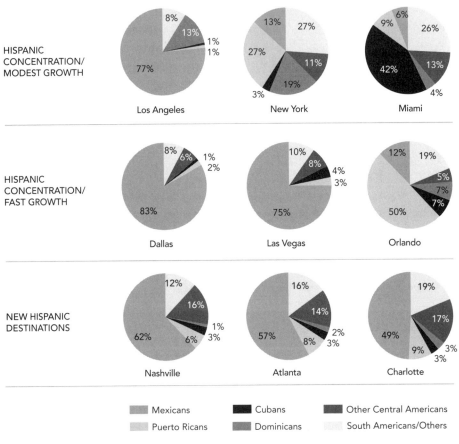

Source: 2010 U.S. census.

85 percent of the metropolitan area's rapid Hispanic growth. In western cities, such as Seattle and Boise; Midwest cities, such as Omaha and Dubuque; and Deep South areas, such as Little Rock, Mexicans contributed the lion's share to Hispanic population growth.

Other areas showing large increases in the Hispanic population are the Hispanic concentration/fast-growth areas. Most of these areas are located in parts of the country that already have large Hispanic populations, and their gains tend to reflect the groups that already live there. For example, in Dallas, the population of Mexican origin constitutes more than four-fifths of the 2010 Hispanic population (see figure 4-4), and Mexicans were responsible for 90 percent of the 2000–10 Hispanic gain for this area. Similar Mexican-dominated populations and growth are evident for many of the established but growing metropolitan areas in the West, such as Phoenix, Riverside, and Las Vegas. The major exceptions to Mexican-dominated growth are in the East, particularly in Florida, where Mexicans are not a dominant part of the Hispanic population. In Orlando, for example, where Puerto Ricans make up one-half of the Hispanic population and Mexicans make up only 12 percent, Puerto Ricans also constitute a plurality of the area's recent Hispanic gains.

Of course, established settlement areas such as Los Angeles, New York, and Miami, whose populations reflect their long Hispanic settlement histories, are not changing dramatically with regard to the origins of their populations. Rather, it is the new destination areas that are seeing rapid Hispanic population growth and growth in the variety of Hispanic groups, drawing immigrants from outside the United States and migrants from established Hispanic population centers elsewhere in the nation. Because many of the new arrivals are low-skilled workers, whether Mexicans, Salvadorans, Guatemalans, or others, the challenges for them and their broader communities will be to develop ways for them, as the leading edge of Hispanic dispersal, to "fit in" better.

# Asians in America
## The Newest Minority Surge

# 5

The most recent dimension of America's diversity explosion involves the growth of the U.S. Asian population, which has mushroomed largely as a result of post-1965 immigration. While Asians often are dubbed the "model minority," the population is composed of many national origin groups, ranging from long-time Chinese and Japanese residents to more recent entrants from India and other countries, which will be increasingly important partners of the United States in the global economy. Although recent immigration of Hispanics from Latin America has increased and decreased along with the ups and downs in the U.S. economy, new immigration from Asian countries has been relatively steady and is likely to increase over time, particularly if future immigration policy places greater emphasis on high skills. Nonetheless, because of its relatively small size and diverse origins, the Asian population seems to have been overlooked in discussions of America's minorities. This chapter focuses on key aspects of the Asian American population as it continues to grow and disperse across the country.

## ASIAN POPULATION EXPLOSION

America's Asian population, although smaller in size than the population of Hispanics or blacks, has grown in size and significance in the past
four decades. In 1970, Asians constituted just 0.8 percent of the U.S.
population—1.5 million people. By 2010, the Asian population had grown
nearly tenfold, to 14.7 million, roughly 5 percent of the population (see
figures 5-1a and 5-1b).[1] These population gains were in great part a result
of the Immigration and Nationality Act of 1965, which opened the door
to immigration from all countries, replacing a quota system that favored
immigrants from northern Europe. The new law instead emphasized
family reunification and employment as criteria for admission.[2] The
opening up to new countries was especially important for Asian immigration, which had been strictly prohibited in earlier legislation such as
the Chinese Exclusion Act of 1882 and the National Origins Act of 1924.
The U.S. military involvement in Vietnam in the late 1960s and early
1970s and the war's aftermath brought additional Asian immigrants as
refugees and asylum seekers. Following these changes, Asian countries
accounted for four of the top-five places of immigrant origin in the 1970s
and 1980s. From 2008 to 2010, the top places of origin, after Mexico,
were China, India, the Philippines, and Korea. In fact, during that period,
which saw a downturn in Latin American immigration, Asian immigrants accounted for two-fifths of all newly arrived immigrants, a share
which has risen since then.[3]

### Early Asian Immigration

Asians clearly are a newer minority than Hispanics. As of 2015, more
than nine in ten U.S. Asians but only two-thirds of Hispanics are
either first- or second-generation Americans.[4] Yet several Asian
groups, particularly Chinese, Japanese, and Filipinos, began settling
in noticeable numbers in the United States in the late nineteenth and
early twentieth centuries. During that period of early immigration,
Asians were hardly treated as the "model minority" that they are
often considered today.[5]

Chinese immigrants, largely unschooled laborers, first arrived on
the U.S. mainland in the mid-nineteenth century, lured by jobs on the

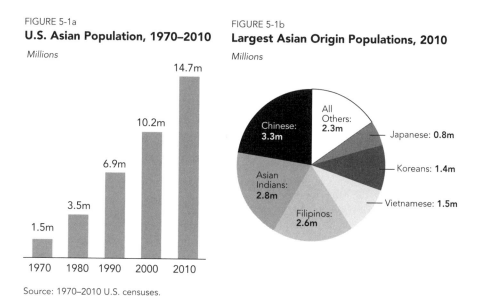

FIGURE 5-1a
**U.S. Asian Population, 1970–2010**

*Millions*

FIGURE 5-1b
**Largest Asian Origin Populations, 2010**

*Millions*

Source: 1970–2010 U.S. censuses.

western frontier associated with the Gold Rush and later with the Transcontinental Railroad. Yet discrimination and resentment on the part of white workers led to the Chinese Exclusion Act of 1882, which restricted immigration and the right of Chinese immigrants to become U.S. citizens. Their population then declined and stabilized for most of the first half of the twentieth century.[6]

Japanese immigrants came later in the nineteenth century, initially to work as farmers. Yet they also bore the burden of discrimination, with immigration restricted by the Gentlemen's Agreement of 1907–08. They experienced further restrictions, also aimed at other Asian immigrants, under the National Origins Act of 1924. Yet because of natural increase, the U.S. Japanese population was the largest population of Asian origin between 1910 and 1960.

Filipinos also made an early appearance, due largely to the U.S. acquisition of the Philippines in 1898. They came to work in domestic and service jobs, but because the Philippines was a U.S. territory, their immigration was not restricted by the 1924 National Origins Act. However, they faced discrimination and hostility from white workers, and in 1934 Congress passed the Tydings-McDuffie Act, which granted commonwealth status to the Philippines but also severely restricted further Fili-pino immigration to the United States.

Although populations from China, Japan, and the Philippines estab-lished some Asian presence in the United States in the early twentieth century, the U.S. Asian population remained relatively small and heavily involved in manual labor and low-skilled jobs. As late as 1960, the Asian population in the United States stood at 878,000, representing only 0.5 percent of the population.[7]

## Post-1965: New Asian Waves

Two aspects of the 1965 Immigration and Nationality Act significantly altered the profile of the Asian population in the United States. The first was the opening of immigration and the opportunity for citizenship to people from all countries, thus abandoning what remained of the restric-tions previously imposed on Asian immigration. Second was the desig-nation of employment and family reunification as major preferences for selecting new immigrants. The new, more lenient law led to a sharp increase in the number of Asians in already established populations—Chinese, Japanese, and Filipinos—and of those from other Asian coun-tries whose U.S. presence was previously small or nonexistent. Among the latter were new Korean and Indian immigrants who took advantage of the emerging economic opportunities in the United States. Some of the attraction had to do with employment preferences and later amend-ments to the immigration law that led to a shift toward high-skilled immigrants from these countries.

Still another development that drew Asian immigrants was the U.S. military involvement in Southeast Asia and the end of the Vietnam War in the early 1970s, which led to waves of Vietnamese, Laotian, and Cambodian refugees. Later, the number of Vietnamese in the United States increased considerably because of immigration in the late 1970s of political refugees from Vietnam, including the "boat people," and immigration in recent decades associated with family reunification in the United States.

The post-1965 Asian immigration waves continue to bring gains in Asian populations. Figure 5-2 indicates the population gains from 1990 to 2010 for the six largest Asian groups. In that 20-year period, the

Chinese population more than doubled, from 1.6 to 3.3 million, while the Asian Indian population more than tripled, to 2.8 million, becoming the second-largest Asian population in the United States. Filipinos, Vietnamese, and Koreans also saw large gains. The only decline shown is that of the Japanese American population, as immigration from Japan has been low and the Japanese population in the United States has been aging. So although the small pre-1965 Asian population was composed predominantly of residents of Japanese, Chinese, and Filipino origins, the current Asian population is more of a kaleidoscope of groups. Together, the six largest groups constituted 85 percent of the Asian population in 2010. The remaining portions of the Asian American population are made up of more than a dozen groups, most growing even more rapidly than the larger groups. Among those with at least 50,000 residents are Pakistanis, Hmong, Cambodians, Laotians, Thais, Bangladeshis, Indonesians, Burmese, and Nepalese.

FIGURE 5-2
**Size of Largest Asian Origin Populations, 1990–2010**

*Millions*

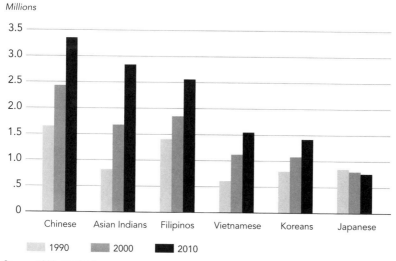

Source: 1990–2010 U.S. censuses.

**A New Image**

The pre-1965 image of Asian immigrants as low-skilled workers, labor-ers, and farmers who arrived without families and had to contend with blatant discrimination has changed with the advent of new Asian immi-grants. In many ways, this change has to do with the employment provi-sions of the 1965 immigration act, which selects immigrants for jobs that there are not enough U.S. workers to fill. Many of these are high-skilled jobs for which Asian immigrants qualify.[8] Other Asians who arrived as students or on temporary work visas were able to become permanent residents because they could perform jobs not filled by other residents. Perhaps even more important is the fact that U.S.-born Asians have shown a penchant for pursuing higher education as a means of achieving upward mobility, often with strong encouragement from their parents.[9] Thus, the Asian American community is often considered a model minority. Although this blanket term glosses over differences within the Asian community, it certainly reflects a more positive image of Asians than the image that predominated a half-century ago.

Table 5-1, with profiles as of 2015, indicates that Asians are in fact distinct in a number of respects from the total population and from the white majority. With regard to education attainment, Asian adults are better educated than the U.S. population as a whole. More than half of all Asian adults have college degrees and seven in ten have some schooling beyond high school. Recent statistics indicate that students from Asia make up well over one-half of foreign students in U.S. institutions and constitute one-third of all holders of doctorates in physical sciences and higher shares of those holding doctorates in math and engineering. It is not surprising, then, that Asian Americans have a high representation in management, professional occupations, and related occupations and have higher-than-average incomes.[10]

These high education attainment levels may seem even more impres-sive in light of the fact that most Asians today are foreign born and are likely to speak an Asian language rather than English at home. Further-more, more than one-third do not profess to speak English "very well." Yet it should be recognized that the Asian population is in a state of flux. Over time, the native-born Asian population will increase, and younger U.S.-born residents who identify as Asian will be proficient in English.

TABLE 5-1

**Social and Demographic Profiles: Asians, Whites, and Total U.S. Population, 2015**

*Percent*

| Profile | Asians | Whites | Total U.S. |
|---|---|---|---|
| *Nativity* | | | |
| Percent foreign born | 66 | 4 | 13 |
| *English proficiency (ages 5+)* | | | |
| Speaks only English at home | 25 | 95 | 79 |
| Does not speak English very well | 34 | 2 | 9 |
| *Age* | | | |
| Under 18 | 20 | 19 | 23 |
| 18–29 | 18 | 15 | 17 |
| 30–44 | 25 | 18 | 19 |
| 45–64 | 25 | 29 | 26 |
| 65+ | 12 | 19 | 15 |
| *Household type* | | | |
| Married couples with children | 33 | 19 | 20 |
| Married couples without children | 27 | 32 | 28 |
| Other families with children | 7 | 8 | 11 |
| Other households without children[a] | 33 | 41 | 41 |
| *Education (ages 25+)* | | | |
| Not high school graduate | 13 | 8 | 13 |
| High school only | 16 | 28 | 27 |
| Some college | 19 | 30 | 29 |
| College graduate | 52 | 34 | 31 |
| *Poverty status* | | | |
| Percent below poverty | 12 | 10 | 15 |
| *Homeownership* | | | |
| Percent owners | 58 | 71 | 63 |

Source: American Community Survey, 2015.

[a]Includes "other family without children" and "nonfamily household" (persons living alone or with nonrelatives).

Asians are also distinct from the rest of the population in their penchant for marrying and forming households composed of a married couple with children.[11] While married couples account for less than one-half of all U.S. households, they account for 60 percent of Asian households. Moreover, one-third of all Asian households but only one-fifth of all U.S. households are "traditional" married households with children. That means that the vast majority of Asian children grow up with two parents, and many Asian households are multigenerational.[12] Despite these traditional families, the proportion of U.S. Asian residents under the age of 18 (20 percent) is slightly less than the proportion for the general population. The median age of Asians was 36.5 years, lower than the median of 37.9 years for the nation as a whole. The reason for this seeming paradox is that more Asian Americans than the general population are in the primary labor force age range (18–64 years). Due to the recency of most Asian immigration, which took place at younger adult ages, there are fewer Asian Americans age 65 and older.

On other economic indicators, Asian poverty rates are lower but not substantially lower than those of the total population, and Asians have rates of homeownership below those of the general population, reflecting their new immigrant status. Clearly the "newness" of Asian residents in terms of their first-generation and recent immigrant status underscores the fact that they are not yet fully integrated socially and economically. What does stand out, beyond their newness, is their high level of educational attainment and traditional family structure.

## DIFFERENT ORIGINS, NEW DESTINATIONS

As was the case with the Hispanic population, the Asian population first planted itself in several traditional settlement areas associated with different national origin groups before they started to spread to other parts of the nation. Yet Asian settlements are distinct in two ways. First, unlike with the Hispanic population, there is not one dominant group (such as Mexicans) but several groups of somewhat similar sizes that began their settlements in different locations. Second, Asians, as a newer, more recently immigrating minority, have not dispersed as widely as Hispanics. Nonetheless, Asian Americans are continuing to spread to new destinations, planting the seeds for new Asian communities in all parts of the country.

### Major Settlement Areas

Major settlement areas for Asian populations differ by national group, although they have some commonalities (see table 5-2). For example, Los Angeles is one of the largest settlement areas for each of the six largest groups of Asian origin. New York and San Francisco also are prominent locations for most of them. Another commonality is the strong concentration of all Asian groups in large metropolitan areas, despite recent dispersion. Still, the geographic locations where groups cluster differ depending on their growth histories within the United States. There is a pronounced western dominance, especially with the locations of the more long-standing Asian groups (Chinese, Filipinos, and Japanese) in light of their original settlements in Hawaii and on the Pacific coast. The 1860 census, the first to enumerate Asians, reported that all Americans of Asian origin resided in the West. In 1960, before the new immigration waves took shape, no other region held as much as 10 percent of the Asian population.[13] Even today, California is still home to the largest number of Asian Americans, more than 30 percent of the U.S. Asian population.

Over time, there has been an expansion of Asian Americans across different parts of the country, particularly toward large metropolitan

TABLE 5-2
**Metropolitan Areas with Largest Asian Origin Populations, 2010**

| Asian origin population | Group population size | Asian origin population | Group population size |
|---|---|---|---|
| **Chinese** | | **Vietnamese** | |
| New York | 649,989 | Los Angeles | 271,234 |
| Los Angeles | 473,323 | San Jose | 125,774 |
| San Francisco | 428,403 | Houston | 103,525 |
| San Jose | 152,860 | Dallas | 71,839 |
| Boston | 110,834 | Washington, DC | 58,767 |
| *Percent in top 5 areas* | 54% | *Percent in top 5 areas* | 41% |
| **Asian Indians** | | **Korean** | |
| New York | 526,133 | Los Angeles | 304,198 |
| Chicago | 171,901 | New York | 208,190 |
| Washington, DC | 127,963 | Washington, DC | 80,150 |
| Los Angeles | 119,901 | Chicago | 54,135 |
| San Francisco | 119,854 | Seattle | 52,113 |
| *Percent in top 5 areas* | 37% | *Percent in top 5 areas* | 49% |
| **Filipinos** | | **Japanese** | |
| Los Angeles | 393,170 | Honolulu | 149,701 |
| San Francisco | 239,232 | Los Angeles | 134,563 |
| New York | 189,058 | New York | 44,391 |
| San Diego | 146,618 | San Francisco | 39,310 |
| Honolulu | 142,238 | Seattle | 27,128 |
| *Percent in top 5 areas* | 43% | *Percent in top 5 areas* | 52% |

Source: 2010 U.S. census.

areas where new employment opportunities developed within ethnic enclaves. Metropolitan New York is now home to the largest number of Chinese Americans, about one-fifth of the total Chinese American population, followed closely by Los Angeles and two other areas in California, San Francisco and San Jose. Chinese Americans are the Asian group that is most concentrated in metropolitan areas; in fact, more than one-half of Chinese Americans reside in just five metropolitan areas. Still, their populations are not regionally isolated; substantial Chinese populations are located in Boston, Chicago, Washington, D.C., Seattle, Houston, and Philadelphia, among other cities.

More of the Filipino population than the Chinese population remains in the West. Nearly half of U.S. Filipinos reside in California and another 7 percent live in Hawaii, where Filipinos have had a long-time presence. Eight of the ten largest metropolitan Filipino populations are located in western cities, led by Los Angeles and then by San Francisco, San Diego, Honolulu, Riverside, Las Vegas, Phoenix, and Seattle. New York and Chicago are home to the largest non-western Filipino populations. The small Japanese American population also is heavily concentrated in the West. California is home to more than one-third and Hawaii to an additional one-quarter of all U.S. Japanese residents. Among metropolitan areas, Honolulu and Los Angeles contain, by far, the largest Japanese American populations. Other areas with sizable Japanese American populations are New York, San Francisco, Seattle, and San Jose.

Among the newer Asian groups, the rapidly growing Asian Indian population is most dispersed across regions outside the West. Its largest metropolitan populations are in northeastern and midwestern areas, including New York and Chicago, and there is a sizable population in Washington, D.C. While California metropolitan areas, including Los Angeles, San Francisco, and San Jose, have sizable Asian Indian populations, so do Dallas, Houston, Philadelphia, Atlanta, and Boston. As discussed in greater detail below, Asian Indians are more highly educated than other Asian groups and therefore are more suited for knowledge-based jobs in science, engineering, and medicine, which are available nationwide. Accordingly, they are somewhat less constrained by national origin networks in their search for employment.

Korean Americans, who also have shown more recent growth, are highly clustered in metropolitan areas, although in different regions. Koreans are one of the most entrepreneurial groups in the country, which explains why they are drawn to large metropolitan areas with existing racial enclaves.[14] Roughly one-half of all Koreans live in five metropolitan areas, dominated by Los Angeles and New York. Washington, D.C., Chicago, Seattle, and Atlanta also are home to significant Korean populations. The Vietnamese population, the first to come as refugees, was initially dispersed to several parts of the country, sometimes under the sponsorship of church and civic organizations. Over time, many of these early arrivals resettled in major settlement areas, such as Orange County, California, which is now part of the Los Angeles metropolitan area.[15] Their current settlement patterns show the largest populations in Los Angeles, San Jose, and Houston, with sizable populations in Dallas, Washington, D.C., San Francisco, and Seattle.

**Dispersing to New Destinations**

As a smaller and more recently arrived population than Hispanics, Asians are less spread out and less prevalent across broad parts of the United States. Still, the Asian population is very much in a state of flux, characterized by fast growth and dispersal to new areas. These patterns became evident in the first decade of the 2000s, when almost all of the nation's 366 metropolitan areas showed gains in the Asian population and nearly one-half showed gains exceeding 50 percent. To place these changes in perspective, map 5-1 displays 113 selected metropolitan areas that can be classed into three categories:

*Asian concentration/modest-growth areas.* These are areas with a sizable Asian presence where the rate of Asian population growth is lower than the national rate.[16] These areas include large traditional settlement locations such as Los Angeles, New York, and San Francisco and smaller areas with established Asian settlements. There are 20 such areas, heavily concentrated in California and the West, and they account for 49 percent of the U.S. Asian population.

MAP 5-1
**Asian Concentration Areas and New Asian Destinations**

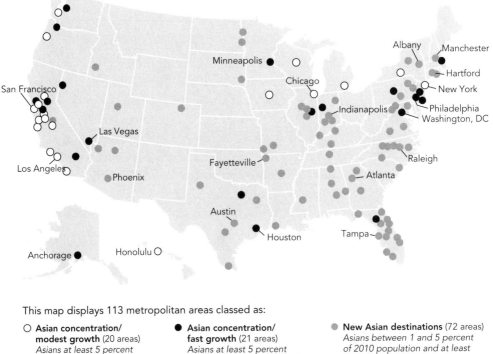

This map displays 113 metropolitan areas classed as:

○ **Asian concentration/ modest growth** (20 areas)
*Asians at least 5 percent of 2010 population and less than 43 percent 2000–10 growth.*

● **Asian concentration/ fast growth** (21 areas)
*Asians at least 5 percent of 2010 population and at least 43 percent 2000–10 growth.*

● **New Asian destinations** (72 areas)
*Asians between 1 and 5 percent of 2010 population and at least 70 percent 2000–10 growth.*

Source: 2010 U.S. census.

*Asian concentration/fast-growth areas.* These also are areas with a sizable Asian presence, but their Asian population growth rate is at least equal to the national Asian growth rate.[17] These are areas that are adding to their already large Asian populations. Examples are Washington, D.C., Houston, Las Vegas, Minneapolis, and Philadelphia. In contrast to the more stagnant Asian concentration areas, these metropolitan areas are spread across the country, including the Eastern Seaboard, the interior West, and Texas. These 21 areas account for 24 percent of the U.S. Asian population.

***New Asian destinations.*** These areas are at the cutting edge of Asian population growth—areas with smaller-than-average Asian populations but with Asian growth rates that far exceed the national Asian growth rate.[18] There are 72 such areas, of all sizes, which together account for just 11 percent of the U.S. Asian population. However, they represent the forefront of Asian growth across the country. Among the larger of such areas are Atlanta, Austin, Raleigh, Phoenix, Tampa, and Indianapolis.

Of particular importance are the fast-growth areas and new destinations. Figure 5-3 indicates that for each major Asian group, the fastest growth is in new Asian destinations and the slowest growth is in the more traditional settlement areas. Particularly noteworthy is the rapid growth of the Asian Indian population, especially in the faster-growing metropolitan areas. In fact, Asian Indians are responsible for a disproportionate contribution to recent population gains in new Asian destinations, and they make up a larger share of Asian populations in these areas than in other kinds of areas.[19] An example is Atlanta, where the Asian population grew by 86 percent between 2000 and 2010 and Asian Indians contributed 35 percent to that growth. As a consequence, Asian Indians now make up 31 percent of Atlanta's Asian population (see figure 5-4). In Raleigh, where the Asian population grew by 130 percent, Asian Indians contributed nearly one-half to that growth. Asian Indians now make up 40 percent of Raleigh's Asian population, up from 32 percent in 2000.

Although Asian Indians are a significant part of growth in new destinations, they are not the major contributor in all cases. In Boise, for example, Chinese and Filipinos make the greatest contributions to Asian population growth, and in college towns such as Durham, North Carolina, and Bloomington, Indiana, Chinese make greater contributions to growth than Asian Indians do. Yet Asian Indians play a key role in the increase of Asian American populations in those areas, where Asian growth is relatively new.

In more established Asian fast-growth areas, however, new Asian population gains are more likely to reflect the mix of existing origin groups or proximity to large Asian settlements in nearby areas.[20] In Las Vegas, for example, where Filipinos constitute a large share of the Asian population overall, they contributed to more than half of the

FIGURE 5-3
**2000–10 Growth Rates for Asian Origin Populations,
Concentrated and New Destination Metropolitan Areas**

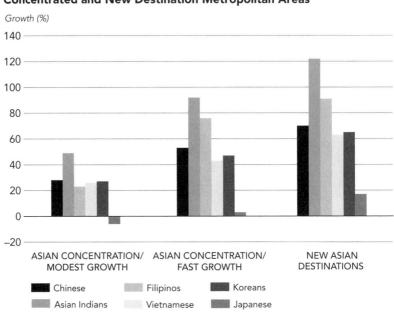

Source: 2000–10 U.S. censuses.

area's substantial Asian population gain in the first decade of the 2000s. Filipinos also made major contributions to Asian gains in Riverside, Stockton, and Sacramento, California, and Reno, Nevada. In Boston, the Chinese made the greatest contributions to Asian gains. Yet even among these metropolitan areas, Asian Indian gains were sufficient enough to increase the Indian share of the Asian population in most areas.

In contrast, the more established, slowly growing Asian settlement areas are typically distinct from one another because of their historical settlement patterns. For example, Chinese and Asian Indians constitute large shares of New York's Asian population while Chinese and Filipinos are major groups in San Francisco. Because population growth rates are lower than average in all of these areas, there is little overall shift in their

FIGURE 5-4

**Asian Origin Populations for Selected Metropolitan Areas, 2010**

*Percent*

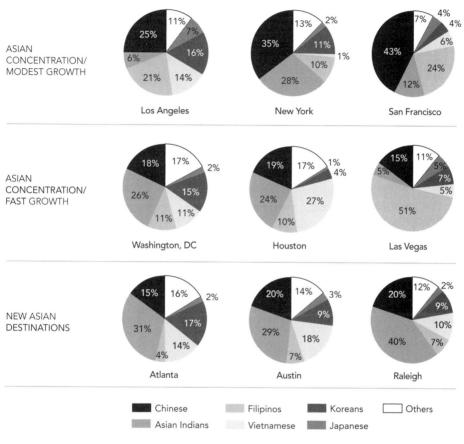

Source: 2010 U.S. census.

Asian nationality profiles as a result of recent changes. When there is substantial change, however, Asian Indians are making the biggest difference. Because of recent growth, the Indian share of the Asian population increased notably in several California areas, including San Jose, San Diego, and Oxnard, as well as in Chicago, where Asian Indians now constitute one-third of the Asian population.

## MODEL MINORITY(IES)

The new image of Asian Americans as a model minority reflects, especially, the higher-than-average education and more traditional families that broadly characterize the group. Yet this umbrella term can be misleading. Because different Asian groups have different origins and immigration histories, their social and demographic attributes differ somewhat, as of 2015, as shown in table 5-3.

All groups, except Japanese Americans, have relatively high percentages of foreign-born members, a result of their recent immigration. Almost six in ten Japanese Americans are native born, reflecting both their long history of settlement in the United States and their relatively low levels of recent immigration. Chinese and Filipino residents also first settled here more than a century ago, but the post-1965 replenishment of their ranks has kept their populations almost "new"—roughly two-thirds are foreign born. High numbers of foreign-born residents also are evident among more recent arrivals—Vietnamese, Koreans, and Asian Indians—whose immigrant population is relatively young.

Both the historic length of settlement and the magnitude of recent immigration affect the age structure of the different Asian groups. Japanese Americans are the oldest group; more than one-quarter are 65 years of age or older, and only 10 percent are under the age of 18. In contrast, 23 percent of Asian Indians are under the age of 18, nearly three times as many as those age 65 and above. The other groups generally fall in between, with populations including relatively high proportions of people of working age.

The household status of different groups reflects both the age structure of each and the tendency of Asian families, in general, to have children within the context of husband-wife families. Accordingly, the Japanese population, as the oldest, has the lowest share of married-with-child households (17 percent) while such households constitute 46 percent of Asian Indian households. Among all groups, married couples with children sharply outweigh the number of other families with children, underscoring the strong prevalence of Asian children growing up in two-parent families.

TABLE 5-3
**Profiles of Asian Origin Populations, 2015**
Percent

| Profile[a] | Chinese | Asian Indians | Filipinos | Vietnamese | Koreans | Japanese |
|---|---|---|---|---|---|---|
| *Nativity* | | | | | | |
| Percent foreign born | 70 | 71 | 66 | 68 | 72 | 41 |
| *English proficiency (Ages 5+)* | | | | | | |
| Speaks only English at home | 19 | 23 | 34 | 14 | 24 | 57 |
| Does not speak English very well | 46 | 20 | 22 | 51 | 41 | 23 |
| *Age* | | | | | | |
| Under 18 | 18 | 23 | 17 | 21 | 16 | 10 |
| 18–29 | 20 | 18 | 16 | 18 | 18 | 12 |
| 30–44 | 22 | 32 | 24 | 23 | 26 | 21 |
| 45–64 | 27 | 19 | 29 | 28 | 27 | 31 |
| 65+ | 13 | 8 | 14 | 10 | 13 | 26 |
| *Household type* | | | | | | |
| Married couples with children | 27 | 46 | 31 | 34 | 26 | 17 |
| Married couples without children | 29 | 28 | 28 | 26 | 29 | 29 |
| Other families with children | 5 | 2 | 9 | 10 | 5 | 5 |
| Other households without children[b] | 39 | 24 | 32 | 30 | 40 | 49 |
| *Education (ages 25+)* | | | | | | |
| Not high school graduate | 17 | 8 | 7 | 26 | 8 | 5 |
| High school only | 14 | 9 | 15 | 23 | 18 | 18 |
| Some college | 14 | 9 | 30 | 23 | 20 | 26 |
| College graduate | 55 | 74 | 48 | 28 | 54 | 51 |
| *Poverty status* | | | | | | |
| Percent below poverty | 15 | 8 | 7 | 15 | 13 | 9 |
| *Homeownership* | | | | | | |
| Percent owners | 62 | 55 | 60 | 66 | 48 | 67 |

Source: American Community Survey, 2011–15.
[a]Average annual values 2011–15 based on American Community Survey, 2011–15, multiyear estimates.
[b]Includes "other families without children" and "nonfamily households" (persons living alone or with nonrelatives).

Asian Indians, by far, have achieved the highest level of education, which reflects, to a large degree, their select immigration to the United States, especially in the past two decades. During that period there was strong demand for high-tech workers reflected, in part, by the establishment of the nation's H-1B visa program, which has seen the largest share of participants coming from India.[21] Nearly three-quarters of Asian Indian adults have received college degrees. Still, roughly one-half of Chinese, Korean, Filipino, and Japanese American adults have received bachelor's degrees or higher; in contrast, just 31 percent of the total U.S. adult population and 34 percent of whites have done so. Vietnamese adults are significantly less likly than other Asian groups to be college graduates, at 28 percent, and 26 percent of Vietnamese adults in America have not graduated from high school.

The population of educated Asian Americans is fairly widespread. Map 5-2 identifies 86 metropolitan areas where more than half of Asian adults held at least a bachelor's degree in 2010. These include modest-sized college towns such as Ann Arbor, Michigan; Bloomington, Indiana; and State College, Pennsylvania, where more than 80 percent of Asians have a bachelor's degree or higher, as well as larger cities, including San Jose, Phoenix, Omaha, Houston, Indianapolis, and Buffalo. In many of these places, Asian Indians are the major engine of recent growth and represent a disproportionate share of the Asian populations. Among large metropolitan areas, Asian education attainment is greatest in high-tech and knowledge-based centers such as Raleigh and Austin, the global city of Chicago, and slowly growing industrial areas such as Pittsburgh and Detroit (see table 5-4). Even in major areas where Asians have relatively low shares of college graduates, such as New Orleans, Las Vegas, Sacramento, and Oklahoma City, more than one-third have obtained college degrees.

There is certainly variability among Asian groups on a number of socioeconomic measures. For example, Vietnamese, Koreans, and Chinese have higher levels of poverty than other groups have (see table 5-3). But overall, their levels are on par with that of the U.S. general population. It is clear that what has been termed a model minority really consists of a collection of distinct groups with varied immigration and settlement histories. The term is intended to be complimentary, highlighting the social and economic achievements made by many Asian Americans today and

MAP 5-2
**Metropolitan Areas with Highest Asian Educational Attainment, Adults Age 25 and Over[a]**

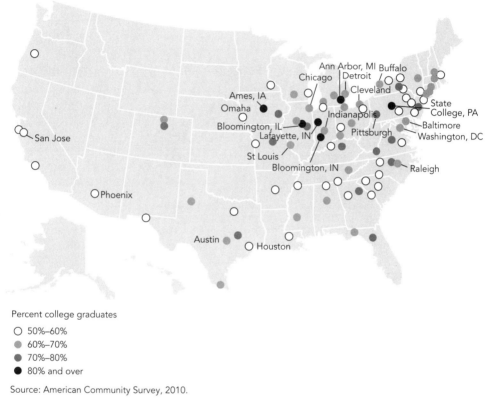

Percent college graduates

○  50%–60%
◉  60%–70%
●  70%–80%
●  80% and over

Source: American Community Survey, 2010.

[a]Map displays 86 metropolitan areas with Asian populations greater than 5,000 and where at least 50 percent of Asian adults have received a college degree or more education

contrasting their situation with the difficult circumstances in which Asian-origin residents found themselves many decades ago. Of course, as mostly first- and second-generation Americans, many residents of Asian origin face the challenges related to language, networking, and other aspects of assimilation that are encountered by all new immigrant minorities. Still, their rapid population growth and continued dispersion to all parts of the country, coupled with their social and economic achievements, signal that Asian Americans are on track to become a central part of the nation's mainstream in the twenty-first century.

TABLE 5-4

**Percent of Asian Adults Who Are College Graduates:
Highest and Lowest Rankings, Large Metropolitan Areas**

| Ranking | Percent college graduates among Asian adults[b] |
|---|---|
| *Highest ranking* | |
| 1  Pittsburgh | 71 |
| 2  Raleigh | 67 |
| 3  Austin | 66 |
| 4  Columbus | 65 |
| 5  Detroit | 64 |
| 6  Cincinnati | 64 |
| 7  Baltimore | 63 |
| 8  Chicago | 62 |
| *Lowest ranking* | |
| 1  New Orleans | 34 |
| 2  Las Vegas | 37 |
| 3  Sacramento | 39 |
| 4  Virginia Beach | 40 |
| 5  Salt Lake City | 42 |
| 6  Minneapolis–St. Paul | 43 |
| 7  Oklahoma City | 43 |
| 8  Providence | 44 |

Source: American Community Survey, 2010
[a]Metropolitan areas with populations over 1 million and with more than 20,000 Asians; official names abbreviated.
[b]Persons age 25 and over.

# The Great Migration of Blacks, In Reverse

# 6

Along with the expansion of new minority populations, important changes in the black population are worthy of attention. Especially significant is the renewed black migration to the South, which is contributing to the continuing distinctiveness of the region. The reversal of the Great Migration out of the South began as a trickle in the 1970s, increased in the 1990s, and turned into a virtual evacuation from many northern areas in the first decade of the 2000s. The movement is driven largely by younger, college-educated, and soon-to-be retiring baby boomer blacks—from both northern and western places of origin. They have contributed to the growth of New Sun Belt and southern metropolitan regions such as Atlanta, Houston, and Dallas. These areas are in the midst of new immigrant growth and white in-migration, which are shaping a region that is welcoming to blacks as well as new immigrant minorities.

This chapter points up major dimensions of this reversal of the historical Great Migration during a period in which a recognizable black middle class has emerged at the same time that a large portion of the black population remains left behind. To place this new southward geographic tilt in context, the next section highlights important aspects of the black population's unique history in the United States

## A LONG WAIT FOR UPWARD MOBILITY

Prior to the recent large waves of Hispanic and Asian population growth, the terms "minority" and "nonwhite" were synonymous with the nation's black population. For most of U.S. history, blacks were numerically the largest minority, representing as much as 19 percent of the total U.S. population in 1790 and at least 10 percent of the population since the beginning of the twentieth century.[1] Although overtaken by Hispanics in the 2000 census, blacks still accounted for 90 percent of the nation's nonwhite population as late as 1960. The black population is still growing more rapidly than the nation's population as a whole and is projected to account for at least one in eight Americans in the next three decades (see figure 6-1).[2]

The primary reason why the term "minority" has been equated with blacks stems from the long history of blatant discrimination and disenfranchisement endured by the nation's black population, which can be traced to the slaves who arrived from Africa well before nationhood in the late sixteenth and seventeenth centuries. Even after slavery was formally abolished, in 1865, by the Thirteenth Amendment to the Constitution, blacks were hardly treated as equals with whites. For much of the century that followed, blacks were denied full participation in the nation's economic, social, and political life. Continuing discriminatory practices kept them segregated from mainstream white society, and they were denied adequate jobs, housing, and educational opportunities and even the right to vote. Their plight was highlighted in 1944 in Gunnar Myrdal's classic work, *An American Dilemma: The Negro Problem and Modern Democracy*.[3] This history created a sharp and virtually insurmountable divide between whites and blacks that persisted late into the twentieth century, and its effects are still felt today.

The 1950s and early 1960s brought little measurable change in the conditions that blacks faced, but the civil rights movement did increase national awareness of them.[4] There was increased activism on the part of

FIGURE 6-1
**U.S. and Black Growth by Decade, 1950–2010**

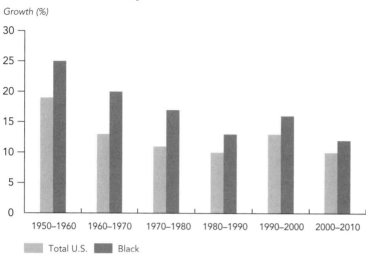

*Growth (%)*

Source: 1950–2010 U.S. censuses.

black organizations in the South, such as the 1955–56 Montgomery, Ala-bama, bus boycott to protest segregated seating, "sit-in" demonstrations, well-publicized confrontations between protesters and state and local officials, and the peaceful, nationally televised March on Washington in 1963, which featured Martin Luther King's "I Have a Dream" speech. Also significant during this period were legal victories such as in the 1954 Supreme Court decision in *Brown* v. *Board of Education,* which declared that maintaining separate schools for black and white students was unconstitutional. Perhaps the most important outcome of this period was the enactment of the landmark civil rights acts of 1964, 1965, and 1968, which outlawed discrimination based on race, color, religion, sex, and national origin with respect to access to public accommoda-tions, employment, voting, and the sale, rental, and financing of housing.

**Post–Civil Rights Era Upgrading**
The civil rights era, which also was fraught with violence and rioting in the South and later in northern and western cities, put a spotlight on the need to eliminate racial discrimination and set the stage for greater access to education, employment, and housing opportunities for new genera-

tions of African Americans. Still, black progress on a series of economic measures has occurred only gradually and, to some degree, generationally.[5] This is evident in shifts in educational attainment, a measure that should track improvements in both secondary and higher education. In 1970, among blacks aged 25 to 34, nearly half had not graduated from high school and only 6 percent had graduated from college (see table 6-1). These young black adults, born before the end of World War II, had hardly benefited from the social changes of the 1960s.

Twenty years later, however, progress was becoming evident among young adult blacks who were of high school age after the major civil rights legislation was passed. By 2015, 89 percent of blacks age 25 to 34 had graduated from high school and nearly three out of five had some post–high school education. Although these are broad measures, blacks show consistent generation-based upward mobility, a pattern that also is evident in occupational measures.[6] Nonetheless, large disparities with whites still exist, particularly in the level of higher education. This trend has a number of explanations, including less access to quality primary and secondary education among blacks. Educational inequality stems from remaining segregated residence patterns, differences in family resources available to finance higher education, and selective admission criteria that, although not blatantly discriminatory, still encourage college admission of whites instead of blacks.[7] Nonetheless, many more blacks in today's younger generation have access to a path to the middle class through postsecondary training opportunities than was the case in decades past.

TABLE 6-1
**Black and White Educational Attainment, 1970–2015: Adults Ages 25–34**
*Percent*

| Educational attainment | 1970 | 1990 | 2010 | 2015 |
|---|---|---|---|---|
| *High school graduate or more* | | | | |
| Blacks | 51 | 77 | 86 | 89 |
| Whites | 74 | 89 | 94 | 94 |
| *Some college or more* | | | | |
| Blacks | 17 | 44 | 56 | 59 |
| Whites | 35 | 57 | 71 | 73 |
| *College graduate* | | | | |
| Blacks | 6 | 12 | 19 | 21 |
| Whites | 16 | 26 | 37 | 40 |

Source: 1970 and 1990 U.S. censuses and American Community Survey, 2010 and 2015.

Unfortunately, education attainment is probably the most positive indicator of progress for many blacks. With regard to other measures more closely tied to the labor market and economic well-being, blacks have made some progress, but the gains have also been volatile. The black unemployment rate, for example, continues to be twice that of whites (or more), reflecting to some degree the hyper-unemployment levels of young black males In 2015, the black unemployment rate was 9.6 percent compared with 4.6 percent for whites.[8]

Moreover, the "last hired, first fired" dictum seems to be at work in the fluctuating unemployment rate for black males, which sank to 8 percent during the tight labor market of the late 1990s but then rose to 16 percent in the aftermath of the Great Recession. In contrast, the white male unemployment rate fluctuated between 3.5 and 8.7 percent in the same period.[9] The average wage of black males took a similar roller-coaster ride, falling to such an extent that the 2010 average wage was less than that of 1997, further widening the gap with whites although both black and white male wages have risen since then.[10]

## Black Families and Poverty

The gap between blacks and whites remains especially wide with regard to family income, which includes wage and nonwage incomes of all family members, in large part because black families are more likely to be headed by a single female and thus include fewer earners.[11] Hence, while black family income has risen since 1970, 2015 income was only about 57 percent of white income, which rose even higher due to its larger share of married couples (see table 6-2). If one examines family income for married-couple households only, black couple income is much closer to white couple income—about 80 percent.

Much has been written about the pervasiveness of female-headed families and single motherhood among blacks, a trend that was evident in some form for decades but has become more prevalent since the 1970s.[12] Although controversial at the time, the 1965 Moynihan Report on the black family called attention to its cultural origins and its correlation with conditions and behaviors associated with poverty in the black community.[13] Since then, observers have attributed the trend to factors such as the geographic isolation of blacks—over several gener-

TABLE 6-2
**Black and White Economic and Family Trends, 1970–2015**

|  | 1970 | 1990 | 2010 | 2015 |
|---|---|---|---|---|
| *Median family income*[a] |  |  |  |  |
| Blacks | $34,648 | $38,170 | $42,486 | $46,360 |
| Whites | $56,482 | $68,131 | $75,851 | $81,545 |
| *Female-headed families*[b] |  |  |  |  |
| Blacks | 28% | 43% | 46% | 46% |
| Whites | 9% | 12% | 14% | 14% |
| PERSONS IN POVERTY |  |  |  |  |
| *All ages* |  |  |  |  |
| Blacks | 34% | 32% | 27% | 24% |
| Whites | 10% | 9% | 10% | 10% |
| *Children in families* |  |  |  |  |
| Blacks | 42% | 44% | 39% | 33% |
| Whites | 11% | 12% | 12% | 12% |

Source: 1970, 1990 U.S. censuses and American Community Survey, 2010 and 2015; "Persons in poverty" and "median family income" from Current Population Surveys, 1970, 1990, 2010, and 2015 (income adjusted to 2015 U.S. dollars).
[a]income adjusted for 2015 dollars.
[b]Families (with or without children) with a female head, as percent of all families.

ations—in economically deprived settings and to the paucity of marriageable men who are able to find suitable employment in such areas.[14] Government welfare programs, in different forms, have focused on the needs of female heads of families.[15] Today, such "nontraditional" families have increased among whites and other minorities as well, suggesting that they are related to class as well as race.[16] Still, female-headed families are most prevalent among blacks, and their poverty rate is four to five times higher than the rate for black married-couple families.[17]

Black poverty has fallen since the pre–civil rights era, but like employment and earnings, it fluctuates with the economy and the gap with whites remains high. Back in 1959, more than half of all blacks lived in poverty, but the black poverty rate has not reached 30 percent since 1994. Still, the 27 percent black poverty rate in the 2009–10 period was the highest since 1996. More significant for the next generation of blacks is the continued high poverty rate of black children, which rose to 39 percent in 2010 after hitting an all-time low of 30 percent in 2001. Back down to 33 percent in 2015, the black child poverty rate is nearly three times higher than that of the white child poverty rate. Poverty among black children—which is tied to the black female-headed family—

remains an important concern. Such families typically have low incomes that shift with the economy. Although a smaller portion than in past, a little more than half of all black children now reside in a female-headed family and about four-fifths of all black children who live in poverty reside in a female-headed family.

### "Disintegration"

Overall, blacks have made tempered progress, but not in lockstep with one other. There is a clearly recognizable black middle-class population, which arose following new black education and occupational advancements and began to be tracked in the 1980s.[18] In 2007, 48 percent of blacks considered themselves part of the middle class, despite sharp gaps with whites in income, homeownership, and especially wealth—gaps that widened during periods such as the Great Recession of 2007–09.[19] At the same time, there is another segment of the black population that falls far short. This segment, still living in areas of high poverty, is characterized by excessive unemployment, large numbers of single parents and out-of-wedlock births, and substantial incarceration rates for young men—the latter being the subject of much discussion about the excessive force and stereotyping in the policing of black men that has given rise to the Black Lives Matter movement.[20]

In his book *Disintegration: The Splintering of Black America,* journalist Eugene Robinson suggests that the American black population is becoming increasingly segmented by class or is at least forming different identities. The two largest groups are what he calls the "mainstream" and the "abandoned."[21] The former represents a solid middle class, which was a minuscule portion of the black population 50 years ago. The latter, because of its pattern of inner-city or rural place of residence, less stable families, and lower incomes, seems to have increasingly less in common with the new black middle class. The "abandoned" population is generally younger than the black population as a whole. There are other segments of today's black population, which, although tiny in comparison with the others, provide a glimpse of the future. One of these, labeled by Robinson as the "transcendent elite," includes the high-flying, well-paid corporate, entertainment, and political elite, including the forty-fourth president of the United States, Barack Obama.

An "emergent" black population that until recently was barely noticed is composed of black immigrants from other countries. These newest blacks, although small in number only three decades ago, now constitute nearly one-tenth of all blacks and differ from native-born blacks with regard to family and socioeconomic attributes; often they fare better (see figure 6-2).[22] They hail largely from Caribbean countries such as Jamaica and Haiti and more recently from African countries, particularly Nigeria, Ethiopia, and Ghana. African-born black Americans in particular rank much higher than native-born blacks on education attainment. Another "emergent" group is the black multiracial population, persons who identify with more than one race. First enumerated on the 2000 census, they were only about 8 percent of the size of the "black only" population in 2010. Still, their numbers should rise, particularly among young people, in light of increases in interracial marriage and the greater willingness of people to report their multiracial heritage today than in the past.[23] Chapter 10 considers this trend in further detail.

## A SOUTHWARD RETURN

The seeds of greater black upward mobility in the 1960s also provided the impetus for new black geographic mobility. Today, the dominant black regional movement, especially among younger blacks, is toward the South—a region that their great-grandparents were anxious to leave. The 2010 census showed that blacks also are moving to the suburbs to a degree not imagined just a few years ago. Both of these movements counter decades of stereotypes and constraints that no longer apply to a broad segment of the black population. What follows is a discussion of the historic reversal of black

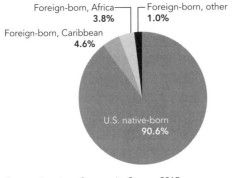

FIGURE 6-2

**U.S. Black Population, by Country of Birth, 2015**

Foreign-born, Africa 3.8%
Foreign-born, other 1.0%
Foreign-born, Caribbean 4.6%
U.S. native-born 90.6%

Source: American Community Survey, 2015.

regional migration—out of and now back to the South—and what it implies for the South and its states and metropolitan areas. Its counterpart migration, the black shift to the suburbs, is discussed in chapter 8.

### Southern Evacuation

The South has always been the primary regional home for blacks. From the beginning of the nation until the start of the twentieth century, at least nine in ten blacks resided in the South, predominantly in rural areas.[24] Although the Thirteenth Amendment gave blacks new freedom to migrate, farm tenancy arrangements, poverty, high levels of illiteracy, and the paucity of opportunities in the North kept black migration from the South at a modest level.[25] All of that changed early in the twentieth century. In the six decades between 1910 and 1970, the Great Migration was under way. In that period an estimated 5 million blacks left the South.[26] The movement was of such magnitude that by 1970, the South retained only a little more than half of the nation's black population (see figure 6-3).

The Great Migration took place in two fairly distinct phases.[27] The first phase, between 1910 and 1930, was triggered by the combination of newly available factory jobs in northern cities, the numbers of which were further increased by U.S. involvement in World War I, and the slowing and eventual government restriction of immigration to the United States. Together, these events caused desperate employers in cities such as New York, Philadelphia, Chicago, and Detroit to look to southern blacks to fill their largely unskilled jobs. Although the pull of northern jobs was a major impetus for migration, there also were strong southern "pushes," including deplorable working conditions, Jim Crow segregation laws, political disenfranchisement, and

FIGURE 6-3

**Percent of U.S. Black Population Residing in the South, 1900–2015**

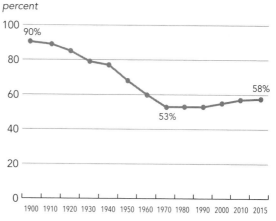

Source: Decennial US censuses and American Community Survey, 2015.

racial violence. Perhaps just as important was the drying up of agricultural employment following farm mechanization and the damage to cotton crops done by the boll weevil.[28]

The second stage took place after a national migration lull during the Great Depression.[29] Again, war was an instigator. The huge increase in manufacturing during World War II brought even more employment opportunities to northern cities and new employment opportunities to western coastal cities such as Los Angeles, San Francisco, and Seattle. The postwar period saw many returning black military veterans settle in northern and western destinations, and even as the South became more urbanized and economically vibrant in the 1950s and 1960s, it continued to experience an out-migration of blacks.

Between 1940 and 1970, roughly 80 percent of all gains in the black population took place outside of the South (see figure 6-4). In contrast to their largely rural settlement patterns at the beginning of the Great Migration, in 1970 eight in ten blacks lived in metropolitan areas, with one in four living in New York, Chicago, Philadelphia, Los Angeles, and

FIGURE 6-4
**U.S. Black Population Gains in the South and Non-South, by Decade, 1910–2010**

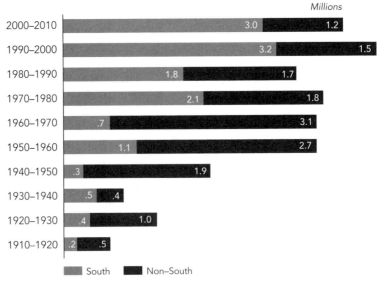

*Millions*

| Decade | South | Non-South |
|---|---|---|
| 2000–2010 | 3.0 | 1.2 |
| 1990–2000 | 3.2 | 1.5 |
| 1980–1990 | 1.8 | 1.7 |
| 1970–1980 | 2.1 | 1.8 |
| 1960–1970 | .7 | 3.1 |
| 1950–1960 | 1.1 | 2.7 |
| 1940–1950 | .3 | 1.9 |
| 1930–1940 | .5 | .4 |
| 1920–1930 | .4 | 1.0 |
| 1910–1920 | .2 | .5 |

South    Non–South

Source: 1910–2010 U.S. censuses.

Detroit. While in 1910 the largest black populations resided in Georgia, Mississippi, and Alabama, the states with the most blacks in 1970 were New York, Illinois, and California (see table 6-3).

**Migration Back to the South**

For the first half of the twentieth century, migration out of the South was not confined to blacks. Because the South was not a prosperous region, in the decades up through 1950 there was also an out-migration of whites, due to new and plentiful employment opportunities in other parts of the country.[30] During the postwar period, however, a favorable business climate coupled with new infrastructure, such as interstate highways, and other improvements, such as the widespread availability of air conditioning, paved the way for the emergence of the "New South." Industries and employers began to head south, and whites were the first to respond, flowing into the region in the 1950s and 1960s.

TABLE 6-3

**Largest State Black Populations, 1910, 1970, and 2010**

| Year/Rank | Black population |
|---|---|
| *1910* | |
| 1  Georgia | 1,176,987 |
| 2  Mississippi | 1,009,487 |
| 3  Alabama | 908,282 |
| *1970* | |
| 1  New York | 2,168,949 |
| 2  Illinois | 1,425,674 |
| 3  California | 1,400,143 |
| *2010* | |
| 1  New York | 3,073,800 |
| 2  Florida | 2,999,862 |
| 3  Texas | 2,979,598 |

Source: 1910, 1970, and 2010 U.S. censuses.

With the deindustrialization that was under way in the 1970s, conditions in the North changed, adversely affecting blacks. Deindustrialization led to the demise or relocation of large numbers of blue-collar jobs, many of which had been filled by urban blacks.[31] At roughly the same time, the "promise" of northern cities was rapidly diminishing. Most blacks resided in less advantaged, segregated city neighborhoods, increasingly isolated from communities where employment opportunities and tax bases were growing as a result of widespread "white flight" to the suburbs.[32] The frustration among blacks over deteriorating employment opportunities, discrimination, and de facto segregation in northern and western cities led to a series of well-publicized urban race riots in the 1960s.[33]

The combined effects of changing "push" and "pull" factors led to the beginning of the black return migration to the South in the 1970s.[34] Figure 6-5 shows the shifts that occurred between five-year migration

FIGURE 6-5

**Black Migration for U.S. Regions, 1965–2010**

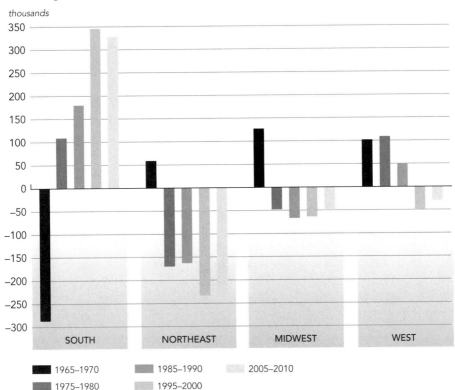

*thousands*

1965–1970
1975–1980
1985–1990
1995–2000
2005–2010

Source: 1970–2000 U.S. censuses and 2010 Current Population Survey, Annual Social and Economic Supplement.

periods in the late 1960s and late 1970s. From 1965 to 1970, the South still lost black migrants to each of the two census-defined northern regions— the Northeast and the Midwest—and to the West. Yet by 1975 to 1980, the South gained black migrants overall, due to its new migrants from both the Northeast and Midwest.

### Reversing State Origins and Destinations

At the state level, the shift was even more dramatic.[35] In the late 1960s, the 14 states experiencing the greatest black exodus were all located in the South, led by the Deep South states of Mississippi, Alabama, and Louisiana. At the same time, nine of the top ten states that gained black populations were located outside the South, led by California and Michigan.

By the late 1970s, however, six of the ten states losing the most blacks to migration were outside of the South—led by New York, Illinois, and Pennsylvania. And although California still led all states in black inmigration, the next six migration gainers were Maryland, Texas, Georgia, Virginia, Florida, and North Carolina. The new black migration gains were clearly favoring southern coastal states and Texas, areas where economies and employment opportunities were on the rise. This was only the first glimpse of a new wave of black migration back to the South, involving both "return" migrants and new migrants who were born in other regions. As figure 6-5 indicates, southern migration gains hit record levels in the 1990s and in the first decade of the 2000s, as did non-southern losses. In the 1990s, for the first time, the South gained black migrants from the West—especially California and the former black destination areas of Los Angeles and San Francisco.

Thus, since the 1990s the South has been gaining black migrants from all other regions of the country. Black migration gains continued to be concentrated in the Southeast and Texas. Georgia led all states in migration gains from the late 1980s through 2010. Among migration losers, New York lost the most black migrants of any state in every period since 1975 and Illinois ranked either second or third in losses during that time frame. Map 6-1 shows the sharp contrast in black migration between the end of the Great Migration and the present. Most of the major Great Migration destination states—such as New York, Illinois, Michigan, and California—have become the greatest contributors to the new southern migration gains. These shifts reflect the changing fortunes of and decisions made by blacks residing in metropolitan areas such as New York, Chicago, Los Angeles, Detroit, and Philadelphia, which have been losing black migrants since the 1970s.[36]

The cumulative effect of recent black migration out of these states and regions has had a profound impact on the overall size of the black population in these previous destinations. The 2010 census reported that, for the first time, the states of New York, Illinois, Michigan, and California registered absolute losses of their black populations (when defined to include only non-Hispanic blacks).[37]

MAP 6-1

**States with Greatest Black Migration Gains and Losses, 1965–70 and 2005–10[a]**

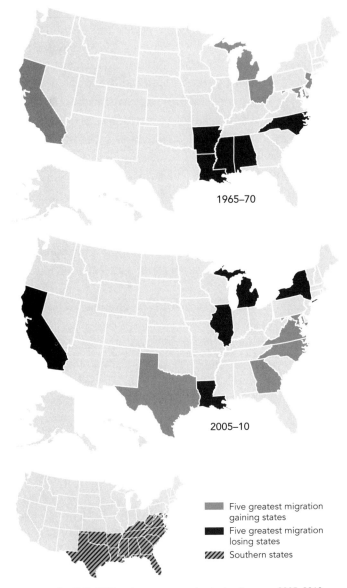

1965–70

2005–10

Five greatest migration gaining states

Five greatest migration losing states

Southern states

[a]Migration for 1965–1970 and average annual net migration over 2005–2010 (multiplied by 5).

Source: 1970 U.S. census; American Community Survey, 2006–10.

*Young Adults, College Grads, and Seniors Lead the Way*

While the volume of new black migration to the South is important, so are the changes that black migrants are bringing to the South with regard to youth and human capital. In the late 1970s and 1980s, the first waves of black North-to-South metropolitan migrants already showed improvements in their immediate social and economic circumstances.[38] While blacks moving to the South exhibit a wide range of family types and income and education levels, it is clear that blacks who migrated to the South in recent decades, especially those arriving in economically prosperous areas, have been disproportionately young and well educated (see figure 6-6).[39] For college-educated and professional blacks, networking opportunities became available in metropolitan areas such as Atlanta, Washington, D.C., Raleigh, and Dallas. Both black and white col-

FIGURE 6-6

**Black Migration Rates, by Age and Education, 2005–10**[a]

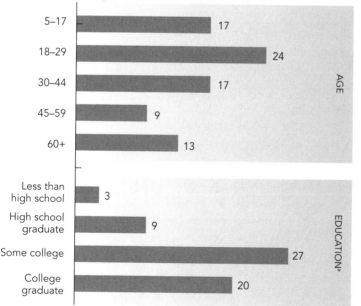

*Net migration per 1,000 South black residents*

Source: 2010 Current Population Survey. Annual Social and Economic Supplement.
[a]Persons age 25 and above.

lege graduates left New York, Illinois, Ohio, Michigan, New Jersey, California, and Louisiana (the latter reflecting, in part, outward movement related to Hurricane Katrina). However, whites moved to a more diverse mix of southern and western regions than did blacks. Black college graduates are heading predominantly for Texas, Georgia, and North Carolina (see map 6-2).[40]

College graduates are not the only migrants. For retirees, many southern Sun Belt areas have both personal and historical appeal (see figure 6-6). The southern pull on black retirees is just beginning to be felt. In the coming decades, millions of non-southern blacks will reach retirement age. Although most retirees do not move long distances, this new, larger senior population will bring more black retiree migrants to the South. Already between 2005 and 2010, migration gains of blacks age 55 and older were greatest in Georgia, Texas, and North Carolina—states that dominated all others. The migration gains of older white adults were less concentrated than those of blacks and were greatest in the traditional "retiree" magnet states—Florida and Arizona leading all others.

### Renewed Southern Ties for Blacks

The draw of the New South is clearly strongest for blacks. Figure 6-7 shows the regional destinations of black and white migrants originating in each non-southern region from 2005 to 2010. In each originating region, the South is the largest destination for both groups. But in each case, black migrants were more likely than whites to select destinations in the South. Among migrants from the Northeast, eight in ten blacks but only five in ten whites chose destinations in the South. Similar patterns are evident for migrants from the Midwest and West. This was the case in the late 1990s and likely earlier periods as well.[41]

Jobs and the South's new economic prosperity are not the only reason that blacks are returning "home." Cultural ties and a large black population are strong draws as well. The cultural and familial bonds associated with residence within the black community were evident in the past. Although the black South-to-North migrants who took part in the Great Migration were less likely to return to the South than were white southern out-migrants during in the same period, they kept in contact with family and maintained kinship networks that helped to promote further

MAP 6-2

**College Graduates[a]: States with Greatest Migration Gains and Losses, Blacks and Whites, 2005–10[b]**

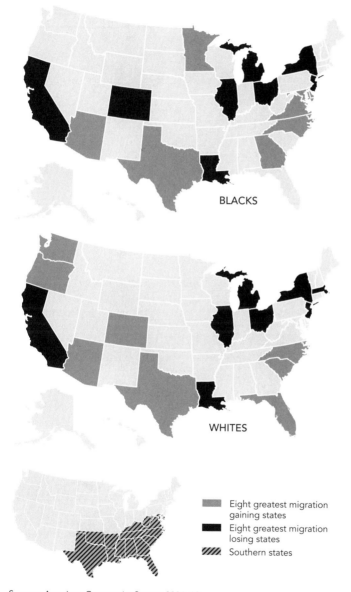

BLACKS

WHITES

Eight greatest migration gaining states

Eight greatest migration losing states

Southern states

Source : American Community Survey, 2006–10.

[a]Among persons age 25 and over.
[b]Average annual net migration over the period 2005–10.

FIGURE 6-7
**Whites and Blacks: Top Regional Destinations of Movers, 2005–10**

*Percent moving to region*

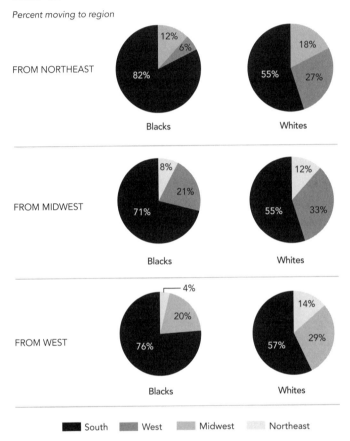

Source: 2010 Current Population Survey, Annual Social and Economic Supplement.

migration out of the South. Blacks' ties to the southern region, whether personal or cultural, also have been evident in the later movement back, especially among northern city residents who did not fare well during the deindustrialization period and found a familiar and welcoming environment among family and friends in the rural South.[42] But there are ties to the region for a broad spectrum of blacks, including retirees with family histories in the South and young professionals who want to join areas with growing middle-class black populations.

Thus, a half-century after the civil rights legislation of the 1960s, new generations of blacks, particularly those with a college education, are moving away from their earlier predominant destinations. Although the initial "reverse" migrants may have been fleeing from deteriorating economic and social conditions in the North, recent younger and privileged migrants are moving to a more prosperous, post–civil rights South that was unknown to their forebears.

## NEW BLACK METROPOLITAN MAGNETS

The migration reversal that has directed mainstream segments of the black population back to the South has changed the hierarchy of metropolitan areas in terms of population size. Most symbolic of this change is the explosion of metropolitan Atlanta's black population over the 1970–2010 period, when it increased more than fourfold. In 1970 Atlanta had the nation's thirteenth-largest black population; in 2010 it had the second-largest, displacing Chicago (see figure 6-8). Atlanta has led all other metropolitan areas in black in-migration for the past three-decades and showed the greatest total black population gains (including migration, natural increase, and immigration) between 1990 and 2010. Atlanta, arguably the capital of the New South, is a transportation hub with a diverse array of industries, educational institutions, and corporate headquarters, and it has been a migration magnet in general and especially for blacks.

Following Atlanta, the next-largest black population gainers in 2000–10 were Dallas, Houston, Miami, Washington, D.C., and Charlotte. Of the 15 metropolitan areas with the largest gains in black population, 11 are in the South. In contrast, earlier black destinations in the North have exhibited out-migration for the last several decades. Many, such as New York, showed black population gains for some of that period, even while experiencing out-migration, due to natural increase. But in the last decade, metropolitan New York, Chicago, Los Angeles, and Detroit sustained absolute losses in their black populations. Table 6-4 compares the areas with the largest black populations in 1970 and 2010. Metropolitan New York, even with its now fairly stagnant population, still ranks first

TABLE 6-4

**Metropolitan Areas with Largest Black Populations, 1970 and 2010**

| Rank/area | Black population |
|---|---|
| *1970* | |
| 1 New York | 2,449,294 |
| 2 Chicago | 1,345,965 |
| 3 Philadelphia | 905,196 |
| 4 Los Angeles | 773,023 |
| 5 Detroit | 760,617 |
| 6 Washington, DC | 749,740 |
| 7 Baltimore | 494,498 |
| *2010* | |
| 1 New York | 3,362,616 |
| 2 Atlanta | 1,707,913 |
| 3 Chicago | 1,645,993 |
| 4 Washington, DC | 1,438,436 |
| 5 Philadelphia | 1,241,780 |
| 6 Miami | 1,169,185 |
| 7 Houston | 1,025,775 |

Source: 1970 and 2010 U.S. censuses.

in black population size. However, Atlanta, Washington, D.C., Miami, and Houston have risen in rank and now are among the seven metropolitan areas that are home to more than 1 million blacks, with Dallas not far behind. Another dimension of black movement to the South is the socioeconomic upgrading of the southern black population due to the selective movement of college-educated and professional blacks to many southern metropolitan areas, discussed above.

Map 6-3 depicts the nation's largest metropolitan areas by the education attainment of their black populations. Southern areas are heavily represented among the areas with the most educated black pop-

FIGURE 6-8

**Metropolitan Chicago and Atlanta Black Populations, 1970–2010**

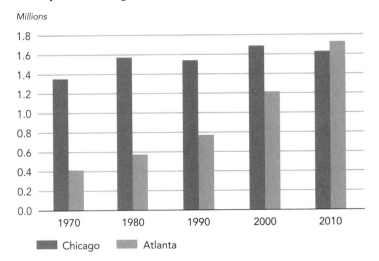

Source: 1970–2010 U.S. censuses.

MAP 6-3

**Black College Graduates: Major Metropolitan Areas with Highest and Lowest Percentages[a]**

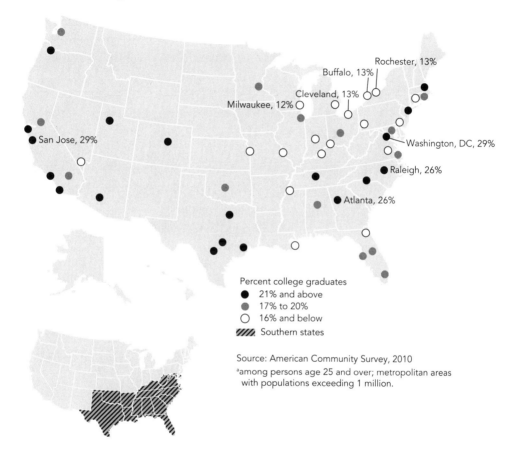

Percent college graduates
- ● 21% and above
- ● 17% to 20%
- ○ 16% and below
- ▨ Southern states

Source: American Community Survey, 2010
[a]among persons age 25 and over; metropolitan areas with populations exceeding 1 million.

ulations, led by Washington, D.C., Raleigh, and Atlanta. San Antonio, Nashville, Austin, and Dallas also are on this list. In addition, southern metropolitan areas including Washington, D.C., Baltimore, and Atlanta rank among the areas with the highest black household incomes. In contrast, northern metropolitan areas rank unfavorably with regard to black educational attainment, household income, and poverty. Among the lowest-ranked areas on those measures are Milwaukee, Cleveland, and

Buffalo.[43] The continuing shift in the migration of blacks to large southern metropolitan areas has changed another long-held stereotype. No longer do blacks in the South constitute a primarily poor, rural population. In 2010, 83 percent of southern blacks resided in metropolitan areas and fully two-thirds of that group lived in large metropolitan areas—both cities and suburbs—with total populations exceeding 500,000.

## THE DISTINCTIVE SOUTH

It is certainly true that more recently arrived minorities, particularly Hispanics, are dispersing to states in the New Sun Belt. Yet due to the continued in-migration and now rising growth of blacks in the South, it is fair to say that much of the South has returned to its roots as a region with predominantly black and white populations. No longer do nine in ten U.S. blacks live in the South, as was the case 100 years ago. But the portion of the nation's blacks in the South has risen from a low of 53 percent in 1970 to 58 percent in 2015 and will rise further as current trends continue. As of 2015, blacks were still the largest minority in the South, constituting nearly one-fifth of its population. Moreover, since 2000 the lion's share—two-thirds—of Hispanic population gains in the South occurred in just two states: Texas and Florida.

So while there is increasing multiracial diversity in large parts of the South, black population gains will continue to ensure that blacks remain the largest racial minority in most southern states and in many large metropolitan areas. Figure 6-9 shows that of the 16 southern states and Washington, D.C., blacks constitute the largest minority in all but Texas, Florida, and Oklahoma. The black populations in each of the remaining states are more than twice as large as the Hispanic populations and more than three times as large in eight states, including the New Sun Belt states of Georgia, South Carolina, and Tennessee. In metropolitan Atlanta, blacks constitute one-third of the population while Hispanics account for just 10 percent. Blacks also are the predominant minority in Charlotte, Raleigh, Nashville, and Washington, D.C., among other metropolitan areas.

FIGURE 6-9

## Minority Percent of Population, Southern States, 2015

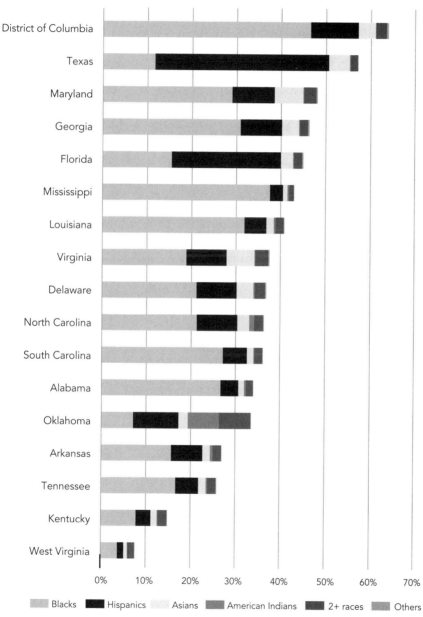

Source: American Community Survey, 2015.

Although it is true that some blacks are dispersing away from traditional settings to fast-growing areas in the Mountain West (for example, Phoenix and Las Vegas) or even toward new destinations in the North (for example, Minneapolis), the South—especially large metropolitan areas within the region—is now the major beacon for new generations of black migrants and homegrown stayers. The South that blacks are moving to has been changing in fundamental ways. Although black neighborhood segregation is still substantial, it has declined noticeably in rapidly growing southern metropolitan areas, faster than in most other parts of the country.[44] And the results of both the 2008 and 2012 presidential elections have shown that the black voting bloc is continuing to make the South more competitive for the major parties.[45] Thus, whether it is because of family connections, cultural ties, or just the "comfort level" in a region that, for better or worse, is familiar and predictable, the South will continue to stand out from the rest of the country by maintaining a large and increasingly prosperous black presence as it also receives other racial minorities.

# White Population Shifts
## A Zero-Sum Game

# 7

Although whites constitute the greatest share of the U.S. population, white growth has slowed to a snail's pace because of low immigration and fertility rates. White gains and losses for different regions and communities depend heavily on migration to and from other parts of the country. Consequently, white population shifts are a zero-sum game. White migrants tend to favor non-coastal, New Sun Belt destinations, similar to those chosen by dispersing minorities. Therefore large metropolitan areas like New York, Los Angeles, and San Francisco are losing whites to areas like Atlanta, Phoenix, and Las Vegas, among others, in growing parts of the South and West.

Yet whites favor smaller metropolitan areas and exurban communities more than dispersing minorities do. The reasons for this new white flight, particularly among young families and retirees, include the cost of living, amenities, and lifestyle preferences instead of the racial antagonism that fueled neighborhood white flight decades ago. Although the white shift represents an initial soft separation from more clustered minority populations, the dispersion of new minorities and blacks, discussed earlier, will close this separation in the near future. At the same time, there appears to be a growing geographic divide within the white population as younger, better-off whites distance themselves from increasingly older, less affluent white populations. This chapter reviews these and other aspects of the nation's ongoing white population shifts.[1]

## AN AGING AND SLOWLY GROWING POPULATION

For most of U.S. history, the white population has been viewed as "mainstream" society, and earlier laws concerning immigration and voting rights and other privileges gave whites priority over other racial and ethnic minorities. For decades, sociologists have viewed the assimilation of immigrants and ethnic minorities into American society as dependent on their adoption of the way of life practiced by the largely white mainstream society.[2] For all of that time, whites were the numerically dominant racial group in the United States. Between 1790 and 1980, whites ranged from 80 to 90 percent of the population, and in 2010, they still constituted 64 percent of the population.[3] On standard social and economic measures, whites fared better as a group than most racial minorities.[4]

However, the image of whites as America's mainstream population is on the wane, in a demographic sense. Population projections based on the 2010 census show that in the 2040s, whites will become a minority of the total population.[5] In 2010 whites were already a minority in 22 of the nation's 100 largest metropolitan areas, and they represented no more than 60 percent of the population in 13 states, including California, Texas, New Mexico, and Hawaii, as well as in Washington, D.C., where they constitute less than one-half of the population. Although some of this change is connected to the rapid growth of the nation's minorities, it also is driven by the slowing growth of the white population. As figure 7-1 indicates, white growth sank to just 1.2 percent for the 2000–10 period. Furthermore, the nation's white population is projected to decline for the first time between 2020 and 2030. The decline is due in part to projected low white immigration and natural decrease in the white population (that is, more deaths than births). Fewer births

FIGURE 7-1
**Past and Projected White Population Growth**

*Growth (%)*

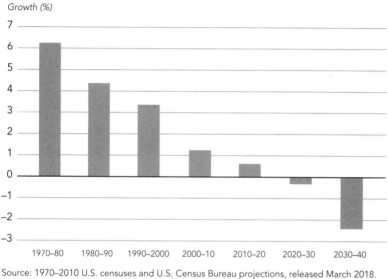

Source: 1970–2010 U.S. censuses and U.S. Census Bureau projections, released March 2018.

and more deaths will be part and parcel of an aging white population. Thus, for most of the lifetime of today's children—nearly one-half of whom already are members of racial minorities—the nation's white population will be in decline.

Yet while the overall white population is headed for decline, the senior population—those age 65 and older—will grow substantially in the next two decades as the large baby boom generation—born between 1946 and 1964—makes its way into the ranks of the senior population. Consequently, the slowly growing white population will begin an accelerated aging process. This contrasts with the experience of the more rapidly growing minority population. With higher fertility rates and greater immigration, the minority population will not age nearly as rapidly as whites. In 2010, 16 percent of the white population already was age 65 or older while just 7 percent of the minority population had reached that age (see figure 7-2). Moreover, that gap will increase: by 2030 approximately 26 percent of the nation's whites but just 13 percent of minorities will be seniors. The disparity between older whites and younger minorities will further magnify the cultural generation gap discussed in chapter 2.

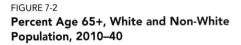

FIGURE 7-2

**Percent Age 65+, White and Non-White Population, 2010–40**

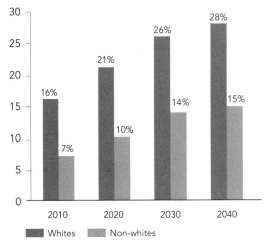

Source: 2010 U.S. census and U.S. Census Bureau projections, released March, 2018.

At the same time that the older portion of the white population is growing, the younger portion will be shrinking. The nation's white population under age 18 had already begun to decline in 2000–10. This decline will continue into the future, as will the decline in the white population under age 65. Between 2015 and 2040, the non-senior white population will be reduced by more than 20 million. Smaller white populations already are evident in institutions that serve youth, such as elementary and secondary schools. The increased absence of large numbers of whites also will soon be seen in the ranks of the labor force, as older, mostly white baby boomers begin to retire in large numbers. Yet the demise of whites as America's mainstream population in terms of sheer numbers should not change its uniqueness in terms of social and economic attributes. Whites are still more highly educated and more likely to have professional, managerial, or "white collar" jobs than the combined minority population, and they are far less likely to live in poverty. Although there are segments within the white population that are doing less well on each of those dimensions, the general trend continues to be that whites do better than the population as a whole on standard socioeconomic measures (see table 7-1).[6]

Even so, the aging of the white population shows up in other ways. There are as many seniors as children in the white population—in sharp contrast with the case of the minority population, which has more than three times as many children as seniors. In addition, the household makeup of the white population is older, more independent, and less child-centric than that of the rest of the population. Despite its higher socioeconomic standing, the older white population reports higher rates of disability. With regard to age, household type, and medical needs, the

TABLE 7-1
**White and Minority Social and Demographic Profiles, 2015**
*Percent*

|  | Whites | Minorities |
|---|---|---|
| *Education*[a] | | |
| College graduate | 34 | 24 |
| Not high school graduate | 8 | 23 |
| *Occupation*[b] | | |
| Management, business, science, and arts occupations | 37 | 29 |
| *Poverty* | | |
| Persons in poverty | 10 | 22 |
| *Age* | | |
| Under 18 | 19 | 29 |
| Age 65+ | 19 | 9 |
| *Household type* | | |
| Household with children | 27 | 42 |
| Childless married couple | 32 | 18 |
| Single person living alone | 29 | 25 |
| *Disability status* | | |
| Disabled | 14 | 11 |

Source: U.S. census and American Community Survey, 2015.

[a]Persons age 25 and over.
[b]Persons in labor force.

slowly growing white population and the nation's growing minorities are at opposite ends of the spectrum.

## GAINING AND LOSING AREAS

The fact that the nation's white population is growing so tepidly means that white population growth and decline across different areas is a zero-sum game. That is, because hardly any demographic cushion is provided by fertility and immigration, white migration is the primary source of growth or loss. Therefore, areas that are gaining substantial numbers of whites are taking growth prospects away from areas that are losing whites. Some areas that are seeing declines in the white population caused by migration—particularly many counties in the Great Plains, Midwest, and parts of the South—also are experiencing a natural decrease in their largely white populations.[7]

At the state level, white population shifts that favor New Sun Belt states are associated with migration flows that have been emerging for several decades.[8] In the first decade of the 2000s, notable white growth occurred in a swath of Mountain West states, including Arizona, Idaho, Nevada, and Utah, and southeastern states such as Georgia and North Carolina. The attraction of these areas, as indicated in chapter 3, lies in their generally low cost of living, the growth of employment in a variety of old and new economy industries, and recreational and environmental amenities that make them attractive to people both in and out of the workforce. Changes in area economies, especially during the 2007–09 recession, led to short-term growth fluctuation in these areas.[9] But the broad trends favoring the interior West and the Southeast are part of the prevailing long-term pattern of U.S. domestic migration, of which whites constitute a major part (see map 7-1).

MAP 7-1
**White Population Growth and Decline, 2000–10**

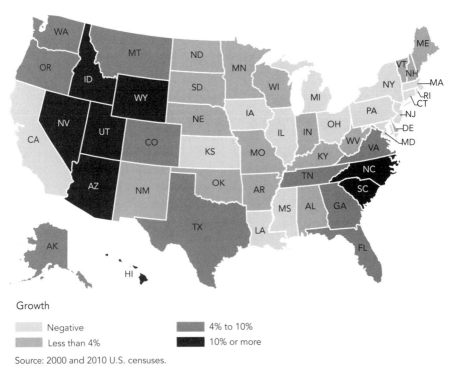

Growth

Negative

Less than 4%

4% to 10%

10% or more

Source: 2000 and 2010 U.S. censuses.

The biggest losers of white migrants are exemplified by two types of states. The first group includes heavily urbanized coastal states with high costs of living where employment growth was less pronounced than in other parts of the country. California, New York, and New Jersey are prime examples of these. The second group includes states where employment slowdowns have spurred major out-migration. Such states, including Michigan, Ohio, and Pennsylvania, are located largely in the Midwest and Northeast. These are among 15 states that registered absolute declines in their white populations in the first decade of the 2000s.

White declines are even more evident in metropolitan areas—areas that more closely represent labor markets. Of the 366 metropolitan areas across the country, the 145 that lost whites in 2000–10 are heavily concentrated in the country's Heartland—in the Northeast, Midwest, and interior South. Yet, as with states, the metropolitan areas losing the most whites are in coastal areas, including metropolitan New York and Los Angeles, each of which lost more than 1 million whites between 1990 and 2010. Also represented among the 11 areas losing the most whites are Heartland metropolitan areas including Detroit, Pittsburgh, and Cleveland (see table 7-2). The metropolitan areas gaining the most whites, on the other hand, are located in the interior West, the Southeast, and Texas, including Phoenix, Atlanta, Raleigh, Charlotte, and Dallas—

TABLE 7-2

**Greatest White Losses and Gains, by Metropolitan Area, 1990–2010**

| Rank | Greatest white losses | | Rank | Greatest white gains |
|---|---|---|---|---|
| 1 New York | −1,179,718 | | 1 Phoenix | 754,565 |
| 2 Los Angeles | −1,116,531 | | 2 Atlanta | 489,191 |
| 3 San Francisco | −323,705 | | 3 Dallas | 403,483 |
| 4 Chicago | −283,282 | | 4 Las Vegas | 377,080 |
| 5 Miami | −271,415 | | 5 Denver | 374,988 |
| 6 Philadelphia | −251,489 | | 6 Austin | 367,598 |
| 7 San Jose | −240,604 | | 7 Portland | 331,197 |
| 8 Detroit | −239,158 | | 8 Raleigh | 307,308 |
| 9 Pittsburgh | −203,823 | | 9 Nashville | 302,187 |
| 10 Boston | −181,839 | | 10 Charlotte | 295,333 |
| 11 Cleveland | −162,429 | | 11 Minneapolis | 254,750 |

Source: 1990 and 2010 U.S. censuses.

areas with diversified economies that include knowledge-based industries. They are attractive for a broad spectrum of migrants who are leaving the expensive coastal areas and northern areas with more depressed economies.

To some degree, whites are gradually shifting from whiter states in the Northeast, Midwest, and Great Plains to economically vibrant states in the South and Mountain West—New Sun Belt states that are now attracting new minorities as well as whites. As depicted in chapter 3 and in maps 3-11 and 3-12, this pattern is especially evident across counties. Over 1,600 of the nation's 3,100 counties are at least 85 percent white, including many in the nation's Heartland and in large numbers of rural and small-town counties. Two-fifths these mostly white counties showed losses in white population from 1990 to 2010. Although many of these counties began receiving some dispersing new minorities in recent years, they represent a large swath of mostly white, declining or slowly growing counties across the country's midsection whose populations are aging more rapidly than the country's population as a whole.

## THE NEW WHITE FLIGHT

The term "white flight" was used to describe the massive movement of white families from cities to newly minted suburban communities in the 1950s and 1960s, a period when suburbs were developing in metropolitan areas across the country. This movement—a result of the post–World War II economic surge, highway development, G.I. Bill–subsidized home loans for returning war veterans, the baby boom, and the rise in family households—allowed families to enjoy the economic and lifestyle benefits afforded by relocation to the suburbs. A wide array of factors led to postwar white flight. Among them was the desire to escape urban congestion, aging housing, deteriorating services, and the high costs of city living by moving to newer, more spacious single-family housing in a more family-friendly environment. Racial attitudes also were an important motivation.[10] Whites often left city neighborhoods because they felt threatened by the increased presence of blacks, from whom they wished to distance themselves. Blacks, then the nation's predominant minority, were effectively barred from moving because of housing restrictions and other forms of discrimination.

As chapter 8 discusses, movement by whites from the city to the suburbs has diminished over time, and the presence of minorities in suburbia has increased, particularly the presence of Hispanics. Yet there is a new form of white flight that is less associated with local suburban movement per se and more associated with movement to outer, smaller areas, especially in the New Sun Belt. This movement is less racially motivated than its predecessor was. But like its predecessor, it is associated with the quest for lifestyle improvements and opportunities in newer communities that are less congested and less expensive than the cities *and the suburbs* of the metropolitan areas that whites are leaving.

### White Flight to Smaller New Sun Belt Areas

The regional and metropolitan dimensions of white flight follow those of the white "winner" and "loser" areas discussed above. The loser areas include the costly coastal areas of the Northeast megalopolis and California. Since the late 1980s, white movement from these areas has included more than just job-related migration, which typically involves the youngest and best-educated residents; it also has included migration by middle-class residents escaping high housing costs for more affordable opportunities elsewhere.[11] This group includes a broad range of people, from families with children to empty nesters and retirees of all education and income levels—the same demographic groups that in earlier generations relocated from cities to nearby suburbs.[12] In addition, metropolitan areas in the less vibrant, northern, middle of the country are bleeding white migrants, particularly young people in search of jobs. The same goes for hard-hit smaller and rural areas.

Unlike the earlier white flight, the new white flight is extra-local and in many cases interregional. Yet its deconcentrated nature is similar to that of its earlier counterpart—that is, it involves movement to newer, smaller, and suburban-oriented metropolitan areas and, within those areas, to outer suburbs and exurbs. Figure 7-3 shows the broad parameters of white population growth in the first decade of the 2000s. There is a pervasive shift from the Northeast and Midwest to the South and West, as has been occurring for many decades, and growth rates are especially pronounced in medium-size and smaller metropolitan areas in the latter regions. Although white numeric gains are greatest in large areas such as Phoenix, Dallas, and Raleigh, the fastest white growth rates are seen in smaller metropolitan areas. Palm Coast, Florida; St. George, Utah; Greeley, Colorado; Wilmington, North Carolina; and Bend, Oregon, each increased its white population by more than 30 percent in 2000–10. Of the 73 metropolitan areas that increased their white population by more than 10 percent, the vast majority are smaller metropolitan areas in the South and West.

### White Flight to the Exurbs

Another part of the new white flight is occurring within the suburbs. Because of decades of postwar white flight, the majority—seven in ten—of metropolitan whites already reside within the suburbs, broadly defined. In recent years, whites, particularly the young, have been shifting from the suburbs of older metropolitan areas to newer, expanding suburbs in metropolitan areas in the Sun Belt, and they have been gravitating from inner to outer suburbs. This trend follows the continuing quest for more affordable single-family homes, perceived greater safety, and a more desirable lifestyle, which requires those in the workforce to commute a bit farther, although many can now telecommute. For retirees, the outer suburbs provide an opportunity for some to take advantage of a small com-

FIGURE 7-3

**White Growth, by Region and Type of Metropolitan Area, 2000–10**

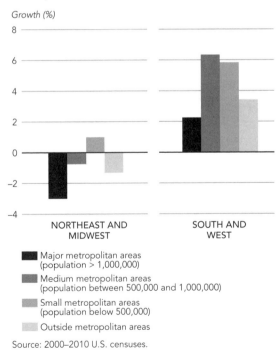

*Growth (%)*

Major metropolitan areas
(population > 1,000,000)

Medium metropolitan areas
(population between 500,000 and 1,000,000)

Small metropolitan areas
(population below 500,000)

Outside metropolitan areas

Source: 2000–2010 U.S. censuses.

munity and less stressful environment in close proximity to natural amenities.

Over 2000–10, the white populations of the outer exurban counties of the nation's largest metropolitan areas grew by a whopping 12 percent. In contrast, white populations grew by only 2 percent in middle and denser inner suburbs and declined by 7 percent in urban core counties.[13] The outward spread of whites within the suburbs is evident in coastal and northern metropolitan areas, which are losing whites overall, and in rapidly growing New Sun Belt metropolitan areas. Map 7-2 depicts an example of each. Although the New York metropolitan area lost more than 500,000 whites between 2000 and 2010, that was not the case for each of its 23 counties, which extend into the states of New York, New Jersey, and Pennsylvania. Three of these counties—Pike County, Pennsylvania; Ocean County, New Jersey; and Hunterdon County, New Jersey—in addition to the Manhattan and Brooklyn boroughs of New York City, showed white population gains. These three counties are the farthest

MAP 7-2

**White Urban and Suburban County Growth: New York and Atlanta Metropolitan Areas, 2000–10**

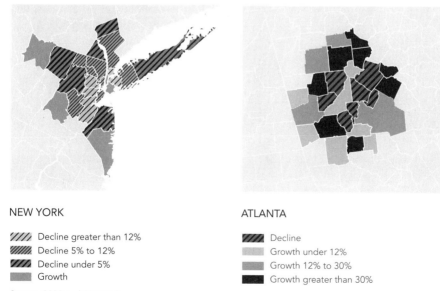

NEW YORK

▨ Decline greater than 12%
▨ Decline 5% to 12%
▨ Decline under 5%
▨ Growth

Source: 2000 and 2010 U.S. censuses.

ATLANTA

▨ Decline
▨ Growth under 12%
▨ Growth 12% to 30%
▨ Growth greater than 30%

flung of the metropolitan area. Of the 18 counties that lost white population, the greatest rates of decline were in Middlesex County, Union County, and Essex County in New Jersey and the New York City boroughs of Queens and the Bronx.

The same spread to the periphery is also evident in Atlanta, a metropolitan area that gained more than 100,000 whites over the decade. Of its 28 counties, the white population grew in all but seven near the urban core. However, the most rapidly growing counties—those registering white growth rates of more than 30 percent—include Forsythe, Paulding, Pike, Cherokee, and Dawson, in the northern and outer suburbs. Their white gains came from migrants originating both inside and outside of the metropolitan area. In this respect, they mirror broader trends that are evident in most of the New Sun Belt.

Of course, not all white gains are occurring in the suburbs and outer suburbs. As shown, parts of New York City—Manhattan and Brooklyn—are havens for young, gentrifying whites and empty nesters. A select group of cities—including Washington, D.C., Seattle, and Denver—exhibited white gains while most inner urban cores were losing whites. The draw of cities for young people during their dating and mating years is not new. In the past, however, they usually moved to the suburbs when children arrived. Yet today's trends in these cities suggest that a countertrend is under way, which could spread to more places, especially as white urban-oriented baby boomers retire and if more millennals embrace the urban lifestyle.

### A "Soft Separation" Between Whites and Minorities

Just as the old city-to-suburb white flight exacerbated the sharp separation between whites and blacks, the new regional white flight to smaller and outer suburban areas is shaping a somewhat softer racial separation. Although Hispanics, Asians, and blacks also are dispersing from traditional urban clusters, their numbers have not reached parity with that of the white population for two reasons: first, the white population was already more heavily located in smaller-sized areas and the suburbs; second, the dispersion of the new, slowly growing white population continues. Thus, although many rural counties are losing whites and gaining some minorities, nearly one-half of the

FIGURE 7-4
**Race Profiles, by Type of Metropolitan Area, 1990–2010**

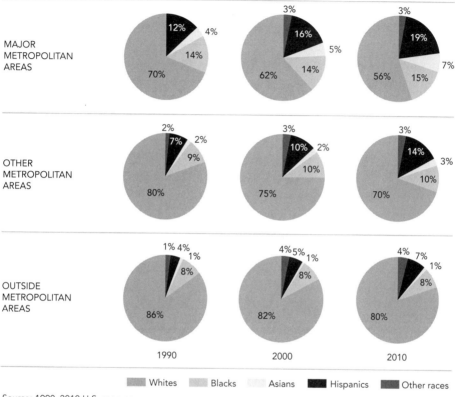

Source: 1990–2010 U.S. censuses.

nation's rural and small metropolitan counties are more than 90 percent white. At the other extreme, 67 percent of Hispanics, 79 percent
of Asians, and 64 percent of blacks still reside in major metropolitan
areas with more than 1 million residents. That is the case for less than
one-half of whites.

Consequently, recent minority gains are still far more prevalent in
major metropolitan areas than in smaller-sized metropolitan areas or
locations outside of metropolitan areas, where white gains prevail.
Between 1990 and 2010, minorities came to constitute 44 percent of the
combined major metropolitan area populations (see figure 7-4). Yet out-

side metropolitan areas, whites still accounted for eight in ten residents. A similar pattern also has occurred within metropolitan areas. Inner-urban-core counties are now majority-minority, although outer-exurban counties are 80 percent white. Over time, the dispersal of younger generations of minorities will close the geographic gap with the nation's aging white population. But in the near term, the different social and political interests of these groups will continue to sustain the gap between them.

## DIVISIONS WITHIN THE WHITE POPULATION

The population shifts of whites from "loser" to "winner" areas over the last two decades have also created social and demographic divisions within the white population. White migration, like most migration, favors young adults and young families. The whites remaining in areas that are losing their white population, particularly rural areas and small towns that have lost their economic magnetism, are older, less privileged, and less educated. That stands in contrast to rapidly growing, white-gaining areas, which are becoming the most youthful. This contrast is demonstrated in the upper panel of table 7-3, which compares 1,164 counties outside metropolitan areas that lost whites between 1990 and 2010 with 587 counties that had at least a 25 percent increase in whites in the same period. These quickly growing counties are located largely in the South and Mountain West (depicted in chapter 3, map 3-11). The former counties have already aged to such an extent that nearly one-fifth of their white population is age 65 or older and close to three in ten households are single-person households.

The faster-growing counties include more children and married couples and fewer seniors. Many are located in the outer suburbs of New Sun Belt metropolitan areas, including places such as Forsythe County in suburban Atlanta, Douglas County in suburban Denver, and Loudon County in suburban Washington, D.C. In each of these counties, married couples with children constitute more than one-third of all white households. Married-with-children households have dwindled to less than one-fifth of white households for the nation as a whole.

TABLE 7-3
**White Demographic Attributes, by Geographic Area, 2010**
*Percent*

| Geographic area | Seniors age 65 and over | Single-person households | Children under 18 years old | Married persons | Persons in poverty | College graduates[a] |
|---|---|---|---|---|---|---|
| *Fast-growing and declining counties*[b] | | | | | | |
| Fast-growing | 15 | 25 | 22 | 58 | 9 | 31 |
| Declining and outside metropolitan areas | 18 | 29 | 20 | 55 | 13 | 19 |
| *Urban-suburban-exurban*[c] | | | | | | |
| Urban Core | 17 | 32 | 18 | 51 | 7 | 43 |
| Mature Suburbs | 16 | 28 | 20 | 54 | 7 | 35 |
| Emerging Suburbs | 15 | 26 | 22 | 57 | 8 | 31 |
| Exurbs | 15 | 23 | 23 | 59 | 10 | 21 |

Source: 2010 U.S. census; American Community Survey, 2006–10.

[a] Among persons age 25 and over.

[b] Counties classed by white growth and decline over the period 1990–2010 as shown in map 3.11 in chapter 3. Fast-growing counties are those where the white population increased by at least 25 percent over the 20-year period; declining counties are those that lie outside metropolitan areas, and registered white population losses.

[c] Counties associated with metropolitan areas with populations over 500,000 and classed by an urban density measure discussed in Brookings Institution Metropolitan Policy Program, "State of Metropolitan America 2010," pp. 16–19 (www.brookings.edu/~/media/Research/Files/Reports/2010/5/09%20metro%20america/metro_america_report.pdf).

The distinctions within large metropolitan areas are shown in the lower panel of table 7-3. Here, white children and married couples are most plentiful in outer-suburban and exurban counties. Inner-urban-core areas, especially those that have sustained decades of white flight, generally house older populations and have a higher proportion of single-person households. For example, in Cuyahoga County, Ohio, which surrounds the city of Cleveland, seniors make up nearly 20 percent of the white population and 36 percent of white households consist of one person. Still, as discussed earlier, some cities continue to attract young singles and childless couples for short periods of their lives and for even longer periods in cities with strong economies and vibrant downtowns.

Disparities within the white population also are evident with regard to social and economic attributes. Rural areas, particularly those with declining white populations, have high levels of white poverty. The highest white poverty rates can be found outside metropolitan areas in the interior Midwest and South. In 2010, more than one-half of white residents in Shannon County, South Dakota, were poor. Within metropolitan areas, poverty among whites is somewhat higher in the exurbs than in much of the metropolitan area because of the outward movement of younger lower-income whites to the far-flung suburbs. Suburban poverty has increased notably during the 2007–09 recession and its aftermath.[14]

Education attainment of the white population is lowest in areas of the country that have experienced a prolonged brain drain—sometimes for decades—of their younger population. Counties outside metropolitan areas with declining white populations are among those that have experienced such a brain drain and therefore fare worse than most other places in the country. Only 19 percent of whites living in these counties obtained a bachelor's degree while 32 percent of whites in the nation as a whole did so. Among the counties with the least educated populations are Clinton County, Kentucky; Morgan County, Ohio; and Roane County, West Virginia, where less than 10 percent of white adults have graduated from college.

The link between local white population growth and education attainment is not strong within metropolitan areas. For example, some of the most well-educated white populations live in urban core areas with modestly growing or declining white populations, such as the Manhattan borough of New York City and the city of San Francisco, in both of which 70 percent of the white adult population are college graduates. These are expensive cities where well-educated, well-paid professionals can afford to live, even if the broader segment of the white population resides elsewhere. Even so, quickly growing white counties, largely in the suburbs, show education levels similar to and sometimes higher than levels for whites overall.

Large metropolitan areas also are seeing a similar education-related population growth phenomenon (see map 7-3). The areas with the highest white education attainment—Washington, D.C., San Francisco, and San Jose—are not the highest in terms of white population gains. But due to the nature of their economic bases—government and knowledge-based

MAP 7-3
**White College Graduates: Major Metropolitan Areas with Highest and Lowest Percent**

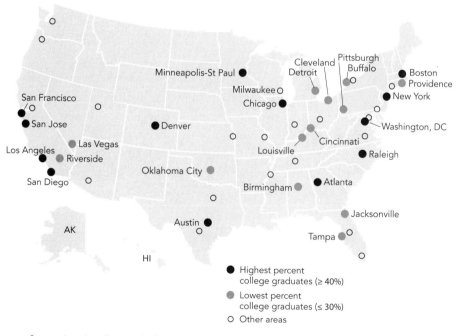

Source: American Community Survey, 2010

[a]Among persons age 25 and over; metropolitan areas with populations exceeding 1 million.

industries—they selectively attract and retain highly educated residents. Other metropolitan areas with high costs of living and strong professional job sectors, such as Los Angeles and New York, have experienced middle-class flight, leaving behind both a largely white, well-educated population and, because of past immigration, a large minority population with less education.[15]

Yet there are metropolitan areas with growing white populations, largely in the New Sun Belt, such as Austin, Raleigh, Denver, and Atlanta, that rank in the top tier of white education attainment. These areas are attracting large numbers of white migrants who are disproportionately young and well educated. They differ from other New Sun Belt areas, such as Las Vegas and Riverside, whose population gains include a broad range of white migrants. In contrast, other metropolitan areas that have been losing whites because of their economic woes, such a Detroit, Buffalo, and Pittsburgh, share the "left behind" syndrome experienced by many rural and small town areas and are home to older, less educated white populations.

The increasing divide between white "winner" and "loser" areas will no doubt continue as America's aging and slowly growing white population continues its shift to popular areas in the New Sun Belt. These are the same general destinations to which young blacks and black retirees are headed, particularly in the South, and where dispersing new minorities—Hispanics and Asians—have been moving, during good economic times in particular.

The remaining parts of the country, where white growth is modest or declining, are gaining population mostly from new minorities (for example, coastal global cities) or are destined to age and decline with their predominantly white populations (for example, rural or industrial areas in the country's interior). In the latter areas in particular, the social, economic, and demographic makeup of the white population is becoming ever more distinct. They represent the extreme of an aging America, where the consumer tastes, service needs, and political preferences of their older white populations will dominate the local social and economic landscape at the same time that the rest of the country becomes relatively younger and more racially diverse.

# Melting Pot Cities and Suburbs

# 8

Perhaps the most visible demographic impact of America's diversity explosion is occurring within urban areas. The classic image of an American metropolis was that of a polyglot city surrounded by mostly white suburbs—the "chocolate city/vanilla suburbs" of the 1950s and 1960s, when white-dominated suburbanization left largely black minority populations stranded in many of the nation's largest cities.[1] The black city/white suburb paradigm has almost entirely broken down. Only in slowly growing northern parts of the country does this stereotype partially hold, and even there changes are afoot as newly arriving Hispanics and Asians contribute to population gains. The old dichotomy stands in sharp contrast to residential patterns in the Melting Pot region of the country, where suburbs and cities alike are receiving large waves of immigrant minorities, often within the context of declining white populations. The old path of white flight to the suburbs is now followed by Hispanics, Asians, and, to a greater degree than ever before, blacks—all aspiring to achieve the suburban American Dream. This chapter explores how America's diversity explosion is playing out within the nation's largest metropolitan areas, especially in the suburbs.[2]

## MINORITIES DOMINATE CITY AND SUBURBAN GROWTH

The rise of new minority populations, the sharp slowdown of white population growth, and the economic gains and increased residential freedom of new generations of blacks are rapidly changing the classic image of suburbanization. Together these trends paint a picture of population growth dynamics in the nation's cities and suburbs that is very different from the one etched in the minds of pollsters, political consultants, and the public at large. Figure 8-1 presents a broad view of racial population dynamics for the nation's 100 largest metropolitan areas during the first decade of this century. What stands out most is that Hispanics are the major source of both city and suburban population gains in those areas

FIGURE 8-1
**Contributions to City and Suburb Population Change, 100 Largest Metropolitan Areas, 2000–10**

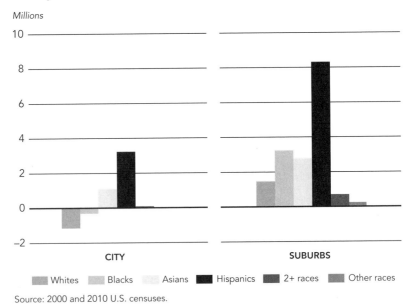

Source: 2000 and 2010 U.S. censuses.

during that period. About one-half of the nation's suburban population gain is attributable to Hispanics, both native born and immigrant. In the cities, Hispanics account for the lion's share of gains, more than making up for cities' loss of white and black residents.

The national picture, then, is one in which the new minorities, Hispanics and Asians, are now the main contributors to city population growth and each of the major minority groups—Hispanics, Asians, and blacks—contributes more than whites to suburban gains. This stands in stark contrast to the white-dominated suburbanization that was a signature trend of the last half of the twentieth century. Of course, the national picture varies greatly across regions of the country, as discussed in chapter 3. This is especially the case for Hispanics, who originally settled in mostly coastal gateway cities in the nation's Melting Pot region and often expanded to their suburbs. Today immigrant as well as native-born Hispanics are dispersing to New Sun Belt suburbs in the Southeast and Mountain West.[3]

The suburbs of all 100 metropolitan areas experienced Hispanic population gains in 2000–10. Areas with the largest numeric gains were Riverside, New York, Houston, and Miami. Yet the fastest Hispanic *growth rates,* all more than 150 percent, are found in the suburbs of the New Sun Belt cities of Nashville, Charlotte, Raleigh, and Provo as well as the Heartland cities of Indianapolis and Scranton. Although overall Hispanic populations are small in the latter areas, their rapid growth indicates where the shifts are trending.

Each central city of the 100 largest metropolitan areas also saw Hispanic gains. As with the suburbs, numeric gains were largest in Melting Pot cities such as Dallas, Houston, and Los Angeles, while growth rates were fast in all parts of the country, including rapidly growing Florida cities such as Cape Coral, Lakeland, and Palm Bay. Hispanics contributed to city population gains (or reduced city losses) more than any other racial group in 76 of the 100 largest metropolitan areas. Asians also contributed to city and suburban population gains in each of the 100 largest metropolitan areas. Asians made substantial contributions to suburban gains in Los Angeles, New York, San Francisco, and Washington, D.C. They contributed more than other racial minorities to city gains in San Francisco, New York, and San Jose. Hispanics and Asians already were responsible for nearly all of the population gains in central cities nationwide in 2000–10. Moreover, these new minorities and their later generations are poised to become the backbone of future suburban growth in ways that will transform the nation.

**The Diminished Role of Whites in Twenty-First-Century Suburbanization**
Chapter 7 demonstrated that whites will play an increasingly smaller role in the nation's population growth. In fact, on the national level, white population loss is projected to occur in less than a decade. This diminished white role is now beginning to play out in U.S. suburbs as well as cities. White population losses in cities are not new. Many of the nation's large older cities showed white losses beginning in the 1950s, during the peak period of white migration to the suburbs.[4] Today, the slowdown in national white population growth is driving white losses in cities more broadly (see table 8-1). Nearly three-quarters (72) of central cities in the nation's 100 largest metropolitan areas lost whites between 1990 snd 2010. Still, the magnitude of those losses has diminished somewhat—a consequence of the renewed attraction of cities for some whites. Fifty of these 72 cities lost fewer whites during the first decade of the 2000s than the decade before, including New York, Los Angeles, Chicago, Boston, and St. Louis. As a group, cities lost one-half as many whites in 2000–10 as in the 1990s.

What is new and likely to be a long-term trend is the slowdown in white population gains in the suburbs. As the white population ages and the childbearing population increasingly consists of minorities, the

TABLE 8-1
**City and Suburb Gains and Losses among 100 Largest Metropolitan Areas**

| Gains/Losses | Primary cities[a] | Suburbs |
|---|---|---|
| *Number with total population gains* | | |
| 2000–2010 | 77 | 96 |
| 1990–2000 | 74 | 98 |
| *Number with white population losses* | | |
| 2000–2010 | 73 | 32 |
| 1990–2000 | 72 | 25 |

Source: 1990, 2000, and 2010 U.S. censuses.

[a]Primary cities of metropolitan areas (include one to three large cities in the metropolitan area)

traditional attraction to the suburbs will be felt more by the latter groups. In addition, the "new white flight," discussed in chapter 7, has directed whites away from the cities *and the suburbs* of many large metropolitan areas in both coastal areas and interior metropolitan areas, especially in the Heartland (see map 8-1).

Nearly one-third of large metropolitan areas experienced absolute declines in their white suburban populations over 2000–10. The greatest white suburban losses occurred in large coastal metropolitan areas like New York, Los Angeles, and San Francisco as well as northern industrial areas such as Detroit, Cleveland, and Buffalo. Nationally, whites contributed only 9 percent to the growth in the suburban population during this decade. Map 8-1 depicts the geography of white population changes in

MAP 8-1

**White Gains and Losses in Cities and Suburbs of the 100 Largest Metropolitan Areas**

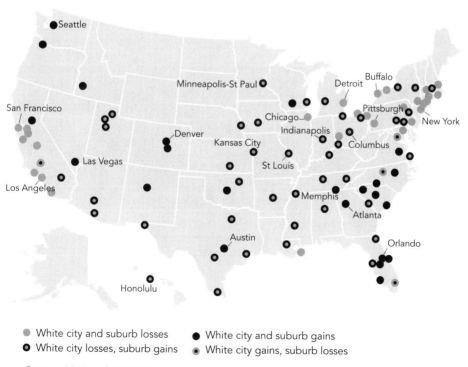

Source: 2000 and 2010 U.S. censuses.

cities and suburbs in 2000–10. More than one-quarter of the 100 largest metropolitan areas experienced white losses in both cities and suburbs. Yet 23 areas recorded white gains in both cities and suburbs. These areas— which include Austin, Denver, Atlanta, and Las Vegas—are located primarily in the New Sun Belt region, and they have been attracting whites from parts of the country that either are more expensive or are in a state of economic decline. There also are 45 metropolitan areas that exhibit the traditional patterns of white flight, including Midwest areas such as Columbus, Kansas City, and Minneapolis–St. Paul. Whites still dominate population gains in a few suburban areas, including Des Moines, Provo, Louisville, and Omaha, but in 78 metropolitan suburbs, such as those of Los Angeles, New York, San Francisco, and Chicago, minorities accounted for most or all of the population gains. In addition, among the 77 cities that gained population during the past decade, minorities contributed to all or most of the gains in 71 of those cities. As new minorities, particularly Hispanics, continue to diffuse across the country, they will increase their presence in suburban communities and cities.

### Black Flight

An important counterpoint to slowing white flight in recent decades is the emergence of "black flight" from major cities with established black populations. Black population losses have been occurring in some cities since the 1970s.[5] However, the magnitude and pervasiveness of black losses in cities during the first decade of the 2000s were unprecedented. As shown in figure 8-1, there was a total decline of 300,000 blacks in the central cities of the 100 largest metropolitan areas, the first absolute population decline among blacks for these cities as a group.

Thirteen of the 20 cities with the largest black populations (including nine of the ten largest) registered declines in their black populations in 2000–10. Among central cities of the 100 largest metropolitan areas, 33 cities experienced declines in their black populations and 68 showed first-time losses, larger losses, or smaller gains among blacks than in the 1990s. Clearly, the black presence, which has been the mainstay of many large city populations, is diminishing.

Three cities with large black declines—Detroit, Chicago, and New York—were among the primary destinations for blacks during the Great

Migration out of the South in the first part of the twentieth century. However, black losses were not confined to northern cities. Southern and western cities such as Atlanta, Dallas, and Los Angeles were also among those losing blacks in 2000–10 (see table 8-2). Much of that population is shifting to the suburbs of these metropolitan areas.

The sharp rise in black suburbanization can be attributed in part to the black population's economic progress in recent decades, especially among younger people aspiring to the suburban lifestyle that eluded their parents and grandparents. Among blacks ages 25 to 34, 19 percent were college graduates in 2010; in contrast, 12 percent were graduates in 1990 and only 6 percent in 1970. Also, a half century has now elapsed since the 1968 Fair Housing Act outlawed racial discrimination in the housing market and made suburban developments open to blacks who have the economic means to move. As discussed in chapter 9, segregation between blacks and whites is now diminishing gradually but consistently across metropolitan areas, with the growing southern and western parts of the country exhibiting the least segregation. Metropolitan areas in these less segregated, growing parts of the country are registering the greatest numeric gains in the suburban black population. The suburbs of Atlanta, Houston, Washington, D.C., and Dallas experienced the largest increases in black population during 2000–10, although Detroit and Chicago also make the list, due in part to large black losses from their central cities (see map 8-2). Among the largest 100 metropolitan areas, 96 showed gains in their suburban black populations. Of those, more than three-quarters had larger increases in 2000–10 than in the 1990s. While delayed for decades, the full-scale suburbanization of blacks is finally under way.

TABLE 8-2

**Cities with Largest Loss of Blacks, 2000–10**

| Rank/City | Change in black population[a] |
|---|---|
| 1  Detroit | −185,393 |
| 2  Chicago | −181,453 |
| 3  New Orleans | −118,526 |
| 4  New York | −100,859 |
| 5  Los Angeles | −54,606 |
| 6  Washington, DC | −39,035 |
| 7  Oakland | −33,502 |
| 8  Cleveland | −33,304 |
| 9  Atlanta | −29,746 |
| 10  Baltimore | −24,071 |
| 11  Birmingham | −22,451 |
| 12  St. Louis | −21,057 |
| 13  Gary | −18,341 |
| 14  San Francisco | −12,010 |
| 15  Dallas | −10,665 |

Source: 2000 and 2010 U.S. censuses.
[a]Non-Hispanic blacks

## MINORITY WHITE CITIES, MELTING POT SUBURBS

The new demographic dynamics affecting the nation's metropolitan areas—substantial Hispanic and Asian population gains, unprecedented slowdowns and losses in white population growth, and an emerging black flight from the city—have already affected city and suburban populations, sometimes dramatically. Two benchmarks tell the story. First, it is now Hispanics, not blacks, who constitute the largest minority group in cities. Second, the white share of the suburban population, 65 percent, in 2010 was nearly the same as the white share of the national population. From a racial standpoint and in other respects, the suburbs are becoming a microcosm of the general American population.[6] Both cities and suburbs are being transformed because of these shifts.

MAP 8-2

**Greatest Black Suburban Gainers, 2000–10**

Gains

- Under 75,000
- Between 75,000 and 150,000
- Over 150,000

Source: 2000 and 2010 U.S. censuses.

### Minority White Cities Are the Norm

Minority white cities are not new. Some major cities, including Washington, D.C., and Atlanta, had fewer whites than blacks by 1960, and several others, such as Baltimore and Detroit, became majority black by 1980.[7] By 2000, with continued white suburbanization and increased Hispanic and Asian gains, central cities in 42 of the nation's 100 largest metropolitan areas had minority white populations. By 2010, more than one-half (58) of the central cities were minority white (see map 8-3). Among the 16 cities that shifted to minority white status in 2010, Hispanics were responsible for 14 of the shifts, including those in rapidly diversifying areas such as Phoenix, Austin, and Las Vegas.

MAP 8-3
**Cities with Minority White Populations[a]**

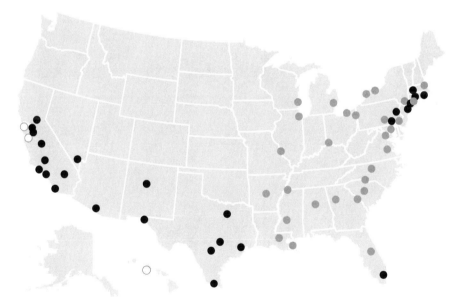

Largest non-white minority
- Blacks
- Hispanics
- Asians

Source: 2010 U.S. census

[a]Map displays 58 primary cities with minority white populations in 2010 among the 100 largest metropolitan areas.

Because of the long history of city segregation and white flight, blacks are still the dominant racial minority in more cities than Hispanics and Asians are, but the latter groups are catching up. In 1990, blacks were the largest minority in 68 of the central cities in the 100 largest metropolitan areas. By 2010 they dominated in only 54 of them, with Hispanics dominating in 41 and Asians in 5. Chicago, a long-standing "white-black" city, has become about one-third white, one-third black, and one-third Hispanic or other races, with an even greater Hispanic presence in the offing. As figure 8-2 indicates, Hispanics dominate all minorities with respect to the nation's city population as a whole, due to their large numbers in Los Angeles and other large

FIGURE 8-2

**City and Suburb Racial Profiles, 100 Largest Metropolitan Areas, 1990–2010**

*Percent*

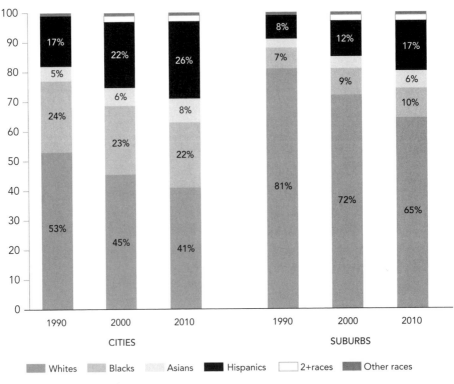

Source: 1990–2010 U.S. censuses.

cities in the Melting Pot region. Yet changes are occurring elsewhere. The rise of Hispanics as the "major city minority" foreshadows tomorrow's urban America. Their rise will affect education, the workplace, commercial life, and patterns of civic engagement.

**The Rise of Melting Pot Suburbs**

More than ever, major metropolitan suburbs reflect the rest of American society. A growing number of suburban areas are achieving what might be termed "melting pot" status. In 36 of the 100 largest metropolitan areas, minorities represented at least 35 percent of the suburban population in 2010, approximately the same as their share of the national population. Within those areas, 16 have majority-minority populations, up from just 8 in 2000. With a few exceptions, such as suburban New York and Chicago, these "melting pot" suburbs are located in the South and West (see map 8-4). Hispanics are the predominant racial minority in most of these suburban areas, an edge that they already held by 1990 and continue to hold despite the increasing share of blacks in the suburbs. Hispanics represent the largest minority group in 25 of these 36 highly diverse suburbs while blacks are the largest group in 9 suburbs and Asians in 2.

Five of the metropolitan suburbs that tipped into majority-minority status in the 2000s were in California: San Francisco, San Jose, Riverside, Sacramento, and Modesto. Others are Houston, Las Vegas, and Washington, D.C. In each of these eight areas, the white share of the population dropped by at least 9 percent. In suburban Las Vegas, the drop was even more dramatic, from 61 percent white in 2000 to 48 percent white in 2010. The racial transitions giving rise to newly majority-minority suburbs also were evident in suburbs nationwide. In the suburbs of all 100 large metropolitan areas, the white share of the population declined over 2000–10. Still, there are wide variations in suburban racial profiles across the country, mirroring regional demographic patterns. For example, the suburbs where Hispanics constitute the largest part of the population—more than 50 percent—are on the Texas border, including the areas of El Paso and McAllen, in addition to the interior California areas of Fresno and Bakersfield. Those with highest black percentages are in the Deep South: Jackson, Mississippi; Virginia Beach, Virginia; and Columbia, South Carolina.

MAP 8-4
**Melting Pot Suburbs**[a]

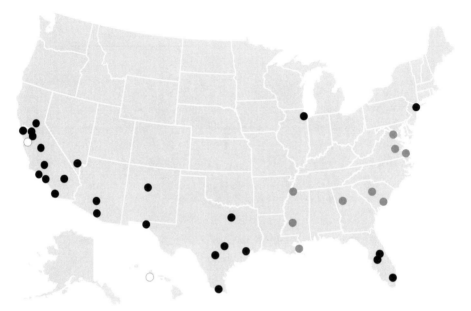

Largest non-white minority
- ⬤ Blacks
- ● Hispanics
- ○ Asians

Source: 2010 U.S. census.
[a]Map displays 36 suburbs with at least 35 percent minority populations in 2010 among the 100 largest
metropolitan areas

The largest Asian shares of suburban populations are in Honolulu and
San Jose.

In many cases the racial mix in the suburbs closely resembles the mix
in the cities. This is especially the case in Melting Pot metropolitan areas
such as Los Angeles (see figure 8-3). Other areas, epitomized by Atlanta,
showed brisk black suburban gains following considerable white suburban growth, creating a sizable black suburban presence. For many southern and western areas, the city-suburb minority gaps are declining as
suburbs become a magnet for all racial groups. At the other extreme are
northern metropolitan areas like Detroit, where decades of nearly exclu-

FIGURE 8-3
**City and Suburb Racial Profiles: Los Angeles, Atlanta, and Detroit**

*Percent*

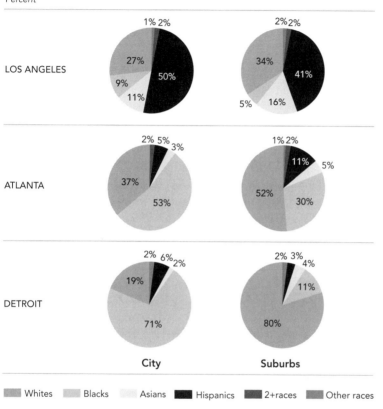

Source: 2010 U.S. census.

sive white suburban growth have only recently been accompanied by a breakthrough in black suburban growth. Detroit shows a substantial city-suburb/black-white disparity that is unlikely to be erased soon, despite new minority growth. Other areas that show similar city-suburb disparities are located primarily in the North. They include Milwaukee and Cleveland—areas with a tradition of high black-white neighborhood segregation that continues today.

Of course, racial shifts are constantly occurring within the suburbs, especially in recent decades and in the inner and middle rings of suburbs. Racial minorities constitute approximately two-fifths of the population of inner and middle suburbs in the nation.[8] Outer exurbs, which constitute only about 10 percent of the metropolitan population, are four-fifths white and are driven largely by white growth. So while Hispanics, Asians, and blacks are now main players in the suburbanization movement, they do not yet have a substantial presence in the outer suburbs and show some clustering in same-race communities, in many cases as a result of quasi-legal exclusionary practices.[9]

Still, demographic forces will continue to diversify the nation's cities and suburbs, with important implications for both policy and politics. Both suburbs and cities face increasing demands for the services needed by new populations, particularly those of different economic circumstances and cultural and linguistic backgrounds. Increasing suburban diversity may cause suburbs to become more "purple" than their traditional red in local and national elections, making them less reliable bases for either Republicans or Democrats, who have depended on demographically homogeneous voting blocs. Similarly, the changing demographics of big cities indicate that success for urban politicians may hinge on cultivating growing Hispanic and Asian constituencies along with traditional black voters and gentrifying whites. The historically sharp racial divisions between cities and suburbs in metropolitan America are more blurred than ever. The shifting social, economic, and political structures of these places will challenge leaders at all levels to understand and keep pace with the consequences.

## ACHIEVING THE SUBURBAN DREAM

For generations, young adults of all backgrounds, but especially racial minorities, viewed a residence in the suburbs as both a means and an end toward achieving the classic American Dream. As far back as the 1920s, when the widespread use of the automobile enabled the development of early suburbs, a move away from the city was associated with upward mobility—a larger, more spacious house, a less crime-ridden community, and a greater distance from neighborhoods composed of disadvantaged and lower-status minority segments of the population.[10] By the end of World War II, many of the nation's older industrial cities already showed

FIGURE 8-4

**Percent of Residents Residing in Suburbs, 100 Largest Metropolitan Areas, 1990–2010**

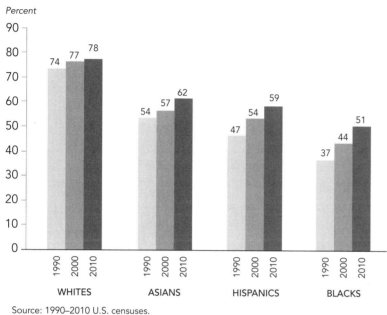

Percent

Source: 1990–2010 U.S. censuses.

sharp city-suburb gaps in their racial profiles as well as in their predominant family types and socioeconomic attributes. Those gaps became far more pronounced after the massive, largely white suburbanization that took place in the immediate postwar years, making the suburbs an even more alluring destination for whites.[11] In contrast, Asians, Hispanics, and particularly blacks dispersed from cities far more gradually. For them, the suburban American Dream was still a goal rather than a given. Hispanics and Asians initially settled primarily in the city's racially circumscribed communities, and until recently, most blacks resided in largely segregated neighborhoods.

As recently as 1980, less than one-half of metropolitan minorities resided in the suburbs.[12] Only beginning in 1990 did more than half of metropolitan Asians become suburban residents, while more than half of Hispanics did not do so until 2000. Moreover, it was not until 2010 that more than half of metropolitan blacks became suburban residents (see figure 8-4). Thus, an important milestone was passed when the 2010 census became the first to show a majority of each of the nation's largest racial minority groups residing in the suburbs. These recent trends were fueled by increased suburban development, especially in growing southern and western parts of the country, and the desire among new minorities to follow the broader postwar trend toward suburban living. For blacks, the substantial rise in suburbanization countered decades of concentration in urban residential neighborhoods fostered by housing discrimination in suburban communities and previously sharp economic disparities with whites.

While suburbs today are far less homogenous in many respects than in the immediate postwar decades, a suburban residence is still a goal for many American households and, for minorities especially, a symbol of "making it" in America. Sociologists have treated the suburban residence of racial and ethnic groups as an outcome commensurate with their achievement of certain other levels of economic and social status.[13] This is consistent with the earlier experience of whites, who were most likely to be suburban residents if they were well educated, had higher incomes, and were raising children.[14] Of course, by now a supermajority of whites resides in the suburbs. White households of all types are far more likely to live in suburbs than cities. But among minority groups, selective suburbanization is still taking place (see figure 8-5). Among each minority group, more than one-half of college-graduate metropolitan residents reside in the suburbs. The likelihood of suburban residence decreases with declining level of education. In fact, among blacks, a suburban residence is likely only for those who achieve at least some post–high school education. Furthermore, although Asians overall are the most suburbanized of the three minority groups, those without a high school diploma are more likely to reside in the city than in the suburbs.[15]

Suburbs also have been the prime destination for families, especially married couples with children, in keeping with the long-held view that the suburbs are better for childrearing. Among Asians, Hispanics, and blacks, married-with-children families are more likely to reside in the suburbs than any other household type. This is significant in light of the fact that minorities will constitute an increasing portion of the nation's

FIGURE 8-5

**Percent of Residents Residing in Suburbs, 100 Largest Metropolitan Areas, 2010**

EDUCATIONAL ATTAINMENT (Persons Age 25 and Over)

*Percent*

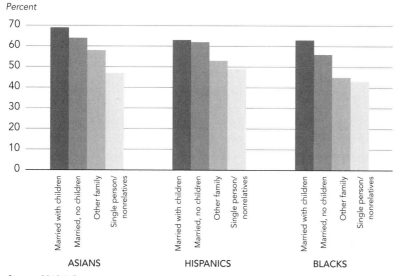

ASIANS        HISPANICS        BLACKS

HOUSEHOLD TYPE

*Percent*

Source: 2010 U.S. census.

child population. From now on, suburban schools and other child-related services will need to become more tailored to a far more diverse child population than in the past. For blacks in particular, there is a sharp difference between married-couple households (with or without children) and other household types with respect to suburban residence. For them especially, there appears to be a clear dividing line between "suburban" middle-class attributes, such as education and marriage, and "urban" attributes associated with lower education levels and other types of households.

Living in the suburbs does not, of course, guarantee a middle-class lifestyle. Communities that develop within the broad "suburban" category can take many forms. Studies on early black and immigrant minorities who were suburban pioneers show that in many cases, their places of residence were only barely an upgrade from the city neighborhoods that they left behind.[16] The experiences of recent minority suburbanites are more mixed, with some residing in racially stable mainstream suburban communities and others in largely minority, less advantaged communities vacated by the new white flight.[17] This pattern will play out as melting pot suburbs proliferate, increasingly in the New Sun Belt and eventually in the Heartland region of the country.

In sum, the first decade of the twenty-first century has set the table for a very different city-suburban racial dynamic, one that stands in stark contrast to what existed in the past. The new minorities, Hispanics and Asians, and others are becoming primary engines of growth in the nation's cities and suburbs in an era when the aging white population will be barely holding its own. There will be hurdles to overcome, including continued racial segregation at the neighborhood level. This is discussed in the next chapter. But for the first time, more of the minority population in the nation's largest metropolitan areas lives in the suburbs than in the city. That is surely an important milestone on the road toward becoming a central part of the American mainstream.

# Neighborhood Segregation
## Toward a New Racial Paradigm

**9**

One of the most intimate settings of American life—one that has an especially important role in shaping community race relations—is the neighborhood. Neighborhoods are where Americans socialize, shop, and attend school and where civic matters have the most impact. Most directly related to the subject of this book is the fact that the racial makeup of a neighborhood can either foster or prevent interactions with other groups. And for many Americans, the term that comes to mind when thinking about race and neighborhoods is "segregation." This term conjures up the image of the stark separation between blacks and whites across broad swaths of American neighborhoods that prevailed for much of the twentieth century, when segregation was hardly voluntary on the part of blacks. It was deeply rooted in the discriminatory forces that denied blacks anything resembling equal access to jobs, adequate schooling, and public services—both before and after the civil rights movement of the 1960s.[1]

A less stark type of segregation, pronounced in the earlier part of the last century, was seen in the separate neighborhoods composed of mostly white ethnic immigrant groups in major cities as they assimilated into American life. The immigrant enclaves of Irish, Poles, Italians, Jews, and others created economic and cultural "comfort zones" for them and their co-ethnics. But compared with black ghettos, these enclaves were relatively transitory, usually lasting no longer than a generation. As emigration from Europe waned in the middle of the twentieth century, these areas became less prominent as later generations voluntarily moved to the suburbs or other parts of the country.[2]

The twenty-first century began with some vestiges of past segregation but also in the midst of the new diversity explosion, which holds the potential to reshape the image of neighborhood segregation and integration as the country moves forward. In the case of blacks, the emergence of a middle class, their continuing flow to prosperous metropolitan regions in the South, and their more widespread movement to the suburbs are driving a shift toward less segregated neighborhood settings than was the norm for much of the last century.

The twenty-first century counterpart to early twentieth-century immigrant enclaves is the neighborhood composed of new minorities—Hispanics and Asians. Yet their recent, more widespread dispersion beyond the traditional melting pots also provides opportunities for greater integration at the local level, although perhaps after an initial period of self-segregation. This chapter discusses the decline of black segregation and the uneven shifts in Hispanic and Asian segregation as these groups disperse across the country. In highlighting the trend toward more multiracial neighborhoods of the future, the chapter also examines specific neighborhood racial profiles today.

## FROM GHETTOS TO THE DECLINE IN BLACK SEGREGATION

The recent decline in black segregation is especially remarkable when viewed in the context of what might be termed the "ghettoization" of America's black population for much of the last century. The rise of black neighborhood segregation in large urban ghettos is one of the most defining and regrettable episodes in America's social and demographic history. Beginning more than a half-century after the Emancipation

Proclamation, black ghettoization was bound up in the separation of most of the nation's black population from mainstream society, which limited blacks' access to schools, public services, private sector amenities, and ultimately opportunities for upward mobility. Black neighborhood segregation continued unabated until 1970, after which it began to loosen over the next two decades, with declines becoming more pervasive as the country approached the new century.

This pattern is depicted in figure 9-1, which shows average black-white segregation levels for U.S. metropolitan areas between 1930 and 2010.[3] Segregation levels are measured by the "dissimilarity index," which, as used here, compares black and white population distributions across metropolitan neighborhoods. It ranges from a value of 0 (complete integration), where blacks and whites are distributed similarly across neighborhoods, to 100 (complete segregation), where blacks and whites live in completely different neighborhoods. Values can be interpreted as the percentage of blacks who would have to change neighbor-

FIGURE 9-1

**Black-White Segregation: Average Levels for Metropolitan Areas, 1930–2010**

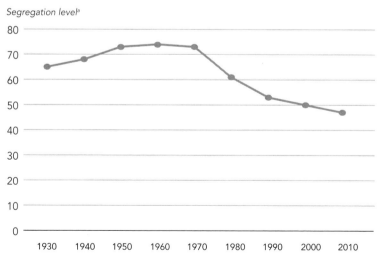

*Segregation level*[a]

Source: Cutler, Glaeser and Vigdor (1999) Appendix A1 for 1930–1980, U.S. Census, 1990–2010.

[a]Segregation levels represent the percent of blacks who would have to change neighborhoods to be completely integrated with whites. Values range from 0 (complete integration) to 100 (complete segregation).

hoods to become completely integrated with whites. Values of 60 and above are considered high; values of 30 and below are considered low.[4]

### The Great Migration and the Rise of Black Segregation

The Great Migration of blacks from the South to northern cities, discussed in chapter 6, was a major factor in the rise of black ghettos, which were later perpetuated by a host of private and public sector forces.[5] The first wave of the Great Migration, between 1910 and 1930, drew large numbers of blacks to northern cities such as Chicago, Detroit, Cleveland, New York, and Philadelphia. However, after arrival they found that they were allowed to live only in certain neighborhoods and parts of the city because of the white backlash against integration. That backlash first erupted as open violence in the form of riots, bombings, and other forms of intimidation to keep blacks from entering all-white neighborhoods. In addition, homeowner associations were formed to work with real estate agents and city planning offices to find ways to restrict black movement. One common device was to attach a restrictive covenant to a deed, which specified that a property could not be occupied by blacks or other groups deemed undesirable for a specified period, such as 99 years. Such covenants were deemed legal by the Supreme Court in 1926, a decision that was overturned in 1948 at the behest of the NAACP.[6]

Even when population pressure made black expansion into white neighborhoods inevitable, coalitions of real estate agents employed a strategy called "blockbusting"—inducing a black family to become the first black occupants in a neighborhood in order to scare resident whites into moving. Blockbusting ensured that black expansion could be restricted to selected neighborhoods as they "turned over" from white to black, and it enabled agents to reap above-market profits from black migrants.[7] In 1940, black segregation already was high and most city blacks lived in almost exclusively black ghettos.[8] A national survey in 1942 showed that 84 percent of whites agreed that "there should be separate sections in towns and cities for Negroes to live in." [9]

The second wave of the black Great Migration took place during the post–World War II period, but for the most part, blacks were excluded from the postwar suburbanization movement. Again, the continued strong resistance among whites to accepting blacks as neighbors led real estate agents to employ discriminatory practices in selling and renting homes, including the "steering" of blacks away from available white neighborhoods or the outright refusal to sell or rent homes to blacks in those locations. Local suburban governments also practiced exclusionary zoning to limit areas where blacks could obtain residences.

Lending practices such as "redlining" also were designed to restrict blacks, continuing a process that began in the 1930s.[10] Their impact was magnified in the postwar period due to the expansion of mostly suburban housing and the availability of federally insured loans that, in practice, were given largely to whites. At the same time, the concentration of poor urban blacks in city neighborhoods was exacerbated by 1960s-era public housing programs that, while eliminating blighted ghetto neighborhoods, re-segregated black residents into large housing complexes.[11]

Although heavily focused on cities in the Northeast and Midwest, these practices occurred in all regions of the country. In 1970, the average black-white segregation level among all metropolitan areas was well above 70. But in the large metropolitan areas where most blacks lived, segregation levels were much higher, with levels of 90 or more in Chicago, Detroit, and Los Angeles. Segregation levels greater than 80 were found in the southern metropolitan areas of Atlanta, Dallas, Miami, and Washington, D.C.

### Segregation Declines in the Decades Following the Civil Rights Movement

On the heels of large urban riots in the 1960s and the Kerner Commission's warning that America was evolving into two racially and spatially separated societies, Congress passed the 1968 Fair Housing Act, a key piece of civil rights legislation that prohibited racial bias in the sale and rental of housing and, by extension, discouraged racial segregation.[12] These events raised awareness of the hardship that extreme racial segregation was imposing on blacks, cities, and society at large. Soon thereafter, as part of the "open housing" movement, additional legislation, court decisions, and government and citizen-initiated efforts were put in action to discourage discriminatory lending and real estate practices. For example, the Home Mortgage Disclosure Act required financial institutions to report information on the race and income of those who obtained or were denied mortgages.[13]

Segregation began to decline between 1970 and 1980, although the greatest declines occurred in modest-sized metropolitan areas in the South and West that housed relatively small numbers of blacks. Unlike with other groups, an increase in income or educational attainment for black households did not translate into access to appreciably more integrated or higher-status neighborhoods.[14] Areas with the largest, most concentrated black populations, including Chicago, Detroit, and Cleveland, remained highly segregated, with minimal black suburbanization. On average, large non-southern metropolitan areas showed declines of fewer than 5 points in segregation between 1970 and 1980.

In *American Apartheid,* published in 1993, Douglas Massey and Nancy Denton argued that the open housing efforts in the immediate post–civil rights years had little impact on the strong institutional forces that maintained segregation.[15] In spite of legislation, an array of informal and quasi-legal discriminatory practices on the part of the real estate industry and financial institutions continued, some of which were documented in housing market "auditing" investigations by the Department of Housing and Urban Development.[16] Yet declines in black-white segregation continued between 1980 and 1990, again with the greatest reductions occurring in southern and western cities—including those with considerable black populations.[17] Between 1970 and 1990, segregation levels declined from 87 to 63 in Dallas, from 82 to 66 in Atlanta, and from 78 to 66 in Houston (see figure 9-2).

Many of these areas were beginning to attract black migrants, part of the emerging reverse black movement to the South. The overall population gains in these areas, part of a general migration to the Sun Belt, helped to trigger increased suburban development and growth. Because substantial suburban growth in these areas took place after the enactment of the Fair Housing Act, the impact of that law in reducing segregation was greater there than in more stagnant areas of the country.

The large northern areas with the highest segregation levels were still most resistant to integration. As of 1990, Chicago, Cleveland, and Detroit continued to show segregation levels above 80, and the majority of their northern counterparts registered levels in the high 70s or above. Most of

FIGURE 9-2

**Black-White Segregation in Selected Metropolitan Areas, 1970–2010**

*Segregation Level*[a]

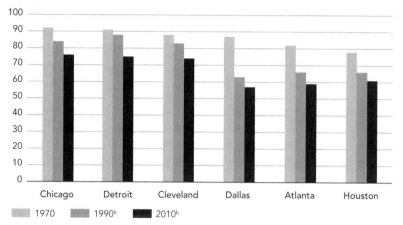

aSegregation levels represent the percent of blacks who would have to change neighborhoods
   to be completely integrated with whites. Values range from 0 (complete integration) to 100
   (complete segregation).
b1970 pertains to all blacks, while 1990 and 2010 pertain to non-Hispanic blacks.

Source: Douglas S. Massey and Nancy Denton, *American Apartheid: Segregation and the
Making of the Underclass* (Harvard University Press, 1993) for 1970; 1990 and 2010 U.S. censuses.

these areas had relatively modest growth and therefore little new housing development compared with their southern and western counterparts. Within them, old stereotypes persisted about which communities
were appropriate for whites and blacks, with whites expressing a strong
distaste for integrated neighborhoods.[18]

**The Beginnings of Black-White Integration**

The 2010 census shows that black-white segregation is still quite evident
in the United States. But it also reveals forces that will lead to an easing
of segregation, well below the ghettoized patterns of the mid-twentieth
century. Among all metropolitan areas, the average segregation level is
47. Among the 100 largest metropolitan areas, including those with the
largest black populations, segregation stands at 55—well below the levels
of 70 or more in the immediate postwar decades. A total of 93 of these
areas showed declines in segregation between 1990 and 2010, making
neighborhoods without any black residents extremely rare.[19]

Some of the trends spurring these shifts were suggested in the 1990s.[20] One is the continued decline in segregation in southern areas that are magnets for both blacks and whites as well as in areas in the West where new suburban housing continues to be constructed. As more of the black population moves to these areas, fewer of the nation's blacks will live in highly segregated neighborhoods.[21] The pattern of declining segregation is beginning to spread outward from Atlanta, Dallas, and other larger southern metropolitan areas. For example, Tampa, Bradenton, and Lakeland, in Florida, are among the cities where segregation has declined markedly since 1990. In the North, black population losses in cities, the destruction of large public housing projects, and increased suburbanization of blacks are contributing to declines in segregation. In Detroit, segregation levels declined from 88 in 1990 to 75 in 2010. Chicago and Cleveland, among others, also experienced marked declines during this period (see figure 9-2).

Another impetus toward less segregation is the growth of the Hispanic and Asian populations. Although all minority groups still show a preference for members of their own group as neighbors, there is also tolerance for other groups, particularly in multiracial settings.[22] That leaves open the possibility that in metropolitan areas where blacks are one of two or more major minority groups, other minorities can serve to "buffer" these divisions. In the 1980s and 1990s, there already was a marked tendency for black-white segregation to decline in multiracial metropolitan areas, especially those in Melting Pot regions such as Houston, Dallas, Los Angeles, and Riverside.[23] The 2010 census shows that some of the lowest black-white segregation scores are in areas with large or growing new minority populations, including Phoenix, Las Vegas, Riverside, Tucson, Stockton, and San Antonio. Several southeastern areas that have had notable recent declines in black-white segregation, such as the cities in Florida cited above, also are home to substantial Hispanic populations. The increased multiracial character of New Sun Belt metropolitan areas, both inside and outside the South, should pave the way for even further attenuation of segregation in metropolitan areas.

Another reason to expect further meaningful declines in black-white segregation is the emergence of the black middle class, discussed in chapter 6, along with the increased ability of blacks to translate economic advancement into housing in less segregated and higher-quality neighborhoods. Because of the refusal of whites to accept any blacks in their neighborhoods, there was scant evidence as recently as 1980 of any translation of improvement in blacks' personal economic circumstances into better neighborhood quality. White attitudes began to change in the 1990s. Although—limited by persistent discriminatory attitudes and social inertia—blacks still are less able to make this transition than Hispanics or Asians, upper-income and more educated blacks are now more able to live in integrated, well-off neighborhoods than blacks who are less well off.[24] Segregation also is less prevalent and becomes even more reduced in metropolitan areas where there is greater convergence of black and white incomes.[25] The upward mobility of a segment of the black population now brings the promise of greater declines in segregation.

The current geography of black-white segregation shows a noticeable regional difference, but segregation scores are generally lower than in 1990 (see map 9-1). Among 87 large areas with at least minimal black populations, 47 areas, located primarily in the South and West, show scores below a "high" value of 60.[26] In contrast, in 1990 only 29 areas registered such scores. Among the new areas with segregation levels below 60 are Atlanta, Louisville, Dallas, Nashville, and Tampa. Three northern areas, Minneapolis–St. Paul, Des Moines, and Providence, also fell below 60. About one-fifth of these areas have segregation scores below 50, including western areas such as Phoenix and Las Vegas and southeastern areas such as Charleston and Raleigh.

Even more revealing is the reduction of segregation in areas with traditionally higher levels. Each of the areas with segregation levels of 60 or more showed declines—by more than 5 points for most—since 1990. In 1990, 27 areas had segregation scores exceeding 70, with five areas (Detroit, Chicago, Cleveland, Milwaukee, and Buffalo) exceeding 80. By 2010, only seven areas reached that level, and only one (Milwaukee) stayed above 80 (see table 9-1). A number of forces—such as increased black suburbanization, demolition of urban public housing, city losses of black residents, and some reduction in the discriminatory practices of financial institutions and real estate agents—are contributing to new reductions in segregation in places where until recently segregation would not budge.[27]

MAP 9-1
**Black–White Segregation, 2010[a]**

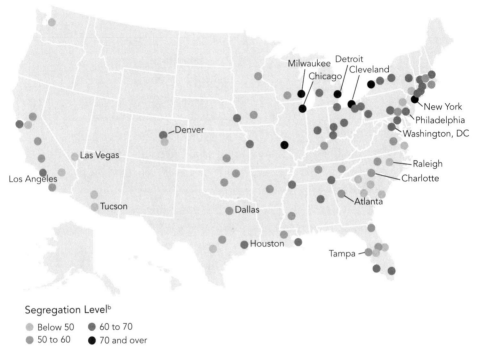

**Segregation Level[b]**

- Below 50
- 50 to 60
- 60 to 70
- 70 and over

Source: 2010 U.S. census.

[a]Segregation for 87 of the largest 100 metropolitan areas where blacks represent at least 3 percent of the total population.
[b]Where 0 indicates complete integration and 100 indicates complete segregation.

The recent widespread reduction in black-white segregation should not in any way be confused with its elimination. Segregation levels in the 50 to 60 range, found in many large metropolitan areas, are still substantial by any standard. Social and demographic inertia, particularly in older, slower growing metropolitan areas, still isolates many black children in high-poverty areas in ways that perpetuate disadvantages across generations and deprive a substantial segment of the black population of the wherewithal to relocate to higher-quality communities.[28]

Yet new forces affecting black-white segregation are ushering in an era that will be quite different from the era of wholesale ghettoization of the black population 50 years ago. The shift of the black population to

TABLE 9-1
**Black-White Segregation Ranks, 2010[a]**

| MOST SEGREGATED | | | LEAST SEGREGATED | | |
| --- | --- | --- | --- | --- | --- |
| Rank/Area | | Segregation level[b] | Rank/Area | | Segregation level[b] |
| 1 | Milwaukee | 82 | 1 | Tucson | 37 |
| 2 | New York | 78 | 2 | Las Vegas | 38 |
| 3 | Chicago | 76 | 3 | Colorado Springs | 39 |
| 4 | Detroit | 75 | 4 | Charleston | 42 |
| 5 | Cleveland | 74 | 5 | Raleigh | 42 |
| 6 | Buffalo | 73 | 6 | Phoenix | 44 |
| 7 | St. Louis | 72 | 7 | Greenville | 44 |
| 8 | Cincinnati | 69 | 8 | Lakeland | 44 |
| 9 | Philadelphia | 68 | 9 | Augusta | 45 |
| 10 | Los Angeles | 68 | 10 | Riverside | 46 |

Source: 2010 U.S. census.

[a]Among 87 of the 100 largest metropolitan areas where blacks comprise at least 3 percent of the total population.
[b]As measured by the dissimilarity index, defined in text.

more prosperous areas in the South, the movement of younger generations of blacks to the suburbs, the general change in racial relations
among blacks and whites, and the substantial period that fair housing
laws and practices have had to take root have dramatically expanded the
opportunities to increase integration. Moreover, the growth and dispersion of new minority groups to all parts of the country, especially to the
New Sun Belt, where all groups are moving, have the potential to ease
the animosities associated with the long-standing black-white divide.
Asian, Hispanic, and soon multiracial groups will serve to buffer those
animosities at the neighborhood and community levels.

## HISPANIC AND ASIAN SEGREGATION IN FLUX

The severity and persistence of black segregation in the twentieth century stand in contrast to the lower, more transitory segregation trends of
earlier white immigrant groups as well as to the current segregation
patterns of Hispanics and Asians. Both Hispanics and Asians owe their
growth to the more open immigration laws since 1965, and like earlier

groups, they have continued to disperse across the country. Hispanic and Asian segregation levels are, on average, markedly lower than those for blacks. Yet as black segregation levels continue to decrease for the majority of metropolitan areas, no similar trend exists for the newer minorities. In fact, among the 100 largest metropolitan areas, average Hispanic and Asian segregation appears flat between 2000 and 2010 after *increasing* somewhat in the 1990s (see figure 9-3). Although this may not appear to follow the transitory paths of ethnic immigrants a century ago, there is an important caveat. Both Hispanic and Asian communities continue to be replenished with new immigrants, whose segregation levels are higher than those of their native-born counterparts. So the average "static" segregation picture for Hispanics and Asians conflates both a turn toward integration among long-term residents and higher segregation levels among new immigrants.

In *Where We Live Now,* John Iceland provides evidence that "spatial assimilation" into more integrated neighborhoods is occurring among Hispanics and Asians who have lived in the United States the longest and among those who were born in the United States.[29] It is also the case that Hispanic and Asian residents with higher incomes and education are able to translate their status into residence in more integrated neighborhoods. These trends play out across individual metropolitan areas that, as discussed in chapters 4 and 5, vary in size, growth, and makeup with regard to their Hispanic and Asian groups. Because there is no typical segregation pattern for metropolitan areas, it is useful to see how they differ.

### Hispanic Segregation across Metropolitan Areas

Hispanic segregation patterns vary across regions of the country, reflecting Hispanic settlement histories and the locations of primary Hispanic groups. Map 9-2 displays Hispanic-white segregation levels in 2010 for 93 large metropolitan areas with a minimal Hispanic population.[30] Segregation levels range from a low value of 25 to a high value of 63. Two kinds of metropolitan areas are positioned at the upper end of the Hispanic segregation spectrum. First are the areas that are home to the largest Hispanic populations and have served as major gateways for Hispanic immigration. Both Los Angeles and New York have segre-

FIGURE 9-3

**Black, Hispanic, and Asian Segregation: Average Levels for 100 Largest Metropolitan Areas, 1990–2010**

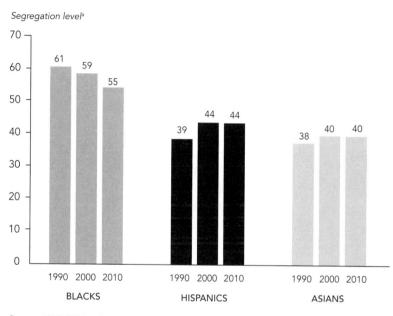

Source: 1990–2010 U.S. censuses.

[a] Segregation levels represent the percent of blacks, Hispanics, or Asians who would have to change neighborhoods to be completely integrated with whites. Values range from 0 (complete integration) to 100 (complete segregation)

gation levels of 62. Miami, Chicago, San Francisco, San Diego, Dallas, and Houston register scores of 50 or higher. Because these areas continue to attract new immigrants, who begin to establish themselves in clustered racial enclaves, segregation in most of these areas did not change dramatically in the last two decades. A second set of areas with Hispanic-white segregation levels above 50 are in the Northeast and Midwest, particularly those areas with large Puerto Rican enclaves. This includes a swath of areas of all sizes in New England and Pennsylvania, including Boston, Providence, Philadelphia, Allentown, and others. Also included in this group are industrial areas such as Milwaukee, Cleveland, and Buffalo.

Metropolitan areas with lower Hispanic-white segregation levels—in the 40s and below—are spread over the country, especially in the South

MAP 9-2
**Hispanic–White Segregation, 2010[a]**

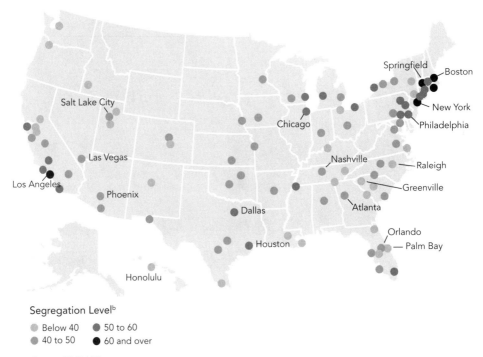

**Segregation Level[b]**

- Below 40
- 40 to 50
- 50 to 60
- 60 and over

Source: 2010 U.S. census.
[a] Segregation for 93 of the largest 100 metropolitan areas with Hispanic populations of at least 3 percent of the total population.
[b] Where 0 indicates complete integration and 100 indicates complete segregation.

and interior West. These tend to be areas where Mexicans are the primary Hispanic group and areas with small or quickly growing Hispanic populations. Among the larger areas in this category are Atlanta, Charlotte, and Nashville in the South and Phoenix, Las Vegas, and Salt Lake City in the West. The smaller areas are located in swaths of New Sun Belt states in the Southeast, Mountain West, and interior California.

One of the reasons that Hispanic segregation, on average, has not declined is that segregation is increasing in many of the new destination metropolitan areas that have attracted Hispanics as part of the larger dispersion phenomenon. As discussed in chapter 4, these areas

TABLE 9-2
**Greatest Increases in Hispanic-White Segregation,1990–2010[a]**

| Rank/Area | Segregation level[b] | |
|---|---|---|
| | 2010 level | 1990–2010 increase |
| 1  Miami | 57 | +25 |
| 2  Nashville | 48 | +24 |
| 3  Scranton | 53 | +23 |
| 4  Indianapolis | 47 | +21 |
| 5  Tulsa | 45 | +20 |
| 6  Memphis | 51 | +18 |
| 7  Raleigh | 37 | +17 |
| 8  Greensboro | 41 | +17 |
| 9  Little Rock | 40 | +16 |
| 10  Birmingham | 45 | +16 |
| 11  Charlotte | 48 | +15 |
| 12  Richmond | 45 | +15 |
| 13  Atlanta | 49 | +14 |

Source: 1990 and 2010 U.S. censuses.
[a]Among 93 of the 100 largest metropolitan areas where Hispanics comprise at least 3 percent of the
 total population.
[b]As measured by the dissimilarity index, defined in text.

have lured Hispanics who are more likely to be foreign born, to be less
fluent in English, and to have lower levels of education attainment than
Hispanics residing in other kinds of areas. As a consequence, these
Hispanics are less likely to assimilate quickly, especially in places where
the Hispanic population is new and subject to indifferent or discriminatory behavior on the part of established whites and blacks.[31] Table 9-2
lists 13 large areas with the greatest increase in Hispanic segregation
between 1990 and 2010. For the most part, these are new Hispanic destinations, located primarily in the South, including Nashville, Memphis,
Raleigh, Charlotte, Greensboro, and Atlanta. New destinations outside
the South, Scranton and Indianapolis, also showed noticeable gains in
segregation.

Overall, 27 of the 93 metropolitan areas showed meaningful (at least
10-point) gains in segregation during the two-decade period. In most
of these areas, the Hispanic population is small, new, and rapidly growing. And in all but three areas (Miami, Scranton, and Memphis), the

2010 segregation levels are relatively low—below 50 and in several cases in the 30s. In Raleigh, for example, the Hispanic population grew more than 150 percent as its segregation level rose from 20 in 1990 to 37 in 2010.

So at present, the Hispanic population is dispersing away from highly segregated areas to new areas that provide greater opportunities than earlier gateway regions. Even though new Hispanic enclaves are making these new destinations more segregated than before, they are still less segregated than the former areas. In addition, if these new residents are able to translate their opportunities into economic mobility for themselves and their children, they will be following the trajectories of earlier immigrant and racial groups toward even greater integration.

### Asian Segregation across Metropolitan Areas

The Asian population has shown more recent rapid growth than the Hispanic population. As discussed in chapter 5, well over one-half of Asians are foreign born and they are far more concentrated in established gateway areas than Hispanics are. But there is still variation across metropolitan areas in Asian-white segregation levels. Among the 45 largest metropolitan areas with minimal Asian populations (shown in map 9-3), segregation levels range from 29 (for Las Vegas) to 52 (for New York).[32]

Metropolitan areas that have served as traditional Asian immigrant gateways tend to have higher levels of Asian-white segregation. New York, Los Angeles, and San Francisco register segregation levels in the 47–52 range, though those levels are markedly lower than the levels for Hispanics. Other areas with segregation levels exceeding the mid-40s tend to be those with large established Asian populations (Sacramento, San Jose, San Diego, Boston, and Chicago), those with quickly growing Asian populations (Houston, Dallas, Atlanta, and Raleigh), and a few older Northeast and Midwest areas (Philadelphia, Detroit and Wichita). Areas with the lowest levels of Asian segregation tend to be located in the Mountain West (Las Vegas, Salt Lake City, and Denver), Florida (Orlando and Jacksonville), interior California (Modesto and Fresno), and "suburban-like" metropolitan areas (Oxnard and Bridgeport) that are near major metropolitan areas.

MAP 9-3
**Asian–White Segregation, 2010[a]**

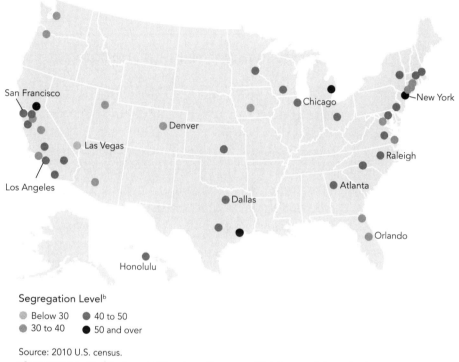

Segregation Level[b]

⬤ Below 30    ⬤ 40 to 50
⬤ 30 to 40    ⬤ 50 and over

Source: 2010 U.S. census.

[a] Segregation in 45 of the largest 100 metropolitan areas with Asian populations of at least 3 percent of the total population.

[b] Where 0 indicates complete integration and 100 indicates complete segregation.

Changes in Asian segregation for individual areas are not as pronounced as changes in Hispanic segregation, although areas experiencing large Asian population increases, including new Asian destinations, experienced higher segregation in 2010 than in 1990. Among areas showing a 20-year increase in segregation of at least 5 points are Richmond, Atlanta, Las Vegas, Dallas, Orlando, and Phoenix. Most of these areas have modest or low levels of segregation. Other areas with established Asian populations, such as Los Angeles and San Jose, showed only small increases in segregation. As indicated in chapter 5, Asians residing in many new destinations have high education attainment, so segregation in these areas does not conform to the low-skilled profile associated with some Hispanic and immigrant groups. Yet if the past experiences of other Asians and other immigrant groups are an indicator, their segregation levels should decline with increased length of residence in their new locations.

## TOWARD NEW MULTIRACIAL NEIGHBORHOODS

The discussion thus far has focused on segregation levels as measured by the dissimilarity index. Although it serves its purpose, in a sense the measure is detached from reality because it does not give an "on-the-ground" picture of the kinds of neighborhoods in which a typical white, black, Hispanic, or Asian will reside. That is because real-world neighborhoods represent several racial groups, not just a pairing between one group and whites. Furthermore, the size of each racial group in a given neighborhood is affected by the overall racial makeup of the metropolitan area.

For example, an average neighborhood in a multiracial metropolitan area like Los Angeles will look very different from an average neighborhood in a much whiter metropolitan area like Minneapolis–St. Paul. Both areas show some segregation between whites and blacks, Hispanics, and Asians. But there are many more minorities in Los Angeles than in Minneapolis–St. Paul, meaning that an average neighborhood where whites live in Los Angeles will be more diverse than an average neighborhood where whites live in Minneapolis–St. Paul.

To illustrate this, figure 9-4 shows the neighborhood racial composition for the average resident of each racial group in Los Angeles. The average white Los Angeles resident does indeed live in a neighborhood that has a healthy smattering of Hispanics and some black and Asian residents. But there are also far more white residents—54 percent—in this neighborhood than in neighborhoods that are home to the average black, Hispanic, or Asian.[33] So segregation still matters in the way that it affects on-the-ground neighborhoods, even in Los Angeles. That is not to say that there are no neighborhoods that are completely white or completely Hispanic in Los Angeles. But, on average, residents of each race are exposed somewhat to members of all races, especially Hispanics. The multiracial character of the Los Angeles region does spill

FIGURE 9-4

**Los Angeles Metropolitan Area: Neighborhood Racial Makeup of the Average White, Black, Hispanic, and Asian Resident, 2010**

*Percent racial groups in neighborhood*

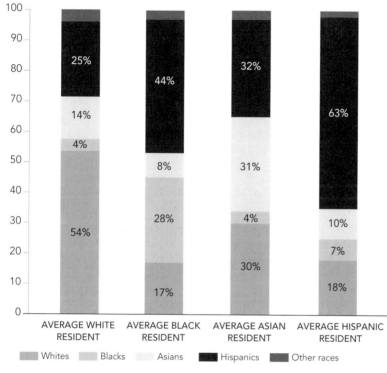

Source: 2010 U.S. census.

over across the area's neighborhoods. Such spillover is also seen in many of the other places in the Melting Pot regions of the country.[34]

Of course, the situation changes in regions that have quite different racial makeups. Both Detroit and Atlanta are areas where blacks are the predominant minority (see figure 9-5). Yet they also differ in important respects. Detroit is a stagnating metropolitan area, located in the nation's Heartland region. It has lost black migrants for decades while registering only modest population gains from other minorities. In contrast, Atlanta has been the primary magnet for black migrants and has also experienced rapid growth in its Hispanic and Asian populations. More-

FIGURE 9-5
**Detroit and Atlanta Metropolitan Areas: Neighborhood
Racial Makeup of the Average White and Black Resident, 2010**

*Percent racial groups in neighborhood*

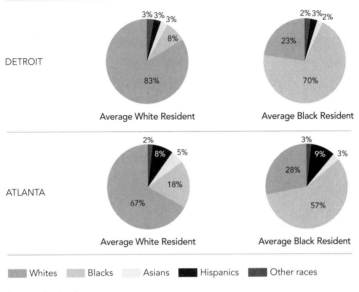

| | |
|---|---|
| DETROIT | |

Average White Resident          Average Black Resident

| | |
|---|---|
| ATLANTA | |

Average White Resident          Average Black Resident

Whites     Blacks     Asians     Hispanics     Other races

Source: 2010 U.S. census.

over, in recent decades, black migration waves included many middle-class blacks and occurred in a post-civil rights environment when new residential development was subject to stricter antidiscrimination regulations. For these and other reasons, Atlanta witnessed a greater decline in black-white segregation than Detroit did.

A comparison of typical white and black neighborhoods in each metropolitan area shows noticeable differences. In both metropolitan areas, the average white person lives in a neighborhood that is mostly white. But in Detroit, whites constitute 83 percent of white resident neighborhoods while in Atlanta whites make up 67 percent of white resident neighborhoods. Blacks in Atlanta also live in neighborhoods that are somewhat more integrated, with greater percentages of whites and Hispanics and smaller percentages of same-race neighbors than one finds in Detroit. Of course, even in Atlanta, there is a high rate of segregation. Blacks, on average, live in neighborhoods that are more than one-half black while whites live in neighborhoods that are two-thirds white. But the segregation in Atlanta is becoming less extreme.

## A NATIONAL NEIGHBORHOOD SNAPSHOT

As indicated in previous chapters, America's racial mosaic is changing in cities, suburbs, states, and regions. Although the broad Melting Pot, New Sun Belt, and Heartland regions discussed in chapter 3 are still somewhat distinct, the dispersion of new minorities virtually everywhere and the continuing southward movement of blacks is leading to shifts that will, for the most part, blur long-maintained spatial divisions, even at the neighborhood level. Therefore, it is useful to observe the kind of neighborhood in which the "average" white, black, Hispanic, and Asian resident lives to provide a benchmark of where things stood at the time of the 2010 census. This picture is given in figure 9-6—which is drawn from all of the neighborhoods in the United States, including those in metropolitan and nonmetropolitan areas of all sizes and in every part of the country—for the "average" resident of each racial group.

The average white resident, for example, lives in a far less diverse neighborhood—one that is more than three-quarters white—than residents of any other group. Nonetheless, the average white person lives in a neighborhood that includes more minorities than was the case in 1980, when such neighborhoods were nearly 90 percent white.[35] Moreover, the average member of each of the nation's major minority groups lives in a neighborhood that is at least one-third white, and in the case of Asians, nearly one-half white. Hence, there is a tendency toward more integrated living among these groups as more minorities relocate to white-dominated or multiracial neighborhoods.[36]

One issue that is especially important is the segregation of minority children into neighborhoods and school districts that often have fewer resources and show poorer overall performance. National statistics comparing neighborhood profiles for average black, Hispanic, and Asian children show them to be decidedly more exposed to members of their own racial group—or having less contact with whites—than is the case

for their adult population (see figure 9-7). In part, that reflects a continuing tendency for white families to choose local areas with better
resources and schools and fewer minorities than the local areas that are
available to minorities.[37] Given today's more diverse youth and their
important role in the future workforce, the inequality of opportunities
associated with their segregation across neighborhoods needs to be
addressed.

Still, overall, population shifts that are bringing Hispanics and Asians
to previously whiter New Sun Belt and Heartland regions will almost
certainly continue to alter the neighborhood experiences of these groups

FIGURE 9-6
**Neighborhood Racial Makeup of the Average White, Black, Asian, and
Hispanic Resident across the United States, 2010**

*Percent racial groups in neighborhood*

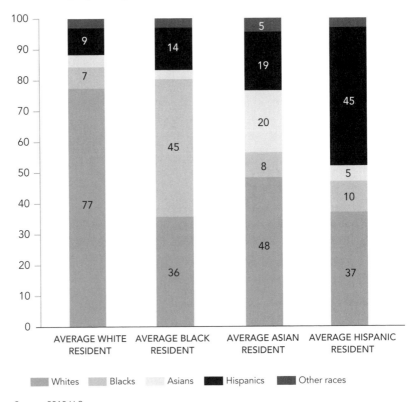

Source: 2010 U.S. census.

by bringing them into more contact with whites than was the case in the past. The nation's blacks have seen a marked shift from a mostly "ghettoized" existence five decades ago to one that more closely follows the path of other racial minorities and immigrant groups as more blacks move to more suburban and integrated communities, particularly in the South. So the broader migration patterns of blacks, Hispanics, and Asians are moving in the direction of greater neighborhood racial integration, even if segregation is far from being eliminated.

FIGURE 9-7

**Neighborhood Racial Makeup of the Average Black, Asian, and Hispanic Child and Adult Resident, 2010[a]**

*Percent of racial groups in neighborhood*

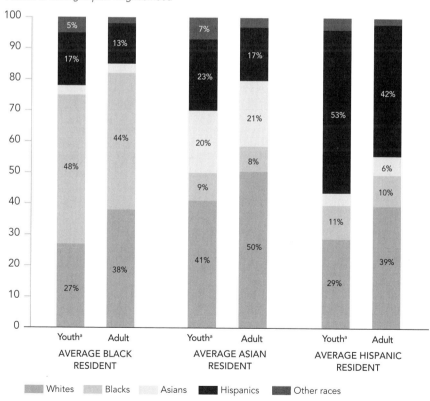

Source: 2010 U.S. census.

[a]Youth pertain to persons under age 18; adults to those age 18 and over

# Multiracial Marriages and Multiracial America     **10**

The usual way that race labels are applied in the United States in everyday parlance and in government statistics belies the increase in multiracial marriages and births, which almost certainly will lead to more blended populations in future generations. As this trend continues, it will bring about a blurring of the racial boundaries that were evident and often inflamed in the last half of the twentieth century. The nation is not there yet. But the evidence for multiracial marriages and multiracial individual identity, as with neighborhood residential integration—another measure of interaction at the local, personal level—shows an unmistakable trend toward a softening of racial boundaries that should lead to new ways of thinking about racial populations and race-related issues.

This chapter first discusses multiracial marriages: marriages between whites, blacks, Asians, Hispanics, and members of other smaller racial groups in the United States.[1] The diversity explosion of the new minorities, Hispanics and Asians, which has affected many aspects of the nation's demography, has also led to a noticeable increase in the number of multiracial marriages across the nation as well as the dispersion of such marriages away from the traditional Melting Pot states. In addition, while still lagging in comparison with new minority multiracial marriages, white-black multiracial marriages also have been on the rise.

Over time, the rise in multiracial marriages will lead to a rise in the multiracial population. In 2000, recognizing that prospect, the federal government for the first time permitted residents to declare on the census that they belonged to more than one race. The responses to the question of racial identity from the past two censuses and their implications for the future of the multiracial population are discussed in the last part of the chapter. Special attention is given to the increase in those declaring themselves simultaneously "white and black" in a country where, for most of its history, the racial boundary between whites and blacks was virtually insurmountable.

## MULTIRACIAL MARRIAGES: STIRRING A NEW MELTING POT?

The long-held ideal of America as a melting pot was manifest in the intergroup marriages among the children and grandchildren of white ethnic immigrants who arrived in the late nineteenth and early twentieth centuries.[2] Initially, fairly sharp divisions existed between these ethnic groups, particularly between "old" European groups such as those from Britain, Germany, and Scandinavia and "newer" groups from Italy, Poland, and Russia.[3] The latter had difficulty assimilating with the existing U.S. population because of their limited ability to speak English, lower levels of education, and less-skilled occupations. They also were viewed as having low status or being morally inferior and therefore not suitable marriage partners for native-born Americans. Of course, several generations later, because of the upward mobility and geographic dispersion of these white ethnic groups, marriages across the groups became much more common. Today, while many Americans take pride in the Italian or Irish heritage of their parents or grandparents, white ethnic origin is hardly the defining—or divisive—trait that it was a century ago.[4]

This "melting pot" marriage experience of white ethnics might be used as a model to gauge the assimilation of the new minorities, Hispanics and Asians, into the American mainstream. Sociologists have viewed multiracial marriage as a benchmark for the ultimate stage of assimilation and acceptance of a particular group into society.[5] For that to occur, members of the group will already have reached other milestones, such as facility with a common language, similar levels of education, regular interaction in the workplace and community, and, especially, some level of residential integration.

Hispanics and Asians differ from the earlier white ethnic groups in many respects. Most important, most Americans view them as racial groups rather than ethnic groups. Because race divisions, especially between whites and blacks, have historically been far less permeable than those between white ethnic groups, the blending of today's new racial minorities through multiracial marriage is breaking new ground. As discussed in chapter 5, native-born Americans have viewed Asian Americans as a race throughout U.S. history. In addition, although the Census Bureau defines "Hispanic" as an ethnic group rather than a race (discussed further below), it is common to view Hispanics—as is done in this book—as a racial group on par with blacks and Asians and as one of the three large minority groups.

Assimilation for these groups into the American mainstream may also mean something different in the future. In the past, the assimilation involved "fitting in" with the largely white core of American society or even with a select part of that core—the "older" European immigrant groups.[6] Yet because the white majority is constantly shrinking in the midst of the much higher growth of new minority populations, today's racial minorities will almost certainly become an integral part of tomorrow's American mainstream.

**Multiracial Marriage Explosion**

Multiracial marriages have been rising dramatically over the past 50 years (see figure 10-1). In 1960, before federal statistics enumerated Hispanics and before the 1965 legislation that opened up immigration to more countries, multiracial marriages constituted only 0.4 percent of all U.S. marriages. That figure increased to 3.2 percent in 1980 (including multiracial marriages for Hispanics and other groups) and to 9.5 percent in 2015. Moreover, nearly one in six newlywed couples are multiracial.

Some of this gain can be traced to the rise in the number of new minorities following the 1965 immigration policy reform and the tendency of some of these minorities to marry other minorities and whites. In 2015, six in ten multiracial marriages were of white-Hispanic or white-Asian couples (see figure 10-2). Yet changes in the racial makeup of the population are not the sole explanation for this shift. The propensity to marry out of one's racial or ethnic group differs by minority group. Blacks, for example, have a much lower propensity to do so than other minorities. Hence, white-black marriages account for only one-half as many marriages as white-Asian marriages, even though blacks make up a much larger share of the marriage-age population.

To better understand the relative propensity of each group to "marry out," it is useful to look at the prevalence of multiracial marriages specific to each racial group. Figure 10-3 shows the prevalence of multiracial marriages among current married couples of different groups.

FIGURE 10-1
**Multiracial Marriages as a Percent of All Marriages, 1960–2015**

*Percent*

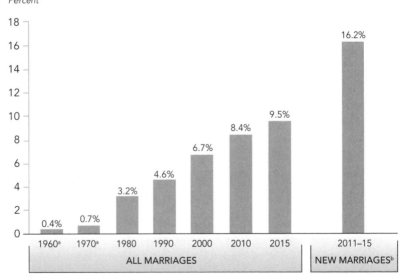

Source: 1960–2000 U.S. censuses; American Community Survey 2010, 2015, and 2011–15.
[a]Multiracial marriages involving Hispanics were not included.
[b]Marriages that occurred in last 12 months.

FIGURE 10-2
**Multiracial Marriages in the United States by Type, 2015**

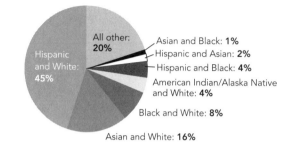

Source: American Community Survey, 2015.

It also shows prevalence trends since 1990 and the multiracial prevalence for recent marriages—those of one year or less in duration. Among the large minority groups, Hispanics and Asians show a markedly higher prevalence of multiracial marriages than do blacks. Among all current Hispanic and Asian marriages, about three in ten are multiracial, and among Hispanic and Asian *recent* marriages, more than four in ten are multiracial. The vast majority of marriages involving American Indians are multiracial marriages. Many of these marriages include spouses who identify as multiracial persons, signaling the extensive blurring of boundaries that has already occurred among the American Indian and white populations.[7]

In contrast to minorities, whites show a small prevalence of multiracial marriages—11 percent of all currently married whites. In part, this low prevalence reflects the relative sizes of the white and nonwhite populations. Because far fewer minority individuals are available as potential marriage partners for whites than vice versa, "blended" marriages are much more visible within the smaller Hispanic, Asian, and black populations. Yet among recently married whites, 18 percent were married to someone of another race. The high prevalence of multiracial marriages for both Hispanics and Asians suggests that as these populations continue to grow rapidly, the number of multiracial marriages will proliferate—emulating the melting pot patterns of early white ethnic groups. Appearing to counter this prediction is the fact that since 1990 there has

FIGURE 10-3

**Multiracial Marriages as Percent of All Marriages for Specified Race Groups, 1990 through 2015[a]**

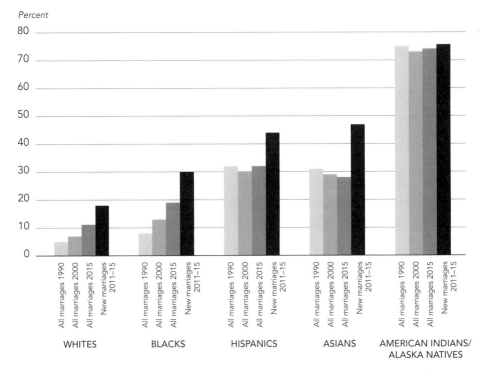

[a] Each race group value indicates multiracial marriages involving that group as a percent of the sum of multiracial and same-race marriages for that group.

Source: 1990–2000 U.S. censuses and American Community Survey 2015 and 2011–15.

been no meaningful increase in the prevalence of multiracial marriages within the currently married populations of either Hispanics or Asians. The multiracial share of each has remained around 30 percent for both groups and, among Asians, has even declined slightly.

One explanation for this apparent cap on multiracial marriage is the fact that new immigrant waves of Hispanics and Asians continue to expand the pool of same-race marriage partners. This expansion provides greater opportunities for in-group marriages, particularly among the first generation, which is not strongly integrated into mainstream society.[8] One could make the case that this would promote greater racial solidarity for these groups, leading to less multiracial blending in the future and solidifying the line between these groups, other minorities, and whites.[9] Yet a more likely outcome is continuing integration and increased long-term out-marriage of the new minorities as more of their members become assimilated with respect to other measures, such as education, income, and improved facility with English. As discussed below, this assimilation will occur with longer residence, generationally, for each group.

America's black population continues to have the lowest prevalence of multiracial marriages. This continues the legacy of black separation from mainstream America on a host of dimensions, which stemmed from the virtual ghettoization of the black population for much of the twentieth century, discussed in chapter 9. Most relevant were the anti-miscegenation statutes, which were prevalent in the antebellum South and persisted in 16 states until 1967, when the Supreme Court declared them unconstitutional in the landmark *Loving* v. *Virginia* decision.[10] It was only after this ruling in the post–civil rights environment that black multiracial marriages began to rise noticeably.[11]

The prevalence of black multiracial marriages is well below that of Hispanics and Asians. Black marriage partners still are often seen as less socially desirable, even among other minorities and those minorities' families and close associates.[12] Even so, the prevalence of multiracial marriages has risen markedly. Among recent, typically younger marriages involving blacks, nearly three in ten were multiracial marriages. These trends signal the onset of an important breakthrough in the long history of black marital endogamy. Especially noteworthy is the rise in white-black multiracial marriages (see table 10-1). In 1960, white-black marriages amounted to only 1.7 percent of all black same-race marriages, but in 2015, they amounted to 14 percent. White-black marriages are still not plentiful, but a clear trend is in the works.

TABLE 10-1

**"White and Black" Multiracial Marriages as a Percent of Black Same-Race Marriages, 1960–2015**

| Year[a] | Percent |
|---|---|
| 1960 | 1.7 |
| 1970 | 1.9 |
| 1980 | 3.5 |
| 1990 | 5.7 |
| 2000 | 8.3 |
| 2010 | 12.3 |
| 2015 | 14.0 |

Source: 1960–2000 U.S. censuses, American Community Survey, 2010 and 2015.

[a]All blacks for years 1960–80 and non-Hispanic blacks for years 1990–2015.

### Who Marries Out?

The future prevalence of multiracial marriages depends, to a large degree, on who is marrying out—particularly, who is marrying a white spouse. If those most likely to marry out are in assimilating demographic segments that are on the rise, then it is likely that a greater blurring of the races is in the offing. One thing is clear: most spouses of out-marrying minorities are white. Figure 10-4 displays the racial profiles of the spouses of those who have out-married among all currently married Hispanics, Asians, and blacks. Whites constitute well over one-half of spouses. Whites are still far more prominent as spouses among Hispanics and Asians than they are among blacks. One reason is lingering attitudes. A 2010 poll indicated that among whites, fewer respondents

FIGURE 10-4

**Race of Spouses for Hispanics, Asians, and Blacks in Multiracial Marriages, 2015**

*Percent of spouses by race*

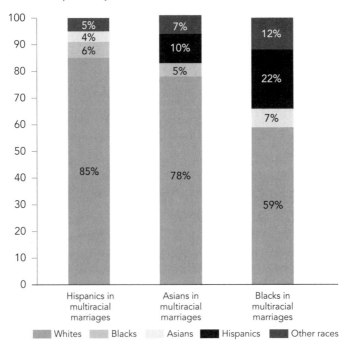

Source: American Community Survey, 2015.

thought that it "would be fine" if a family member married a black spouse than thought so if the relative married a Hispanic or Asian spouse—although, among younger whites, the vast majority would be fine with any of the three groups as spouses.[13]

There is a noteworthy gender difference regarding white and black multiracial marriages. The majority of white-black marriages—seven in ten—involve white women and black men, a pattern that has increased since 1970.[14] This helps to explain a higher overall out-marriage rate among white women than white men and a lower out-marriage rate among black women than black men.

The tendency to marry whites, especially among new minority groups, is an important gauge of assimilation. This is particularly the case if it occurs among the more highly educated and advantaged members of the group—signaling their further incorporation into mainstream society as more of them achieve the American Dream. This is clearly happening for Hispanics and, for the most part, for Asian Americans. As shown in table 10-2, the percent of Hispanics married to whites rises at higher education and family income levels. The percent of Asians married to whites also rises according to income and, to a lesser extent, education. Asian women are more likely to out-marry than Asian men, but both follow similar patterns.

TABLE 10-2
**Percent Married to a White Spouse, by Education and Income: All Married Hispanics, Asians, and Blacks, 2015**
*Percent*

| Demographic attributes | Hispanics | Asians | Blacks |
| --- | --- | --- | --- |
| *Education* | | | |
| College graduate | 34.6 | 13.1 | 8.1 |
| Some college | 24.9 | 17.4 | 7.0 |
| High school only | 13.4 | 12.7 | 5.5 |
| Not high school graduate | 4.4 | 6.8 | 3.9 |
| *Family income* | | | |
| Upper quartile | 36.9 | 15.0 | 8.3 |
| Second quartile | 20.4 | 13.9 | 6.4 |
| Third quartile | 10.5 | 13.3 | 5.6 |
| Bottom quartile | 5.8 | 7.1 | 5.2 |

Source: American Community Survey, 2015.

Perhaps even more important for longer-term blending are the higher out-marriage rates to whites for native-born Hispanics and Asians than for both longer-term and more recently arrived foreign-born immigrants (see figure 10-5). There is always the possibility, discussed earlier, that continued new waves of Hispanics and Asians—who are less assimilated with regard to status measures—may hold down the overall out-marriage rates for their groups.[15] Yet over time, the native-born populations—including the second and third generations and beyond—will greatly outnumber their foreign-born counterparts, allowing further blurring to take place.[16]

Among the mostly native-born black population, out-marriage rates also rise with education and family income, for both black men and women. This contrasts with earlier periods and suggests that further blending between blacks and whites should occur with the upward mobility of younger generations of blacks. Furthermore, white-black relationships are more prevalent among recent cohabiting couples than they are among married couples.[17] Some may view this as a temporary phenomenon related to the hesitation to "legitimize" these relationships through marriage because of family or peer disapproval. However, it can also signal a trend that could lead to greater acceptance of white-black marriages overall, especially among members of the younger generation who are more tolerant of both cohabiting relationships and multiracial marriages.

FIGURE 10-5
**Percent Married to a White Spouse by Nativity:
All Married Hispanics and Asians, 2015**

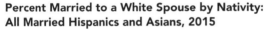

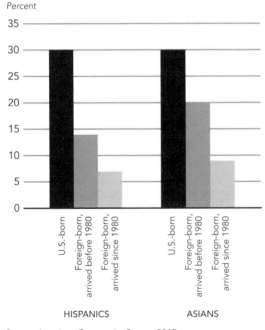

Source: American Community Survey, 2015.

## Geographic Dispersion of Multiracial Marriages

The geographic dispersion of new minority populations from traditional Melting Pot regions to the New Sun Belt states in the South and Mountain West—and into the largely white, interior Heartland states—sets the stage for the dispersion of multiracial marriages as well. As discussed in chapter 3, the states in the Melting Pot region tend to have the highest concentrations of Hispanic and Asian populations and therefore a higher prevalence of multiracial marriages. But multiracial marriages are beginning to spread.

The highest prevalence of multiracial marriages is found in Hawaii, where one-third of all marriages are multiracial, followed by Oklahoma and Alaska, where nearly two in ten marriages are multiracial (see map 10-1). These states have long-standing populations of Asians, Alaska

MAP 10-1

**Multiracial Marriages as a Percent of All Marriages, 2015**

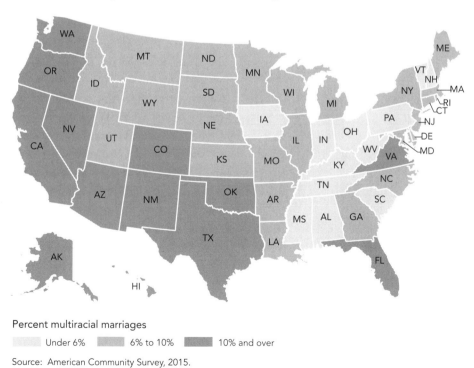

Percent multiracial marriages

Under 6%          6% to 10%          10% and over

Source: American Community Survey, 2015.

Natives, and American Indians, respectively. Beyond these is a mix of states where earlier Hispanic and Asian immigrants have maintained a long-term presence and more recent immigrants are becoming established, including Nevada, New Mexico, California, Washington, Arizona, Colorado, Oregon, Texas, Florida, and Virginia. At least one in ten marriages in these states is multiracial, and the largest portion of multiracial marriages in these states—and for that matter in most states—is white-Hispanic marriages. However, the mix varies within each state. In California, nearly one-half of all multiracial marriages are white-Hispanic, while white-Asian marriages constitute one-fifth. In New Mexico, white-Hispanic marriages make up seven in ten such marriages. At the other end of the spectrum are 12 states where multiracial marriages account for less than 6 percent of all marriages. They are located largely in New England, the industrial Midwest and Great Plains, and parts of the Old South. In Mississippi, only about 3 in 100 marriages are multiracial.

More relevant for the future is the dispersion of multiracial marriages to the quickly growing parts of the country, which serve as new destinations for Hispanics and Asians. Using the regional typology introduced in chapter 3, it is clear that multiracial marriages are growing rapidly outside of the Melting Pot states. Growth is especially strong in the New Sun Belt, in states such as Georgia, North Carolina, Utah, and Nevada—states with rapid growth in their Hispanic populations as well as growth in largely white-Hispanic multiracial marriages (see table 10-3). Several Heartland states, such as Minnesota, Pennsylvania, Connecticut, and Indiana, are also experiencing rapid growth in multiracial marriages.

Although many new Hispanic migrants to these regions are less assimilated than elsewhere with regard to measures such as English language proficiency and education, they are

TABLE 10-3
**Growth in Multiracial Marriages, 2000–15**
*Growth (%)*

| Region/selected states | Multiracial marriage growth |
| --- | --- |
| *Melting Pot* | |
| Texas | 54 |
| Florida | 51 |
| California | 26 |
| New Mexico | 5 |
| *New Sun Belt* | |
| Georgia | 86 |
| North Carolina | 72 |
| Utah | 64 |
| Nevada | 53 |
| *Heartland* | |
| Minnesota | 89 |
| Pennsylvania | 71 |
| Connecticut | 69 |
| Indiana | 48 |

Source: 2000 U.S. census; American Community Survey, 2015.

likely to have substantial interaction with the larger non-Hispanic populations in these states, which may lead to higher multiracial marriage rates. For example, in Georgia and North Carolina, the prevalence of multiracial marriages among Hispanics is 37 and 39 percent, respectively. In Idaho and Utah, the prevalence is 49 and 44 percent. These rates stand in contrast to rates of 28 and 22 percent in the more mature Melting Pot states of California and Texas.

## The Future of Multiracial Marriage

Overall, the evidence suggests a continuing surge in multiracial marriages in the United States. In some ways, the trends mirror those pointing to greater racial residential integration, discussed in chapter 9. For Hispanics and Asians, the new minorities, both multiracial marriage and residential integration are more prevalent among the more assimilated members of each group—those with higher education and incomes and those who have been in the United States the longest. The greatest "blending" of marriages, as with neighborhoods, may occur in new destination regions of the New Sun Belt and eventually in the Heartland regions of the country as the new minorities continue to disperse outward. Therefore, as Hispanics and Asians continue to become more established generationally, more assimilated economically, and more dispersed geographically, multiracial marriages among them will continue to rise.

The increase in black multiracial marriages parallels the increase in residential integration. That is, there have been rises in both multiracial marriages and residential integration in the post–civil rights era—rises that tend to be most marked for those who are upwardly mobile (in terms of education and social status) and geographically mobile (in terms of moving toward the suburbs and the South, for blacks). Clearly, white-black marriages are still less common than white marriages with Hispanics or Asians, but the gap is moving in the direction of closure. The new trend toward increased multiracial marriage is coupled with the greater acceptance of such marriages by younger generations. A 2011 Pew survey showed that young adult millennials were most accepting of multiracial marriage, with 60 percent saying that it was a change for the better, while only 47 percent of generation Xers and just 36 percent of baby boomers had the same view.[18]

## MULTIRACIAL AMERICANS

An obvious consequence of a rise in multiracial marriages would be an increase in multiracial children, which would lead to a greater share of the population claiming a mix of racial backgrounds. The marriage of individuals from various European immigrant backgrounds led to the melting pot that characterizes much of today's white population. It would seem only natural to anticipate a similar boom of multiracial persons in the years ahead. Yet in the case of multiracial marriages, national and cultural boundaries are not the only lines being crossed. New ground is being broken, pushing back against long-standing social and even legal constraints that often subjugated multiracial persons—particularly those with white-black ancestry—to second-class status. In many cases, individuals who could "pass" as white tried to do so in order to become part of the mainstream.[19]

The racial divide in the United States has been so stark that it was not until recently that nationwide federal statistics were collected for persons identifying with "two or more" races. The historical practice, which was to divide whites from blacks and other nonwhites, began in the early years of nationhood, when the slave population was counted separately.[20] For a long period, persons were identified as blacks according to the "one drop" rule, which stipulated that if they had any black ancestors, they could not be classified as white. The classification for American Indians, for some periods, was also bound by similar standards.[21]

Although classifications in later censuses included Chinese, Japanese, Filipino, and Hindu, there was little attempt to think of these largely "racial" categories as subject to mixing. This stands in contrast to the collection of information on parental birthplace and ancestry or national origin, which was widely used to study the blending of white ethnic populations.[22] Thus, although multiracial populations emanating from multiracial marriages certainly existed, they were not well documented in national statistics.

### Census Classification of Multiracial Persons

Beginning with the 2000 census, federal guidelines mandated that when U.S. government statistical agencies collect information on race, they must provide options for persons who identify with more than one race.[23] The impetus for this change came initially from a well-organized grassroots effort by people who thought of themselves as multiracial and wanted to be recognized as such in government statistics. There also was widespread recognition of an increase in the population that could be defined in terms of two or more racial groups. Therefore, an earlier 1977 set of federal standards for the collection of racial information was revised in 1997 to allow people to identify with two or more races.[24] The 2000 census was the first decennial census to take this approach, which was continued with minor revisions in 2010. Table 10-4 presents the 2010 census results for persons identifying with two or more races. It is important to note that the census distinguishes between "racial" groups—such as whites, blacks, Asians, and American Indians/Alaska Natives—and Hispanics, who are considered an ethnic group. Strictly speaking, because the census responses of "two or more races" apply only to racial groups, Hispanics are not counted in this classification.[25]

The census permits identification of combinations of up to six specific racial categories, including "some other race," a catch-all category for those races not specifically identified. Those identifying as "white and black" make up the largest single group—a population that more

TABLE 10-4
**Multiracial Populations Reported in 2010 Census**
*Percent*

| Multiracial group | Size | Percent change since 2000 | Percent of 2010 U.S. population |
|---|---|---|---|
| Two races[a] | 8,265,318 | +30 | 2.7 |
| White and black | 1,834,212 | +134 | 0.6 |
| White and Asian | 1,623,234 | +87 | 0.5 |
| White and American Indian/Alaska Native | 1,432,309 | +32 | 0.5 |
| White and Some Other Race | 1,740,924 | −21 | 0.6 |
| Black and American Indian/Alaska Native | 269,421 | +48 | 0.1 |
| Black and Asian | 185,595 | +74 | 0.1 |
| Three races | 676,469 | +65 | 0.2 |
| Four, five, or six races | 67,286 | +41 | 0.0 |
| All multiracial groups | 9,009,073 | +32 | 2.9 |

Source: 2000 and 2010 U.S. censuses.

[a] The specific two-race combinations shown do not include all possible two-race combinations.

than doubled over 2000–10, especially among the young. For every 100 black toddlers under age five, 15 toddlers are identified as both white and black—a sharp rise since 2000 (see figure 10-6). Other groups with populations nearly as large are those identifying as "white and Asian" and "white and American Indian or Alaska Native." Another large group includes those identifying as whites and the catch-all "some other race," although many of these individuals may have been attempting to identify their Hispanic status as a race, confounding the race-ethnicity distinction that the census tried to preserve.[26]

A question of interest to advocacy and political organizations representing the concerns of a racial group is how much of a racial group's national population might be "inflated" by including multiracial persons who declare that particular race as one of their backgrounds. The answer to this question differs by group (see table 10-5).

FIGURE 10-6

**Persons Identified as "White and Black" as a Percent of Black Persons, by Age, 2000 and 2010**

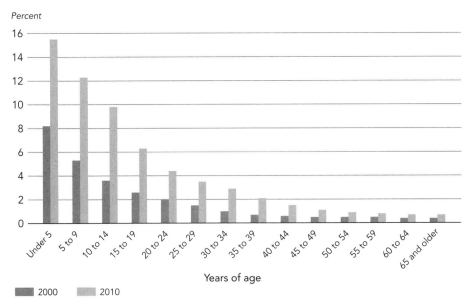

Source: 2000–2010 U.S. censuses.

TABLE 10-5
**Multiracial Population as Percent of Single-Race Population, 2010**

| Group | Population | | Multiracial as percent of single-race population |
|---|---|---|---|
| | Single-race | Multiracial[a] | |
| Black | 38,929,319 | 3,091,424 | 8% |
| Asian | 14,674,252 | 2,646,604 | 18% |
| American Indian/Alaska Native | 2,932,248 | 2,288,331 | 78% |

Source: 2010 U.S. census.

[a] Includes multiracial persons for whom one race is the designated group's race.

In 2010, the black population would have increased by 8 percent and the Asian population by 18 percent if multiracial persons were included in each separate racial category (that is, if multiracial Asians were counted as Asian and multiracial blacks were counted as black). Yet the American Indian/Alaska Native population would increase far more substantially—by 78 percent—if multiracial populations that included some American Indian or Alaska Native ancestry were counted as such. This reflects their longer history of multiracial marriages, particularly with whites, and the increased awareness of and pride in their Native American heritage of many formerly "white-only" citizens.[27] Because early advocates for racial minorities raised this issue, federal guidelines allowed certain multiracial minority combination populations to be added to their counterpart single-race populations for purposes of monitoring and enforcing civil rights legislation.[28] The question of whether persons who identify as multiracial wish to be classified with single-race populations is an open one and should be less likely to arise in the future as these multiracial populations become larger in size.

Overall, the census statistics with regard to multiracial persons show a rise in this population—by one-third over 2000–10. In states such as Hawaii, Alaska, and Oklahoma, they represent a share of 6 percent or more of the total population and of nearly 5 percent in California, Nevada, and Washington.[29] Yet overall, the share of the U.S. total population that is multiracial—2.9 percent—is surprisingly small in light of the pervasiveness of multiracial marriages and the general public perception that a larger multiracial population exits.

### A Larger Multiracial Population

There are several reasons to believe that the census numbers markedly understate current and likely future multiracial populations. One such reason is that the census does not include Hispanics in its count of multiracial persons because they are considered an ethnic rather than a racial group. It can be argued that the distinction between race and ethnicity, as the Census Bureau has applied it to the Hispanic population, is an artificial one. In an earlier era, race categories in government statistics were often identified by a person's physical traits. That has not been the case since at least 1970, when the census was first sent by mail and individuals were asked to self-identify their race. Over time, the broad race categories used to refer to minorities in civil rights legislation, mainstream media, and the public at large considered Hispanics on par with blacks, Asians, American Indians, and others. These categories pertained to major minority groups with distinctive social and cultural identities.

After the 2010 census, the Census Bureau began investigating alternative questionnaire formats that included Hispanics along with the other traditional racial categories in a single self-identification question—or, in practical terms, treating Hispanic as a race.[30] It allowed for multiple responses such as "white and Hispanic" or "black and Hispanic" along with the other multiracial categories used in earlier censuses. This change led, in one scenario, to a rise in the multiracial share of the population to 6.8 percent, well above the 2.9 percent in the 2010 census. Moreover, earlier projections using a similar approach by non-census researchers show the U.S. multiracial population reaching 10 percent in the year 2020 and 18 percent in the year 2050.[31]

A second reason why the multiracial population may be larger than enumerated in the 2010 census is that the single racial status or multiracial status of children is often determined by the adult who fills out the census form. Other surveys suggest that in identifying the race of their children, multiracial couples often select single-race identities that they believe will be more socially acceptable or will better prepare their children for success.[32] This, of course, may change as these children come of age and find that many of their peers also are multiracial.

A similar bias also occurs among the reports of adults of multiracial heritage, particularly adults who think that it is more desirable to be associated with a single race. For example, President Barack Obama, the child of a multiracial marriage, announced through his spokesperson that he identified himself as "black" rather than "white and black" on his 2010 census form.[33] It is likely, however, that younger and future generations of Americans with a multiracial heritage of any type will be more likely to embrace their multiracial heritage as it becomes more commonplace.

## SOFTENING THE WHITE-BLACK DIVIDE

The foregoing discussion makes clear that the racial lines are softening at the personal level between whites and the newer minorities—Asians and Hispanics—as well as American Indians and Alaska Natives. This trend is evident when examining the high prevalence and growth of multiracial marriages, signaling greater gains in multiracial populations. Yet even more significant from a historical standpoint is the clear and steady softening of the white-black racial divide. The rise in white-black marriages is unmistakable, as are the gains in the population that identifies itself as "white and black," especially among the very young. For further evidence that the white-black divide is eroding, it is useful to look to the South, the region historically most resistant to change. Because of past prejudices and customs, the white-black population, as a percentage of all blacks, is still considerably lower in southern states than in other parts of the country (see map 10-2). In a slew of states from Maryland to Texas, "white and black" populations amount to less than 5 percent of the black-only populations; in Mississippi and Louisiana, "white and black" populations constitute only 1 percent. In contrast, in a handful of states with sparse black populations in the West, Great Plains, and New England, the population of "white and black" persons is more than 20 percent of the black-only population.

Yet, as discussed in chapter 6, the South is attracting blacks in large numbers, including multiracial blacks, from all parts of the country.

MAP 10-2
**Persons Identifying as "White and Black" as a Percent of Black Persons, 2010**

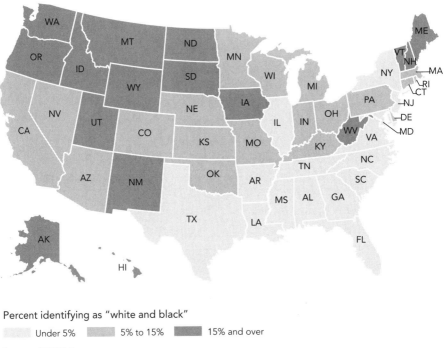

Percent identifying as "white and black"

▒ Under 5%        ▒ 5% to 15%        ■ 15% and over

Source:  2010 U.S. census.

It is significant, then, that when states are ranked by the growth in their "white-black" multiracial populations in the first decade of the 2000s, the southern states led all others (see table 10-6). In that period, the Carolinas, Georgia, Mississippi, and Alabama more than tripled their white-black multiracial populations, while Tennessee, Florida, Arkansas, Louisiana, and Kentucky were not far behind.

In fact, southern states as a whole accounted for 41 percent of the nation's decade-long gain in the "white and black" multiracial population. Responsible for this gain is a combination of the following factors: children born to multiracial parents, migration from other regions, and an increase in individuals' willingness to identify with a multiracial heritage in a region where it was long discouraged and penalized. The fact that the white-black divide was etched in stone by laws, public and private institutions, and even the ways in which population statistics were collected makes these shifts—incremental as they may seem—a major breakthrough toward the blurring of the nation's racial boundaries. These changes, coupled with the continued growth and intermingling of new minorities, are a further sign that integration at the personal level is part of the new racial reality in the twenty-first century.

TABLE 10-6

**States with Greatest Growth in Persons Identifying as "White and Black," 2000–10**

*Growth (%)*

| Rank/Area | Growth |
|-----------|--------|
| 1  South Carolina | 248 |
| 2  North Carolina | 232 |
| 3  Georgia | 223 |
| 4  Mississippi | 220 |
| 5  Alabama | 209 |
| 6  Tennessee | 196 |
| 7  Florida | 192 |
| 8  Arkansas | 183 |
| 9  Louisiana | 181 |
| 10  Kentucky | 180 |

Source: 2000 and 2010 U.S. censuses.

# Race and Politics

## The Cultural Generation Gap in Presidential Elections

# 11

The sweeping diversity explosion that is now under way in the United States will continue to change the social and demographic personalities of all parts of the country in ways that would not have been anticipated 20 or 30 years ago. Its impact on presidential politics is one of these. This is nothing new. Since the nation's founding, significant episodes of demographic change have shaped and reshaped regional interests and voting blocs in unforeseen ways.[1] The country is now well in the midst of one of these episodes. The election and re-election of the nation's first black president, Barack Obama, a progressive Democrat, would have been unthinkable to voters in the Reagan Republican–dominated 1980s. Obama's election, largely on the shoulders of a growing young and minority electorate—in some previously Republican-leaning New Sun Belt states—was probably the most visible symbol of how the diversity explosion has already made its mark.

Yet, the 2016 election of Republican baby boomer Donald Trump makes plain that young minority and other progressive voting blocs are not yet substantial enough to prevail uninterruptedly into the future. In fact, the racial demographics that brought about the election of both presidents Obama and Trump are still evolving in a way that makes it difficult to predict future election outcomes. To a large degree, they reflect the broader "cultural generation gap" between old and young that was discussed in chapter 2.

The "browning" of America from the bottom of the age structure upward has already been manifested in the politics of the younger millennial generation whose members tend to hold more progressive political views and skew Democratic in presidential elections. Yet their views are being countered by the more conservative and Republican leanings of an aging, mostly white senior population whose size will mushroom as the large baby boom generation ages.

This generational dynamic was apparent in the 2008 and 2012 elections of Obama as well as the 2016 election of Trump. In all three of these elections, younger and minority voters prevailed to give the Democratic candidate (including Hillary Clinton in 2016) the national popular vote advantage. Yet, unique to the 2016 election was the emergence of a geographic version of the cultural generation gap—separating older and whiter northern battleground states where voters favored Trump from several more diverse South and West states that have been trending Democratic. It is this geographic version of the cultural generation gap that led to Trump's 2016 Electoral College victory.

This chapter examines the impacts of the nation's new racial demographics on presidential politics with an emphasis on how they affected the elections of Barak Obama and Donald Trump. It is clear from these experiences that racial minority voters will play an important—though not necessarily decisive—role in future elections.

## A MORE DIVERSE ELECTORATE—WITH A DELAY

The increased growth of new minorities—Hispanics and Asians—described in earlier chapters has begun to make its mark on the nation's electorate by reducing the white portion of total voters. As recently as the 1980 presidential election, whites constituted 90 percent of all voters; in contrast, just 73 percent of voters were white in 2016. Yet even with these shifts, the 2016 voting population was "whiter" than the total U.S. population, then just 61 percent white.

The large discrepancy between whites' share of voters and their share of the total population can be seen as a "voter representation gap" between whites and minorities. A substantial part of this gap for Hispanics and Asians is attributable to the fact that smaller portions of their populations are eligible to vote. Greater percentages of these groups than of whites are under 18 years of age and therefore too young to vote. And among those who are old enough to vote, larger percentages do not have citizenship, even if they reside in the United States legally, and therefore cannot vote.[2] Consequently, the portion of all Hispanics and Asians who are eligible to vote—citizens of the age of 18 and above—constitutes only about one-half or less of their total populations. As a census survey taken after the 2016 election shows, among all Hispanics in the U.S. population, only 46 percent were eligible to vote (see figure 11-1). Furthermore, among all Asians, only 55 percent were eligible to vote. This contrasts with blacks and whites, of whom

FIGURE 11-1
**Share of Population Eligible to Vote, 2016**

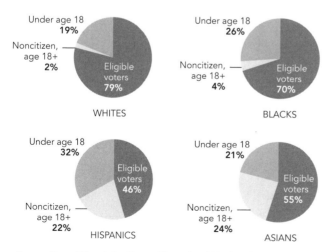

Source: Current Population Survey, November 2016 Supplement.

70 percent and 79 percent of their respective populations were eligible to vote.

Figure 11-2 illustrates the lag for Hispanics and Asians in translating their representation in the total population (left panel) to their representations in the eligible voter population (middle panel). While the Hispanic portion of the total population increased from 14 to 18 percent between the 2004 and 2016 elections, the Hispanic portion of eligible voters remained lower for both elections, increasing from just 8 to 12 percent. Asian representation among eligible voters also remained lower

FIGURE 11-2

**U.S. Total and Eligible Voter Population by Race, 2004–16**

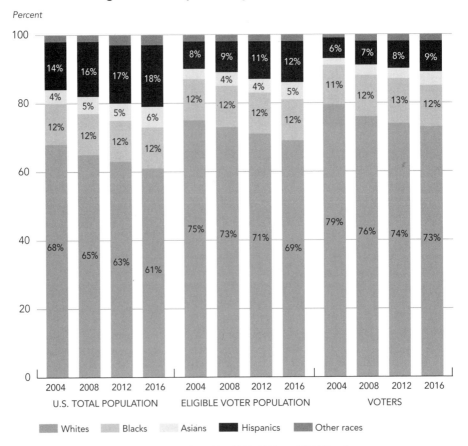

Source: Current Population Survey, November 2004, 2008, 2012, and 2016 Supplements.

than among the total population. Blacks maintained the same share, 12 percent, among eligible voters and among the total population for all four elections. In stark contrast, whites continue to be more highly represented among eligible voters than among the total population (69 percent versus 61 percent in 2016) because of their older age structure and higher citizenship rates.

The representation gap for Hispanics and Asians is further widened among actual voters (figure 11-2, right panel) because fewer Hispanics and Asians than whites and blacks who are eligible to vote actually turn out at the polls. Often, because of their recent residence status or lack of information, Hispanics and Asians are less likely to register to vote and cast ballots.[3] As a result, Hispanics represented only 9 percent of voters in the 2016 presidential election despite constituting twice that share of the total population. Furthermore, although the white share of the population continues to shrink, whites are far more highly represented among voters (73 percent in 2016) than in the population as a whole.[4]

The representation gap should eventually close as new minority groups age and become eligible for citizenship.[5] Among Hispanics this will occur fairly gradually in the near term due to their somewhat higher fertility and more youthful immigration. Yet as the Hispanic population ages, the "too young to vote" portion of its population is projected to decrease over time. Over the past several years, as more Hispanics turn 18 years of age, they added over 800,000 new voting-age citizens annually, a trend that is projected to continue.[6]

New minority voter participation will increase for two additional reasons. First, there will be higher rates of naturalization among Hispanic and Asian permanent residents who are eligible to become citizens. Naturalized citizenship rates have increased in recent years, although there is room for further growth. This is especially the case for Mexicans, who constituted 37 percent of the more than 9 million lawful immigrants who met eligibility requirements in 2015 and have one of the lowest naturalization rates. A survey conducted by the Pew Research Center indicates that language, administration, and financial barriers are keeping Hispanics from naturalizing.[7] These barriers are likely to be overcome with increased assistance as more public and nonprofit services become available.

Second, voter turnout rates among Hispanics and Asians, discussed below, will increase as members of these communities—particularly those in new destinations—become more familiar with registration and voting practices with the help of local government and civic organizations.

Nonetheless, there was concern during recent presidential elections that overly stringent voter identification legislation, proposed in some states, was intended to prevent uninformed minorities from registering to vote. Furthermore, there were accusations that voting opportunities and poll station hours were deliberately restricted in some minority-populated areas.[8] These and other voter suppression practices can and will make a difference in election outcomes, especially in closely contested states. They deserve attention and should be monitored by local citizenship groups, civil rights organizations, and government authorities. Yet over the long haul, the effects of any such attempts to suppress voters will pale in comparison with the larger demographic sweep of minority groups that will shape the nation's civic decisionmaking.

## RACE AND PRESIDENTIAL ELECTIONS: THE POPULAR VOTE

Although the nation's electorate still lags behind its total population with respect to racial makeup, there is no doubt that racial minorities made the difference in the national popular vote for Democrat Barack Obama's 2008 and 2012 wins. And while Republican Donald Trump won the 2016 election in the Electoral College, the popular vote was won by his Democratic opponent, Hillary Clinton. Blacks, Hispanics, Asians, and other minorities showed their electoral clout in each of these elections in ways that were rarely evident in the past. A prominent feature of this clout rests with their concentration in the younger part of the electorate. How have minorities been impacting the national popular vote for the president? What does this more diverse electorate imply for future presidential elections?

**The Minority Vote in Recent Elections**

Presidential elections are affected by a myriad of forces—such as the mood of the country, the national economy, the particular candidates chosen to run, and the demographic makeup of the electorate. The electorate's multifaceted demographic makeup has been subject to millions of dollars of research by political pollsters and strategists in an attempt to garner a voting margin advantage among the various demographic segments for their respective candidates. The changing racial demographics of the American electorate, coupled with distinct race-specific voting margins and turnout patterns, were central to recent election outcomes.

### Racial Voting Trends

Race-related voting patterns in presidential elections—with minorities favoring Democrats and whites favoring Republicans—have been evident since at least the mid-1960s. The nation's black population has shown the most consistent voting pattern, having voted for Democratic presidential candidates since the 1936 second-term election of Franklin D. Roosevelt. Yet it was during the 1960s that Democratic tendencies among black voters intensified, influenced by the passage of civil rights legislation by the Democrat-controlled White House and Congress. Since the election of Lyndon B. Johnson in 1964, no Republican candidate has received more than 15 percent of the black vote.[9]

Hispanics also favor Democrats in presidential elections but not nearly as overwhelmingly as blacks do. Since 1980, the percentage of Hispanics favoring Democratic candidates has ranged from 56 percent to 71 percent.[10] Despite a general rise in Hispanic support for Democrats in recent years, there have been fluctuations. One occurred in 2004, when only 58 percent of Hispanics voted for Democrat John Kerry and 40 percent voted for George W. Bush—the narrowest Democratic margin for Hispanics (18 percent) in 32 years. More than previous Republican candidates, Bush made a special effort to court Hispanics on issues such as immigration reform. That said, the Hispanic vote is hardly monolithic, given the different national origins of its components. Traditionally, Cuban Americans have tended to vote Republican, though that may be shifting. Protestant—particularly evangelical—Hispanics, a relatively small group, also lean Republican. Surveys based on the 2016 election, show strong Democratic votes cast by Dominicans, Mexicans, and Central and South Americans.[11]

The Asian population has only recently shown a sizable national presence in the electorate. Its voting record has changed since the 1990s, moving more decidedly to the Democratic column in recent presidential elections. In both 1992 and 1996, when many older Asian Americans sided with the pro-business and anticommunist positions of the Republican Party, Asians voted for Republican candidates George H. W. Bush and Bob Dole instead of Bill Clinton. The more recent swing toward Democrats is connected to the growth of younger and more diverse Asian populations that have more progressive views on social and economic issues. In the 2016 election, surveys showed substantial support for Democrat Hillary Clinton, among all Asian groups, although it was least solid among Chinese and Vietnamese voters.[12]

In contrast to racial minorities, white Americans favored Republican candidates in every presidential election after 1964, when they favored Lyndon B. Johnson over Barry Goldwater. Since then, white Republican voting margins (the percent voting Republican minus the percent voting Democratic) have varied from values of higher than 30 in the landslide wins of Richard Nixon in 1972 and Ronald Reagan in 1984 to values of under 5 in 1976, 1992, and 1996, when Democrats Jimmy Carter and Bill Clinton (twice) won despite white support for the Republicans. Whites, of course, are not a monolithic group, and they change voting preferences over time. For example, well into the 1960s, working-class or blue-collar whites were the backbone of the strong, union-based Democratic constituency. That has changed, especially since 1980s, as this group eschewed the "cultural changes" associated with the socially progressive positions that the Democratic Party adopted in the aftermath of Johnson's Great Society agenda. Over time they began to embrace the lower-tax, smaller-government message of the Republican Party.[13]

Yet since then, Republicans have done less well—although they still often win—among educated whites, especially women, and white unmarried women.[14] Given this scenario, the recent goal of Democrats has been to minimize their losses among the white working class and increase their appeal to educated whites, particularly college graduate women and single women.

## Obama's 2008 and 2012 Victories

The long-term trends in presidential voting, showing minorities skewing toward Democrats and whites favoring Republicans, may very well have reached a point where the minority electorate itself has become critical to a Democratic victory. It was in the election of Barack Obama in 2008—and especially his reelection in 2012—that the minority population, through its size, turnout, and voting preferences, demonstrated its considerable heft.

Obama's victories came on the heels of the 2004 election, in which George W. Bush was reelected by a net of 3 million votes—gaining 16 million white votes and losing 12.9 million minority votes (see table 11-1). In the subsequent two elections—Obama versus John McCain in 2008 and Obama versus Mitt Romney in 2012—Obama was a victor with net gains of 9.5 million votes and 5 million votes, respectively, over his Republican opponents. This was because the size of Obama's support from minorities mushroomed to 21.2 million in 2008 and 23.5 million votes in 2012. At the same time, his Republican opponents received smaller white vote gains of 11.7 million in 2008 and 18.6 million in 2012.

Obama's continued gains in the minority vote were attributable, in part, to the rise in the portion of eligible voters who were minorities (shown in figure 11-2). But it was also attributable to an increase in Dem-

TABLE 11-1
### Presidential Popular Vote Outcomes: 2004 through 2016
*Thousands of votes*

| Group | Net vote difference: Democatic minus Republican candidate (1,000s)[a] | | | |
|---|---|---|---|---|
| | 2004 | 2008 | 2012 | 2016 |
| Total | −3,012 | 9,549 | 4,985 | 2,868 |
| Whites | −16,008 | −11,676 | −18,555 | −18,502 |
| Minorities | 12,996 | 21,225 | 23,540 | 21,370 |
| *Democratic candidate* | Kerry | Obama | Obama | Clinton[b] |
| *Republican candidate* | Bush | McCain | Romney | Trump[b] |

Source: Author's analysis of national popular votes reported in David Leip's *Atlas of U.S. Presidential Elections,* and margins reported by the National Election Pool Media Consortium, Edison Research as reported in CNN Election Center (www.cnn.com/election).

[a]Difference equals votes for Democratic candidate minus votes for Republican candidate (positive value indicates Democratic advantage; negative value indicates Republican advantage).

[b]In 2016, Trump won the presidency through the electoral college while Clinton receieved the most popular votes.

ocratic voting margins and voter turnout rates for minorities. This can be seen, first, by comparing Democratic voting margins (the percent voting Democratic minus the percent voting Republican) for blacks, Hispanics, and Asians in the three elections, 2004, 2008, and 2012 (see figure 11-3). As in previous elections, blacks exhibited the largest Democratic margins in each election. Yet the magnitudes of those margins were higher in both of the Obama elections than in the 2004 Bush-Kerry election. A similar trend is apparent for the lower, but still solid, Democratic margins among Hispanics and Asians. In fact, for each of these groups, the Democratic margins in 2008 and 2012 were as high as the margins in any previous election. Clearly, the support for the first minority candidate, Obama, was accentuated by the voting preferences of all three groups.

Perhaps even more important for Obama was the rise in voter turnout rates among black, Hispanic, and Asian eligible voters in his two elections. As indicated above, the turnout of eligible minority voters has typically been well below that of whites. But if more minority voters could be ener-

FIGURE 11-3

**Democratic-over-Republican Margin, by Race, 2004 through 2016 Presidential Elections**

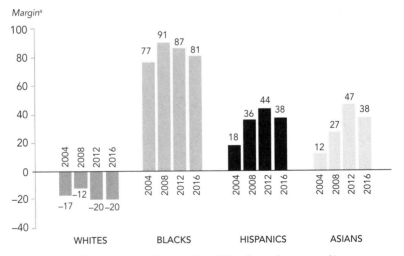

Source: National Election Pool media consortium, Edison Research as reported in CNN Election Center (www.cnn.com/election).

[a]Margin is defined as percent voting for Democratic candidate minus percent voting for Republican candidate.

gized to vote by civic organizations or political campaigns, they would amplify the impact of the groups' collective voting clout. That was the case for all three major minority groups in the 2008 and 2012 elections.

As shown in figure 11-4, black voter turnout increased so that nearly two-thirds of black eligible voters cast ballots in 2008 and 2012. Along with the decline in white voter turnout, this resulted in black voter turnout exceeding white voter turnout in 2012, for the first time since such statistics have been recorded.[15] Although lower than the black voter turnout, Hispanic and Asian turnouts were higher in both Obama elections than in 2004. A combination of greater enthusiasm and a dedicated campaign to turn out the vote enlarged the size and effect of these minority groups on the final election outcome.

The increased influence of minorities was important in both of Obama's victories but especially so in 2012, when the white Republican vote advantage swelled beyond its 2004 level. That advantage was smaller in the 2008 election because of lower white turnout and a lower

FIGURE 11-4

**Voter Turnout, by Race, in the 2004 through 2016 Presidential Elections**

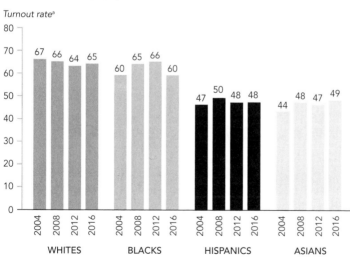

*Turnout rate*[a]

Source: Current Population Survey, November 2004, 2008, 2012, and 2016 Supplements

[a]Turnout rate is defined as percent of eligible voters who voted.

Republican vote margin among whites who did vote. This election was held during a time when overall Republican support hit a low point due to the onset of the financial crisis in September 2008 and general dissatisfaction with the economy and the Iraq and Afghanistan wars. Therefore, at a time when minority support for the first minority presidential candidate was on the rise, enthusiasm for the Republican candidate, McCain, was declining among several key white voting blocs.

In 2012, the economy continued to fade, and there were increasing expectations that Obama might not be reelected. Yet this time the story was mixed. White voters who actually cast ballots rang up the largest Republican voting margin since 1984 (figure 11-3), when Ronald Reagan beat Walter Mondale. However, the voters who did cast ballots were part of an extremely low white turnout—a decline from the previous two elections.

Therefore, the rising demographic clout of minorities demonstrated its true heft in the 2012 election. In earlier elections when Democrats won while whites voted Republican (1976, 1992, and 1996), minorities were able to make a difference because the white Republican margins were small. But in 2012, when whites generated one of the largest Republican margins in 30 years, the combined minority population still prevailed to elect a Democratic president. Although it is true that Obama's reelection was the result of several factors operating together—more minorities in the electorate, high voter turnout, and strong Democratic voting margins—the results demonstrate the strength of the minority vote in American politics.

### The Trump-Clinton 2016 Popular Vote Contest

In the 2016 election pitting Donald Trump against Hillary Clinton, minority contributions to the Democratic candidate were noticeably smaller (at 21.3 million) than in 2012. The white contribution to the Republican candidate was nearly the same (at 18.5 million) as in the previous election. Nonetheless, the Democrat, Clinton, gained the popular net vote advantage at 2.9 million (see table 11-1). Although Clinton lost the election in the Electoral College, her popular vote victory followed the same general pattern displayed in Obama's two wins. In each of these elections, the Democratic candidate showed vote gains among minorities exceeding 21 million, while the Republican candidate showed vote gains among whites ranging from 11.7 to 18.6 million.

The 2016 downturn in Democratic support among minorities reflects two components—lower minority turnout and lower Democratic voter margins. As shown in figure 11-4, lower turnout was especially evident among blacks in 2016—dropping from the all-time high of 66 percent in 2012 to 60 percent. Likewise for black voters, the Democrat minus Republican voting margin in 2016—while still high at 81 percent—was down from 91 and 87 percentages in the prior two elections (see figure 11-3).

Hispanic and Asian voter turnout in 2016 was not reduced from 2012. Yet for both groups, the voting margins for Democrats dropped below 2012 levels. In fact, it was the somewhat less enthusiastic minority support for Democrat Clinton that had led to the lower overall Democratic popular vote advantage in 2016. This can be expected because both turnout and Democratic voting preferences were extraordinarily high for Obama, the first minority presidential nominee from a major party. Still, with minority support Clinton did win the popular vote with relatively similar race dynamics at play as was the case for the previous two elections.

## Racial Voting Blocs and Future Elections

The 2008, 2012, and 2016 elections validated the importance of minorities on the national political stage. But they were also extremely polarizing elections. In the three elections combined, Republican candidates gained nearly nine of their ten votes from whites, while Democratic candidates captured nearly eight of every ten minority votes. In addition to their potential for increasing racial divisions, future elections that follow these trends will not be demographically sustainable. The projected rise in the minority portion of the electorate—from 34 percent in 2020 to 40 percent in 2032—demands that both parties cross the racial divide to succeed in the future (see figure 11-5).[16] Hispanics will contribute the most to this gain as they overtake blacks among eligible voters in 2020—two decades after Hispanics overtook blacks in the total population.

Both parties have recognized the need to reach out to crossover voting blocs. Republican strategists such as Karl Rove, who engineered George W. Bush's relatively strong showing among Hispanics in 2004, have long advocated for greater GOP outreach to minorities, Hispanics

FIGURE 11-5
**Projected Eligible Voter Population by Race 2020–32**

*Percent*

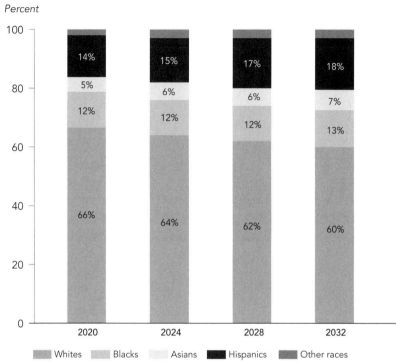

Source: William H. Frey, Ruy Teixeira, and Robert Griffin, "America's Electoral Future," Center for American Progress, Brookings Institution, and American Enterprise Institute, February 2016.

in particular.[17] After its loss in the 2012 presidential election, the Republican party issued what was termed an "autopsy report," highlighting the need to campaign specifically to reach Hispanics, African Americans, and Asian Americans.[18] Such initiatives were not emphasized in the failed 2008 and 2012 presidential bids of Republicans John McCain or Mitt Romney or in the 2016 campaign of Donald Trump. But they are likely to be revisited in the future if the GOP attempts to expand its reach to minorities. If so, they may find some openings. A 2016 Pew Research Center survey indicates that for both blacks and Hispanics, those under age 35 were more likely than their elders to call themselves independents and less likely to identify as Democrats.[19]

Democrats, for their part, have continued to eye potentially winnable segments of the white electorate. In their 2002 book *The Emerging Democratic Majority,* John B. Judis and Ruy Teixeira show that although the Democrats have lost their advantage with the white working class, their focus on progressive issues increased the party's appeal to rising white demographic segments in a postindustrial economy—professionals and women who, along with minorities, could reinvigorate the party's base.[20] More recently, political writer Ronald Brownstein coined the term "coalition of transformation" to identify key growing voting blocs that Democrats could cultivate to their advantage. These include minorities, white college graduates—particularly women—and the younger millennial generation.[21] Although minorities are clearly a cornerstone of the party's future, Brownstein points out that white college graduates are demographically significant where white college graduate women could become a solid Democratic constituency.

The millennial generation, in its overlap with minorities and educated whites, could hold the most long-term promise for Democrats. They are the most minority-dominant generation, and Pew Research Center polls show them to be more socially tolerant, liberal, open to larger government, and inclined to vote Democratic.[22] If this generation continues to hold fast to those attitudes as they advance into middle age, Democrats would benefit greatly.[23] Yet not all generations have held onto their youthful visions, as evidenced by many early baby boomers, who shifted politically to the right as they aged.[24] The challenge for Democrats will be to retain the loyalties of millennials over the long term.

## The Cultural Generation Gap

Given these trends, the country is on the cusp of an emerging generation gap in voting patterns and in politics more broadly. As discussed in chapter 2, the browning of America, starting with the younger generations, has caused a cultural generation gap between the young and the old. That became evident in past debates over immigration reform and in the competition for government resources between the young and the aged, as the largely white older generation feels disconnected from the increasingly diverse younger population. These kinds of divisions have already emerged in national politics and may continue in future presidential elections. Although the new racial shifts introduced by the millennial generation may very well drive current and future Democratic vote advantages, the national electorate will also include a large and growing senior population as the baby boom population continues to age.

The importance of the youth and minority voting blocs for Democrats is evident from the 2016 Democratic voting margins by age, shown in figure 11-6. Among all voters, it was the more youthful 18- to 29-year-old segment that gave Democratic candidate Hillary Clinton her greatest popular vote margin, and within this age group, minorities clearly were the biggest contributors. Although young whites voted slightly against Clinton, they showed the lowest Republican margin of all age groups among whites. The more heavily minority younger age groups not only formed the largest basis for Democratic support in 2016, but they also provided the strongest support for Barack Obama in both the 2008 and 2012 elections.

In contrast, older voters, especially older whites, favored the Republican candidate, Donald Trump, most heavily in 2016. It is within older age groups—including the baby boom generation and the older "silent generation"—that Republican-leaning, blue-collar whites who do not hold college degrees are prominent. A Pew Research Center survey shows that, even before 2012, both of these cohorts favored Republican candidates, expressed reservations about the changing face of America, and generally

FIGURE 11-6

**Democratic-over-Republican Margin, by Age Group, 2016**

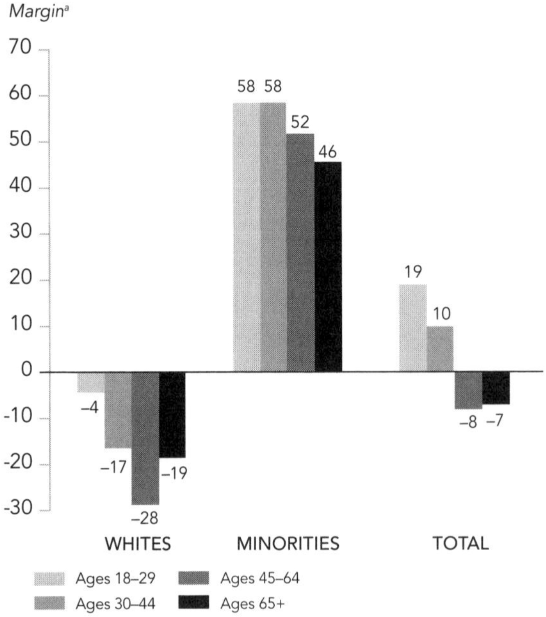

*Margin*[a]

Source: National Election Pool media consortium, Edison Research as reported in CNN Election Center (www.cnn.com/election).

[a]Margin is defined as percent voting for Democratic candidate minus percent voting for Republican candidate.

wanted a smaller government with fewer services—with the exception of Social Security, for which they favor Democratic more than Republican approaches.[25] More important from a demographic standpoint is the fact that these older generations of whites will continue to have staying power in the electorate. This is evident in figure 11-7, which depicts eligible voters in 2016 and the projected eligible voters in 2028 for each age group.

There will clearly be a browning of the 18- to 29-year-old and 30- to 44-year-old segments of the electorate as the large millennial generation begins entering middle age in 2028. By then, minorities will constitute nearly one-half of young adult eligible voters and more than 40 percent of those ages 30 to 44. They represent voting blocs that are ripe for Democratic retention if current race and generational political affinities persist. During the same period, the large, mainly white group of voters age 45 to 64 will lose some of its white baby boom population as the latter advances into a sharply rising senior electorate. Votes from these two

FIGURE 11-7

**Projected Eligible Voters, by Race and Age, 2016 and 2028**

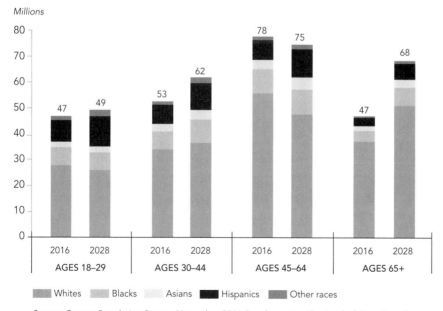

*Millions*

Source: Current Population Survey, November 2016 Supplement; author's calculations based on U.S. Census Bureau projections.

older groups will be easier for the Republican Party to retain if current generational voting affinities continue. Even if these trends do continue, there will still be a contest. That is, in 2028 the eligible voter population age 45 and above will be 29 percent larger than the population of eligible voters under age 45—a disparity that will be further widened by the higher turnout of older eligible voters.

Of course, today's racial and generational proclivities are not necessarily destined to continue in a straight-line fashion. Democrats could make greater strides with key white voting blocs, including white college graduates—both men and women—who will increasingly dominate post-boomer generations of white voters. Republicans could make gains among Hispanics and other minorities. Furthermore, both parties will do their best to garner the favor of the growing, high-turnout senior population, which will be increasingly composed of baby boomers. In fact, the greatest challenge for both parties will be to meet the often conflicting needs of voters on both sides of the cultural generation gap. To do so, they will have to persuade seniors that the key needs among striving young minorities—education, affordable housing, and steady employment—will work to benefit the Social Security and medical care programs that seniors will need in retirement.

## RACE AND THE ELECTORAL COLLEGE VOTE

It might seem safe to assume that the popular vote scenario presented for future presidential elections will easily translate into actual election outcomes. But in two recent presidential elections, 2000 and 2016, this was not the case. The 2016 election in which Donald Trump lost the popular vote but won the Electoral College and the presidency was especially significant. This is because it occurred on the heels of two elections when, because of demographic shifts, it looked as if Democrats were trending toward long-term Electoral College dominance.

This potentially Democratic friendly scenario is set out in the discussions below of the growth of minority voters in long-standing Republican-leaning New Sun Belt states and their importance in electing Barack Obama as president in 2008 and 2012. They are followed by an analysis of the demographic underpinning—a state-level cultural generation gap—which served to elect Donald Trump as president in 2016.

## The New Sun Belt as a Battleground

For many elections prior to 2008, much of the New Sun Belt—swaths of states in the Southeast and Mountain West—voted reliably Republican. But this began to change when several of the region's states became political battlegrounds as minorities were increasingly represented there.

The dispersal of the overall minority population, documented in early chapters, is also occurring in the eligible voter population. Map 11-1 portrays the racial makeup of eligible voters by state at the time of the 2016 election. Clearly, minorities are a sizable presence in many states, including those that are not in traditional coastal settlement areas. Minorities constitute nearly one-half or more of the electorate in Hawaii, New Mexico, California, Texas, and Washington, D.C., and at least one-third or more in a swath of additional states in the South and interior West.

Hispanics account for a substantial and increasing portion of the electorate in many western states as well as in Texas, Florida, New Jersey, New York, and Illinois; in the latter states, they may soon approach blacks in electoral clout. Minorities constitute more than one-quarter of the electorate in most southern states, where blacks are the largest group (Florida, Texas, and Oklahoma excepted). Blacks still dominate the small minority populations in whiter Heartland states such as Michigan, Ohio, and Pennsylvania, although their smaller Hispanic populations are rising, as in other parts of that region. Therefore, although the nation's electorate is still divided somewhat between whiter Heartland states and heavily minority coastal states, states in the New Sun Belt stand at the forefront of electorate change. These include fast-growing western interior states that are receiving Hispanics and other minorities and prosperous southern states that are attracting blacks along with Hispanics from other regions.

This trend is illustrated in the minority contributions to the growth in eligible voters between the 2004 and 2016 elections in selected fast-growing states (see figure 11-8). In each of these states except Texas, minorities contributed more than two-thirds to the growth of their electorates. Hispanics contributed to nearly one-half of eligible voter growth in Florida

MAP 11-1
**Minorities as Percent of Eligible Voters, November 2016**

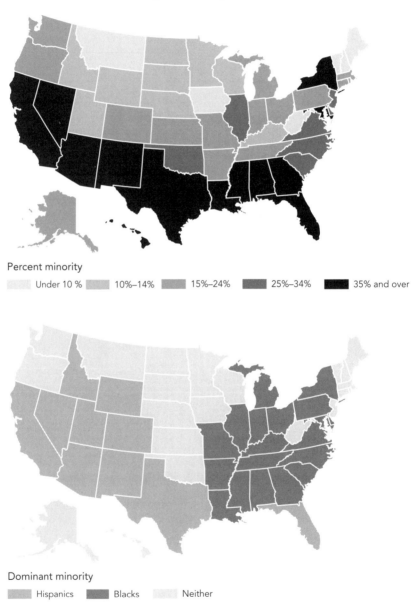

Percent minority

Under 10 %    10%–14%    15%–24%    25%–34%    35% and over

Dominant minority

Hispanics    Blacks    Neither

Source: U.S. Census Bureau, Current Population Survey, November 2016 Supplement.

and Arizona and more than one-fifth to growth in the other states. In Georgia, blacks contributed to more than half of new eligible voters between 2004 and 2016, and in Virginia, Asians and other races contributed to more than one-third.

The geographic dispersion of new minorities and the southward migration of blacks work to the advantage of the Democrats by enlarging the number of battleground states and allowing Democrats to cut into electoral turf that Republicans held steadily over a long period. In the 2004 election, as in the election four years earlier, George W. Bush won by making a nearly clean sweep of the interior West and South, along with Great Plains and several northern states—most notably

FIGURE 11-8
**Growth in Eligible Voters, by Race Contributions, 2004–16**

*Growth rate*

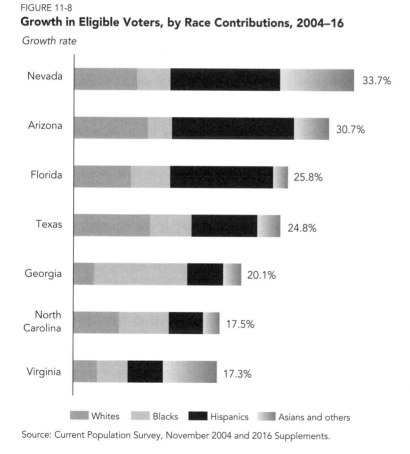

Source: Current Population Survey, November 2004 and 2016 Supplements.

Ohio—which were then dubbed battleground states (see map 11-2). This Sun Belt sweep was not new to Republicans. Although they lost some Sun Belt states when southerner Bill Clinton ran in the three-way elections of 1992 and 1996 and when southerner Jimmy Carter ran in 1976 and 1980, the Republicans have held fairly firm control of the South since the civil rights years, when white southerners started voting in large numbers for Republican candidates.[26] With very few exceptions, the mostly white conservative-leaning interior West states voted for Republicans continuously from 1968 to 2004, aside from the three-way elections of the 1990s.

The Democratic strongholds for the two elections prior to 2008 consisted of urbanized, racially diverse coastal states such as California and New York and a swath of states in New England, the Northeast, and the Midwest with industrial or farming histories. Although these states' constituencies reflected both the new and the old strengths of the party—minorities, union workers, progressive professionals, and women—they did not represent the most rapidly growing parts of the country.

### State Racial Demographic Shifts and Obama's Electoral College Wins

The political map changed with both the 2008 and 2012 elections due to the changing racial demographics of a number of New Sun Belt states.[27] This change can be seen in map 11-2, which shows that, in contrast to the Democratic performance in 2004, Obama won the new West and South battleground states of Nevada, New Mexico, Colorado, Virginia and Florida in both of his elections and, in 2008, North Carolina.

The impact of demographic changes along with the new enthusiasm for Obama is illustrated in Nevada. In 2004, Nevada's voters were 80 percent white, 8 percent Hispanic, 6 percent black, and 6 percent Asian or another race. Nevada's white share dropped to 73 percent in 2008 and to 67 percent in 2012, when the Hispanic share rose to 15 percent, the black share to 9 percent, and the share of Asians or another race also to 9 percent. Aside from demographics alone, the Democratic voting margins increased, especially for Hispanics—from 21 in 2004 to 54 in 2008 and 47 in 2012.

Shifts in this direction were evident in most of the other Sun Belt states that Obama won in 2008, where a rise in the minority Democratic

MAP 11-2

**States Won by Democratic and Republican Candidates, 2004, 2008, and 2012**

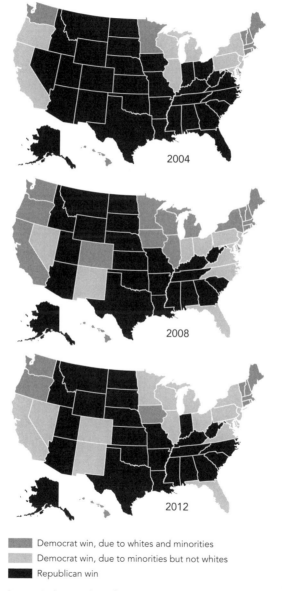

2004

2008

2012

| | Democrat win, due to whites and minorities |
|---|---|
| | Democrat win, due to minorities but not whites |
| | Republican win |

Source: Author's analysis of National Election Pool media consortium, Edison Research as reported in CNN Election Center, (www.cnn.com/election/2012/results/main).

vote overcame the Republican white vote.[28] For most of these South and West battleground states (North Carolina was the exception), Obama's minority support was strong enough to overcome an increased white Republican margin in 2012. That was especially crucial in Florida, where the white Republican margin increased from 14 to 24 between 2008 and 2012. But due to a larger minority turnout and increased Democratic margins, Obama won this key battleground state again.

As shown in table 11-2, minorities were responsible for winning five South and West battleground states in both 2008 and 2012, defeating the white Republican advantage for those states. It appeared as if that the growth of Hispanics and other new minorities and the southward migration of blacks were opening the door to greater future Democratic prospects in the Sun Belt—perhaps including previous Republican bastions such as Texas, Georgia, and Arizona, whose U.S.–born populations under age 18 are dominated by minorities.

Still, it should not go unnoticed that minorities also were responsible for winning battleground states for Obama in the slowly growing Heartland, such as Ohio and Pennsylvania (see table 11-2). Voters in both of these states were primarily white (83 and 85 percent, respec-

TABLE 11-2

**Battleground States Where Minorities Were Responsible for Obama's Win, 2008 and 2012[a]**

| Region | 2008 | 2012 |
|---|---|---|
| *Northeast and Midwest* | Ohio | Ohio |
| | Pennsylvania | Pennsylvania |
| | Indiana | Wisconsin |
| *South and West* | Florida | Florida |
| | Nevada | Nevada |
| | New Mexico | New Mexico |
| | Virginia | Virginia |
| | North Carolina | Colorado |
| *Electoral votes for these states* | 117 | 110 |
| *Obama's total electoral votes*[b] | 365 | 332 |

Source: Author's analysis of National Election Pool media consortium, Edison Research as reported in CNN Election Center (www.cnn.com/election).

[a] Battleground states for each election that were won by Democrats in which whites voted Republican or split the vote. (Battleground states include those defined by pollsters before the election or those that showed a Democratic margin of less than 7 percent.)

[b] 270 needed to win.

tively,) with modest recent minority gains. Obama won these states for two reasons: both Democratic margins and the turnout of their small minority populations, especially blacks, were high; and the white Republican voting margins were smaller than in other states.[29] Even so, these were among the closest states in the 2012 election and, even then, pointed up a potential geographic fissure that could make Democrats vulnerable. That is, although Democrats may have become more successful at garnering fast-growing populations—millennials, minorities, and college graduates—as they open new geographic opportunities in the Sun Belt, the older, whiter, slowly growing battleground states could become more open to Republican messages if the right candidate came along.

### The Geographic Cultural Generation Gap and Trump's 2016 Victory

That candidate did come along in 2016 in the person of Donald Trump.[30] Not a conventional politician, Trump made his reputation as a real estate mogul and reality television personality. In the primary election campaigns against more conventional Republican candidates and in the general election against Hillary Clinton, Trump stood out as a populist anti-establishment candidate promising to "drain the swamp" in Washington, D.C., and focus on the interests of non-elites. In promising to bring back jobs to voters in parts of the country that have been hit hard in the post-recession economy, his appeal was especially directed to older working class whites, many of whom felt disconnected from the new economy. However, a key part of his slogan to "Make America Great, Again" was pitched to one side of the cultural generation gap: many of these same potential voters who were uncomfortable with the nation's growing immigrant populations, political correctness, trade agreements, and other aspects of America's emerging demographic change. He promised to lower immigration levels, build a wall along the U.S.-Mexican border, and institute more U.S. friendly trade policies.

Rather than following the advice of the Republican National Committee's autopsy after the 2012 election, Trump did little to reach out broadly to younger, growing racial minority populations in his appeals to what he called the "forgotten" American.[31] In contrast, Hillary Clinton's slogan

"Stronger Together" was an explicit appeal to the same Democratic base that elected Barack Obama—especially young people, minorities, and the college educated. Thus, the two candidates focused their efforts heavily on different sides of the cultural generation gap.

As indicated above, Clinton won the 2016 popular vote by 2.9 million. However, Trump won the presidency in the Electoral College by 304 to 227. As shown in map 11-3, he did so by winning five northern battleground states in the Heartland that Obama won in both 2008 and 2012—Iowa, Michigan, Ohio, Pennsylvania, and Wisconsin—as well as the two southern battlegrounds, Florida and North Carolina. Obama won all of these states (except Iowa) in 2012 by gaining more votes from racial minorities than he lost to whites. Trump won by gaining more whites than he lost to racial minorities.

MAP 11-3

**States Won by Donald Trump (Republican) and Hillary Clinton (Democrat), 2016 Election**

Clinton (D) win—due to whites and minorities

Clinton (D) win—due to minorities but not whites

Trump (R) win

Source: National Election Pool media consortium, Edison Research as reported in CNN Election Center (www.cnn.com/election).

The five northern states, with their combined seventy Electoral College votes, more than made the difference toward Trump's victory. Pennsylvania and Michigan had not voted Republican in a presidential election since 1988; Wisconsin had not done so since 1984. The Trump-Republican takeover of these older, whiter battleground states helped to form a geographic cultural generation gap separating them from the more diverse southern and western battlegrounds—including Virginia, Nevada, New Mexico, and Colorado—that have recently trended Democratic, including in 2016.

There were several key factors associated with Trump's win in these states. One was an extraordinarily high vote among largely older whites who did not have a college degree, beating Clinton by 66 percent to 29 percent, nationally—the biggest Republican margin for this group in decades. Such voters comprised especially high shares of voters in these northern battlegrounds (though they also made a difference in Florida and North Carolina).[32] These voters were directly targeted by Trump's campaign often with a strong social media effort.[33]

A second reason why Trump took these states was the reduced turnout and Democratic-voting among racial minorities, especially blacks. Black voters, in particular, were key to Obama's winning the states of Michigan, Ohio, Pennsylvania, and Wisconsin in both his elections, with high voter turnout and Democratic voting preference. Yet, as was the case nationally, black turnout and Democratic voting preference were smaller and contributed to a worse Democratic showing in these states for 2016. This was also the case for a reduced Democratic vote contribution of blacks in North Carolina and of blacks and Hispanics in Florida.[34]

A third dimension of Trump's win in these northern states, and to some extent nationally, is the sharper Republican-Democratic division between rural America and large cities than existed in either of the Obama elections. Trump's targeted older, white, and blue-collar "forgotten" American voters, who were prevalent in small towns and rural parts of the states he won, responded strongly with their votes. Clinton performed well in large metropolitan areas with their racially diverse urbane demographic voting blocs, nearly matching Obama's gains there. But she performed much more weakly than Obama did outside of these areas.[35]

Table 11-3 shows the dominant impact that small town and rural voters had on Trump's victories in key battleground states. It documents that voters in nonmetropolitan counties—those residing outside of the state's metropolitan areas—made the difference in each of the five northern battleground states except for Ohio, where metropolitan area voters also voted for Trump. This was the case as well for Florida and North Carolina. In each of these states, except Iowa, nonmetropolitan residents comprised substantial minorities of the state's population. But the outsized voting preference for Trump, among these voters, overwhelmed Clinton's advantage among those in metropolitan areas. In Pennsylvania, for example, nonmetropolitan residents made up only 12 percent of the state's population, but their net 287,000 votes for Trump bested Clinton's net 242,000-vote advantage in metropolitan areas.

The geographic racial generation gap can be illustrated by contrasting the attributes of all U.S. residents living in the mostly small counties that voted for Trump versus the mostly large urban counties that voted for Clinton. (See figure 11-9.) The counties that Trump won are clearly whiter and older. Even young people living in these counties are predominantly white, despite the fact that the national child population is close to one-half racial minorities. The populations in counties where

TABLE 11-3
### Trump Minus Clinton Vote Differences in States Won by Trump, 2016 Election

| Region/<br>state | Nonmetropolitan<br>share of state<br>population | Trump minus Clinton vote difference[a] | | |
|---|---|---|---|---|
| | | Nonmetropolitan<br>voters | Metropolitan<br>voters | Total<br>voters |
| *Northern states* | | | | |
| Iowa | 41% | 170,005 | −22,691 | 147,314 |
| Michigan | 18% | 228,151 | −217,447 | 10,704 |
| Ohio | 20% | 419,649 | 27,192 | 446,841 |
| Pennsylvania | 12% | 287,288 | −242,996 | 44,292 |
| Wisconsin | 26% | 142,895 | −120,147 | 22,748 |
| *Sun Belt states* | | | | |
| Florida | 3% | 114,111 | −1,200 | 112,911 |
| North Carolina | 22% | 194,216 | −20,901 | 173,315 |

Source: Author's analysis of votes compiled in David Leip's *Atlas of U.S. Presidential Elections* and U.S. census population estimates, 2016.

[a]Net difference: votes for Trump minus votes for Clinton.

Clinton prevailed are decidedly more racially diverse. In these counties, as a group, racial minorities outnumber whites in all ages under 45 and are not far behind in the 45 to 54 age group. Age and race are fundamental indicators of how these counties differ. However, counties where Trump won are also less likely to be home to foreign-born residents, single persons, and white adults with college degrees than is the case for counties that voted for Clinton.[36]

Trump's Electoral College win in 2016 clearly reflects a cultural generation gap in terms of voting patterns and geography. While Clinton, like Obama, won the popular vote on the basis of strong youthful and minority support, nationally, the distinctly different racial demographic profiles of several northern battleground states made them ripe for a message that favored older, disconnected white voters whose numbers and enthusiasm for Trump were enough to make a difference.

FIGURE 11-9
**Population Profiles of Counties that Voted for Trump and Clinton[a]**

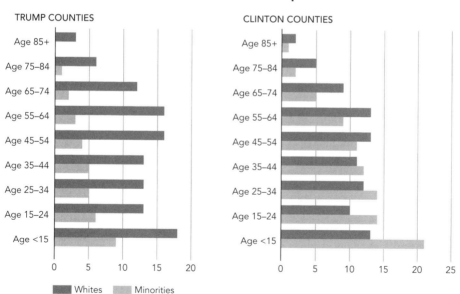

Source: Author's analysis of David Leip's *Atlas of U.S. Presidential Elections in 2016* and U.S. census population estimates, 2015.

[a]Refers to total populations (in millions) residing in counties that voted for Trump or Clinton.

## FUTURE PRESIDENTIAL ELECTIONS

The Obama elections of 2008 and 2012 and the Trump election of 2016 point up how the nation's changing racial demography will, at least in the short term, make the forecasting of future presidential election outcomes a precarious exercise. There is no doubt that the browning of the electorate from younger to older age groups—coupled with current Democratic and Republican race and age voting proclivities—should work to the Democrats' advantage in winning the popular vote. This occurred in three straight presidential elections—including 2016, even with a strong older white Republican vote.

However, because it is the Electoral College that determines the presidential victor, the nation is still in the middle of a regional demographic transformation that will not always ensure a Democratic win. This transformation is one where many growing South and West states are gaining more blacks, Hispanics, and Asians—enough to switch them from reliable Republican states to competitive battlegrounds. Taking advantage of these demographic shifts, Obama made a clean sweep of six such states—Nevada, New Mexico, Colorado, Florida, Virginia, and North Carolina in 2008 and all but the latter in 2012. This helped him win those elections because, at the same time, he held onto long-standing northern battleground states. Clinton tried to replicate Obama's feat in 2016 but lost two of his Sun Belt states (Florida and North Carolina) along with fully five of his northern battlegrounds.

One might say that Obama's wins were propelled by unusually high minority turnout and voting preference for the first racial minority candidate, both in the Sun Belt and in the industrial North—providing, in 2012, barely enough to win in critical states like Ohio and Pennsylvania. Conversely, Clinton's losses in some of those states, by small margins, were due to super-sized Trump-Republican voting by older, white blue-collar voters, coupled with lower Democratic enthusiasm among minorities.

It is possible to make the case that both Obama's and Trump's Electoral College wins were deviations from longterm trends. That is, because Obama's youthful minority base overperformed, he won more than the expected number of states in both the North and Sun Belt. Similarly, Trump's extraordinary support among mostly older, blue-collar whites netted him several states he might have otherwise lost.[37]

Despite these deviations, long-term racial demographic trends should favor Democrats in the Electoral College, as well as the national popular vote, if current voting proclivities continue. Trump's Republican-leaning voting blocs such as rural, largely older blue-collar whites represent shrinking shares of the electorate, both nationally and in most states.[38] While Trump has shown that a strong appeal to such voters can lead to modest victories in enough older, white battleground states to win the Electoral College, it is not a long-term winning strategy for the Republican Party. Reaching out to younger, Hispanic, and other minority voting blocs will be essential for its future competitiveness in presidential politics. By the same token, the 2016 election made clear that Democrats cannot hitch their hopes primarily to their younger, minority, and urban base. Older baby boomers will remain a formidable voting bloc in key parts of the country and need to be a part of any long-term winning Democratic coalition. In essence, it is in both parties' interests to make efforts to close the current cross-party cultural generation gap in their policies and messaging in order to stay relevant in light of the nation's changing racial demographics.

# America on the Cusp

# 12

The diversity explosion that the United States is now experiencing is ushering in the most demographically turbulent period in the country's recent history. By using the term "turbulent" I am not referring to political divisions related to immigration and racial issues that came to the fore after the 2016 presidential election. In fact, I do not believe that the nation will experience continuing sharp conflicts over its growing diversity. As American citizens and their leaders come to understand the magnitude and significance of this new diversity for its demographic and economic future and for its interconnectedness in an increasingly global village, they will seek to find ways to both embrace and nurture this diversity. This demographic turbulence, rather, offers the vibrancy, hope, and promise associated with young generations of new minorities from a variety of backgrounds interacting with older minorities and white Americans in their pursuit of opportunities in a country that is in dire need of more youth. As discussed in chapters 1 and 2, the growth of young, new minority populations from recent immigration and somewhat higher fertility is providing the country with a "just in time" infusion of growth as the largely white U.S. population continues to age.

The nation is benefiting from the healthy growth that these minorities are creating in the nation's workforce—growth that is needed in many U.S. peer nations. In contrast to the labor force–age population of Italy, Japan, Germany, and the United Kingdom, countries with generally older populations, lower fertility, and lower immigration, the U.S. labor force–age population is projected to grow nearly 5 percent between 2015 and 2035 (see figure 12-1). Yet were it not for new minorities—Hispanics, Asians, and multiracial Americans—the country's labor force would decline by almost 7 percent. Moreover, within the labor force, new minorities add needed youthfulness that brings with it innovation and an entrepreneurial spirit. Projections of the labor force–age population show that in 2035, 56 percent of new minorities but under half of the rest of the labor force–age population will be under the age of 40.

FIGURE 12-1
**Projected Growth in Labor Force–Age Populations, Selected Countries, 2015–35ᵃ**

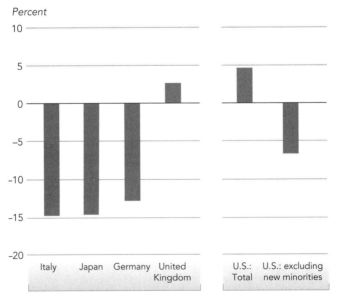

Source: United Nations, "World Population Prospects: The 2017 Revision"; U.S. Census Bureau projections, released March, 2018.
ᵃLabor force–age populations defined here as ages 15–64.

The significance of new minorities in the U.S. economy is already being felt in the private sector. The buying power of the Hispanic population was $1.4 trillion in 2016, a 181 percent gain since 2000, while that of the Asian population was $916 billion, a 222 percent gain. In fact, the combined buying power of the Hispanic and Asian populations in 2017 was 16 percent of the U.S. total—a figure that will continue to rise.[1] These growing markets will follow the population from the "bottom up" of the age structure, racing to accommodate the shifts in demographics of different minorities as they age and become a larger part of mainstream America. A good example is the shift in strategies to reach new segments of the Hispanic market. Not long ago, that meant exclusively Spanish-language television, radio, and advertising in general. More recently, some advertisers believe that to target the younger segments of the Hispanic market, English "with a Spanish accent" could attract the growing numbers of young, U.S.-born, English-speaking Hispanics.[2]

Of course, these are the same audiences targeted by public institutions such as schools, social service agencies, and medical clinics, which will be catering to Hispanics and Asians of different national origins. Furthermore, although the emphasis right now is on the youngest age groups, the future focus will move to more mature markets as these diverse generations begin to age. This trend is illustrated in table 12-1, which indicates the "minority white" tipping point years for different age groups. Based on current projections, the child population will tip in the year 2020, the 18 to 29 year old population will tip in 2027, the 30-something age group will tip in 2033, and the 40-something group will tip in 2041. In each of these "tipping years," whites will make up less than one-half of that age group's total population, Hispanics will constitute about one-quarter, and the sum of new minorities—Hispanics, Asians, and multiracial persons—will represent about one-third. And for all ages below each "tipping" age, minorities

TABLE 12-1

**Minority White "Tipping Points" for Different Age Groups**

| Age group | Year when age group becomes "minority white"[a] |
|---|---|
| Under age 18 | 2020 |
| Age 18–29 | 2027 |
| Age 30–39 | 2033 |
| Age 40–49 | 2041 |

Source: U.S. Census Bureau projections, released March, 2018.

[a]Year indicates first year when the size of the age group's white population is superceded by that of the age group's nonwhite population.

will make up even larger portions of the population. Therefore, marketers of age-related products to teens, homebuyers, young singles, families, and parents will be tracking these changes closely, as will political strategists targeting desired voting blocs.

The demographic turbulence also has a geographic dimension. As discussed in chapters 3 through 7, the rapidly growing new minorities have been spreading outward from Melting Pot areas—the original Hispanic and Asian immigrant gateways—to growing New Sun Belt areas in the nation's Southeast and Intermountain West. This is occurring while the slower-growing black population continues shifting to the South and the soon-to-be-declining white population shifts modestly to the New Sun Belt. The advent of high-growth new minority populations brings a demographic turbulence to parts of the country—suburbs, smaller metropolitan areas, and smaller towns—where, until recently, their presence was little known or nonexistent. These outward shifts bring needed new workers to prospering, rapidly growing labor markets in the New Sun Belt and population infusions to stagnating economies in the nation's slowly growing Heartland.[3] In fact, were it not for new minorities, more than 500 counties, most located outside the Melting Pot region, would have experienced population losses rather than gains in the first decade of the 2000s. The outward shift of new minorities to these areas slowed during the Great Recession of 2007–09, but after a long recovery it reemerged, further contributing to the growing, diverse workforce that is a necessary part of prosperity in all regions of the country.

The new minority pioneers, especially those in the New Sun Belt, will continue to make their presence known. New trends toward greater minority suburbanization, more multiracial marriages, and a changing, more diverse electorate—discussed in chapters 8, 10, and 11—are especially pronounced there. Furthermore, rapid growth in Hispanic and Asian buying power is projected in many New Sun Belt states.[4] Although neighborhood segregation between Hispanics and whites has risen in many of these new Hispanic destinations as more newcomers arrive (discussed in chapter 9), overall levels of segregation in these areas are lower than in more traditional settlements, providing the potential for greater interaction among racial groups.

So there is much reason to celebrate the percolating—if turbulent—upward and outward spread of America's new minorities as a means of reinvigorating and replenishing a national population that would otherwise be stagnating. This is not to say that older minorities are not also poised to contribute to the nation's future. As shown in chapters 6, 8, and 9, more black Americans have entered the middle class and black college graduates and black traditional families, in particular, are making inroads in suburban communities and in growing metropolitan areas of the South. At the same time, neighborhood segregation, though still substantial in many areas, is declining. Clearly, there is more progress to be made, but there also is cause to look at America's demographic future with optimism.

## A DEMOGRAPHIC FRAMEWORK FOR CHANGE

As a demographer, I believe that in periods such as the present, the phrase "demography is destiny" is especially relevant. The United States undoubtedly is becoming more racially diverse than at any other time in the country's history, and new minorities will be a welcome tonic to what would otherwise be a more slowly growing, quickly aging population. The generational dynamics now at work ensure that the diversity explosion will percolate from the youngest generation upward though the age structure. This will occur irrespective of shifts in immigration levels.[5] There is also reasonable certainty that the outward spread of Hispanics, Asians, and multiracial persons from the nation's traditional melting pots, which has already begun in earnest, will continue—reinvigorating both the growing New Sun Belt and the stagnating Heartland. Yet the destiny that these demographic shifts foretell depends, in large part, on the near and long-term progress made by members of younger, rapidly growing racial groups within the millennial generation and its highly diverse successor generations. Their outcomes depend not only on their own initiative as individuals and groups but also on the opportunities for advancement that become available to them. Their outcomes depend on how their local communities receive them, how they fare in the workplace, and how they are affected by future government programs and policies.

These powerful demographic forces will strongly shape the nation's destiny in the decades to come. Because of the ongoing diversity explosion, those communities, organizations, and institutions that hope to improve the well-being and ease the integration of new minorities into mainstream society must understand the key areas in which change will be most effective. To exact maximum change, they need to focus on the younger generations, new minority destinations, and ways to narrow the cultural generation gap.

### Preparing New Generations

This book's mantra, "Diversity is America's future," is best exemplified by arrival of the first minority white birth cohort in 2011. Of that year's cohort, Hispanic newborns constituted 26 percent and other new minorities—Asian and multiracial newborns—constituted a combined 11 percent. Those newborns will continue to age into the country's elementary and secondary schools and eventually into its workforce. As discussed in chapter 2, the success of these new minorities—with respect to their contributions to the labor force and broader economy as well as their general assimilation into the American mainstream—will affect the nation's future considerably. But to be productive workers and citizens, the next generations will require suitable formal schooling and other training consistent with the nation's long-term needs.

That is true for all members of the coming generations, but particular attention should be paid to young Hispanics. Roughly one-half of today's Hispanic children are second-generation Americans, and a plurality have parents with only a high school education or less.[6] Hispanics continue to make progress in completing high school and in pursuing postsecondary education, a pattern that improves for second-generation Hispanics and for immigrants the longer that they stay in the United States.[7] Yet to make progress requires overcoming a number of barriers, including segregated schools and lack of access to affordable postsecondary training.

Despite the ongoing dispersion of Hispanics to new destinations with lower residential segregation levels, a plurality of Hispanic students attend urban school systems that are highly segregated by race and income. Studies by Gary Orfield, a longtime observer of U.S. school segregation trends, showed that, as of 2010, 80 percent of Hispanic students attended majority nonwhite schools and more than two-fifths attended schools in which whites constitute less than 10 percent of the students. Attendance at schools segregated by race and income reflects other barriers to improved education outcomes, including less qualified teachers, high levels of teacher turnover, and inadequate facilities and learning materials. Between 2003 and 2013, rising shares of black and Hispanic students, more so than whites, attended high poverty schools.[8] Less exposure to whites is, to some degree, affected by the decline of whites in the school-age population. Yet the persistence of Hispanic segregation in public schools also reflects the intention of white and high-income parents of other races to locate to more exclusive communities where school quality is superior. Whites are also opting to withdraw their children from public schools and place them in private schools.[9] Segregated schools are a barrier to Hispanic children, and they have been a continuing barrier for a substantial number of black children who, in past decades, lived in highly ghettoized residential environments. Although black-white residential segregation has begun to decline, many black children remain isolated in segregated schools located in poverty-stricken areas.[10]

Apart from segregated schools at the K–12 level, broader access to training for the future U.S. workforce is an issue. It is projected that the plurality of new jobs—and those that are highest paying—will require postsecondary training. But once again, the trajectory typically followed by Hispanics and blacks contrasts sharply with the one followed by whites. Blacks and Hispanics are far more likely to enroll in two-year colleges and less selective four-year colleges and to have lower rates of completion.[11] Financial considerations certainly explain part of this trajectory. Among the reasons given by young Hispanics for not pursuing a postsecondary education, financial pressure to help support a family is cited most often.[12]

Segregation in low-quality schools and the inaccessibility of postsecondary education and training are just two of the barriers faced by Hispanics, blacks, and other children in today's diverse young student population.[13] Clearly, improved access to education is tied to the future well-being of minorities and, in fact, the nation. These areas are highlighted because, as with many other areas in which barriers to minority success exist, solutions for improvement are best focused on children and young families.

**Preparing New Destinations**

The spread of Hispanics and Asians to destinations in the New Sun Belt and the Heartland presents opportunities for economic gains in areas that already are growing and in areas that are in need of reinvigoration. Initially, Hispanic and Asian population growth was heavily confined to Melting Pot areas, usually large cities, but eventually spread to the suburbs and then to new regions, as discussed chapter 3. The new minority arrivals start out heavily dependent on same-race enclaves for social and economic support and often are viewed with suspicion by long-term residents of a community—a reaction that is self-defeating with respect to the long-term benefit of the community itself.

Spreading out to new areas has become even more of a challenge for Hispanics, who often are conflated with undocumented immigrants by some long-term residents. Particularly in the early 2000s, many communities reacted by proposing punitive immigration laws designed to restrict access to housing or employment. Some states made special efforts to empower local police to enforce federal immigration laws or otherwise punish residents who could not present legal documentation to authorities. In other states, there were efforts to restrict access to public services, education, and voting by imposing strict voter registration and identification rules. More recently, in light of greater federal efforts to deport undocumented immigrants, many places with a history of attracting foreign-born residents have declared themselves "sanctuary cities," promising not to cooperate with federal deportation efforts. Yet such declarations are less prevalent in immigrant "new destination" areas.[14]

Although most of these laws focused only on undocumented immigrants, they often signal an unwelcoming attitude to the broader Hispanic community and new minorities in general. Such measures were more pervasive in the New Sun Belt and Heartland regions where the immigrant and Hispanic presence is new and growing.[15] As discussed in chapter 4, Hispanics in new destinations are more likely to be foreign born, are less fluent in English, and are less educated than Hispanics in more traditional Melting Pot areas. As a result, they face even greater challenges in "fitting in."

In the New Sun Belt and Heartland areas in particular, new minority integration into the community is most important. The long-term economic and demographic foundations of these areas can be put in place if existing residents take steps to accommodate new minorities just as these minorities are beginning to establish their presence. This involves providing for their needs with regard to schools, social services, employment assistance, and civic engagement by mounting specialized outreach efforts. A key element in many areas is English language training by public, private, and nonprofit organizations, along with partnerships that match employment opportunities with both high- and low-skilled residents, following the models established in Melting Pot areas.[16]

### Closing the Cultural Generation Gap

Perhaps the biggest demographic fault line in the coming decades is the cultural generation gap—the lack of intimate connections between an increasingly diverse young population and the mostly white older population. As discussed in chapter 2, this gap is already evident, demographically, in New Sun Belt states such as Arizona and Nevada in that children are a much more racially diverse group than seniors are. But this gap increasingly will spread, along with the dispersal of youthful minorities, to other parts of the New Sun Belt and beyond.

The older generation of whites—today's baby boomers and senior citizens—spent their youth and in some cases early adult years in a nation in which most of the population was white and in which blacks, then the largest minority, resided in heavily segregated neighborhoods. Racially different immigrant groups were few, as most immigrants then were whites from different countries who arrived in the first part of the twentieth century. The older U.S. population, particularly residents of areas outside of Melting Pot cities, has met the growth of new minorities with skepticism. This was already evident in 2011 from a Pew Research Center survey that asked white adults of different ages to judge whether various demographic shifts represented a change for the better or for the worse or whether the shifts had not made much difference (table 12-2).[17]

Although a substantial number of responses to all questions fell in the "did not make much difference" category, the responses of older white adults were the most negative. That is, about 45 percent of older whites saw the growing population of immigrants as a change for the worse and

TABLE 12-2
**Percent of White Adults Responding "Change for the Worse" about Demographic Trends**[a]

| Demographic trend | White adults | | | |
|---|---|---|---|---|
| | Age 18–29 | Age 30–44 | Age 45–64 | Age 65+ |
| A growing population of immigrants | 38 | 39 | 47 | 45 |
| A growing population of Hispanics | 15 | 23 | 31 | 29 |
| A growing population of Asians | 6 | 10 | 17 | 15 |
| More people of different races marrying each other | 5 | 5 | 13 | 22 |

Source: Analysis of Pew Research Center for the People and the Press, "October 2011 Generations Survey."
[a]Possible responses include "Change for the better," "Change for the worse," "Hasn't Made Much Difference," "Mixed Changes," and "Don't Know."

nearly 30 percent thought the same of the growing population of Hispanics. Negative responses were not nearly as large with regard to the growing population of Asians or the gains in multiracial marriages. Of course, whites constitute a much larger portion of the overall older population than of the younger population. In addition, minorities—especially younger minorities—had far more positive reactions to demographic changes in the United States.

Although attitudes about immigration have improved over time among the population as a whole, a generational gap still remains. In a 2017 Pew survey, nearly eight in ten adults in their 20s and early 30s agreed that immigrants strengthen the country because of their hard work and talents. However, among baby boomers and other seniors, only a little more than half agreed with this view.[18]

These assessments reflect the young-old gaps on other issues and related voting patterns discussed in chapters 2 and 11. The younger population, now heavily composed of minorities, is more likely to favor larger government and support programs such as those that improve education, make housing more affordable, and create jobs.[19] The older boomer population is wary of a bigger federal government (except to preserve the solvency of Social Security) and favors lower taxes. These issues help to explain the sharply divergent voting patterns between seniors and young adults in the 2008, 2012, and 2016 presidential elections, in which whites and older adults voted Republican while minorities and young people voted Democratic. These issues have also played out at the local level in referendums on expenditures for public schools and for social services for older people.[20]

The emerging political divide between the "gray and the brown," as political writer Ronald Brownstein has described it, will be counter-productive in the long run.[21] That is because the older, largely white population will need the future minority-dominant adult population to be productive workers, taxpayers, and consumers if the nation's economy is to continue to grow and produce revenues and services that benefit both the young and the old.[22] Both public and private sector planning should strive for win-win solutions when interests appear to clash.[23] More important, political, religious, and community leaders in all parts of the country should strive to educate both the young and the old about the need to accommodate each other as part of the emerging demographic transformation.

### Millennials as a Bridge

Members of the millennial generation, born in the 1980s and 1990s, have already made an indelible imprint on the nation, as evident from the tremendous publicity they receive and the consumer base they represent. Yet their most lasting legacy may well be their success in serving as a social, economic, and political bridge to the next racially diverse generation and toward closing the young-old cultural generation gap.

Racial minorities make up 44 percent of the millennial population nationally and more than half its population in ten states and in thirty of the largest metropolitan areas.[24] As shown in figure 12-2, millennials follow much "whiter" older age groups that include Gen Xers, Baby Boomers, and older seniors. In so doing, they face the challenges of becoming integrated and accepted into America's mainstream, but they also serve as role models and provide ladders of success for younger, even more highly diverse generations.

Millennials have already made an impressive start by holding more tolerant attitudes than earlier generations.[25] Compared with their elders, both white and minority millennials are more likely to hold the view that American culture and way of life have changed for the better, that immigrants strengthen the country, and that America's best days lie ahead. Nearly one in seven millennial marriages are interracial

FIGURE 12-2
**U.S. Race-Ethnic Profiles for Age Groups, 2015**

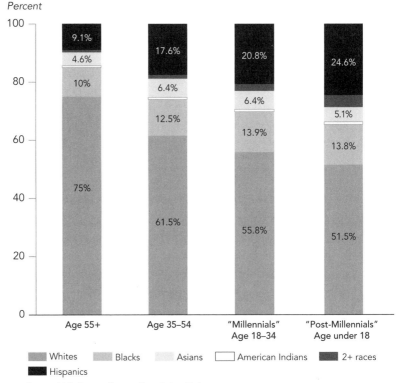

*Percent*

Source: U.S. Census Bureau Population Estimates.

compared with one in twenty among Baby Boomers the same age. As a generation, millennials are also the most educated of all those that came before them, which should bode well for their future success.

Despite their slow start out of the gate—in the aftermath of the 2007–09 Great Recession and accompanying housing market crash—they are optimistic. This is especially the case for racial minority members of this generation. Hispanic, Asian, and black millennials are more likely than whites to say that they personally will do better financially than their parents and that the life of their generation will be better than that of their parents.[26]

As a bridge generation between a whiter, older America and the more multihued country of the future, millennials can play an important role toward achieving their own success and that of subsequent generations. In the process, they will need assistance in overcoming and closing the cultural generation gap in national and local politics where mostly older voters have been reluctant to embrace younger generations in terms of providing much-needed investment and support for them.

By example and as advocates, millennials of all racial backgrounds can make the case that investing in a more inclusive America is essential to the nation's economic success and will, as well, benefit older populations. In this regard, the millennials' population size is important as it already comprises the largest generation of eligible voters.[27] Beyond that, as they move into middle age, millennials will represent the new face of America in politics, in business, and as the nation's image to the rest of the world.

## RACE AND "FITTING IN" WITH THE AMERICAN MAINSTREAM

"Fitting in" with American society is an important goal for both new minorities and old minorities in light of the cultural generation gap and other social and political fissures that may develop as the nation's racial fabric continues to change. Historically, racial minorities have encountered far more difficulty fitting in than other groups. This is especially the case for blacks, who were relegated to separate but unequal status for most of the nation's history. Yet as racial minorities become a larger and more influential presence than ever before, the new demographic dynamics now at work can soften long-standing barriers. Trends discussed in earlier chapters point to areas in which boundaries are becoming blurred, including the rise in multiracial marriages, the more pervasive presence of minorities in the suburbs and elsewhere, and—for blacks in particular—the continued decline in still high levels of neighborhood segregation. Moreover, younger generations of minorities and whites are more open to the idea of racial mixing and to policies that are less racially divisive.

Despite this optimism about the mainstreaming of new minorities, it is important to recognize the continuing sharp social and economic divides that exist between many racial minority group members and the generally more advantaged white population, discussed in earlier chapters. Among Hispanics—especially Mexicans and groups of Central American origin—the gaps with whites are still wide in the areas of education attainment and poverty. Although Asians have been dubbed the model minority, that is not the case for all Asian groups. Most members of Asian nationalities are first-generation Americans, many of whom need to overcome language and other obstacles in order to translate their training into successful careers. Furthermore, although some strides have been made by new generations of blacks in entering the middle class, a substantial portion of the black community, particularly blacks who are located in isolated residential communities, is still affected by high levels of poverty and unemployment.

The economic disparities between whites and racial minorities, attributable to broader society-wide income and wealth inequalities, were exacerbated during the Great Recession of 2007–09 and its aftermath, despite recent improvements in the economy.[28] For many members of racial minorities, then, there are still major economic barriers that must be overcome if they are to fully assimilate into the American mainstream. Racial discrimination continues to exist, although often in subtler forms than in the past. The landmark 1960s civil rights legislation, enacted during a time of extreme racial discrimination, helped blacks and other minorities improve their economic standing and living conditions to a substantial degree. Given the growing, more diverse racial populations that are central to the nation's future, it is imperative that the kinds of laws and policies put in place to ensure equal access to employment, housing, education, and voting are enforced, monitored, and—where necessary—augmented to accommodate new groups and needs, including the integration of immigrants and their families.

Yet, in the long run, I believe that the demographic die is cast in a way that will ensure that the coming generations of what are now thought of as racial minorities will not just "fit in" but will hold sway in important ways in both public and private sector decisionmaking. The economy will wax and wane, as will immigration flows. But through it all, today's minorities—both new and old—will have considerable demographic clout in the nation's politics and economy.

At the time that civil rights legislation was enacted in the 1960s, the mostly black racial minority population accounted for just 15 percent of the total U.S. population and was geographically concentrated in the South and in large cities, mostly in the North and on the West Coast. By 2020, the combined minority groups—including blacks, Hispanics, Asians, American Indians, multiracial individuals, and others—will constitute 40 percent of the U.S. population. These groups already constitute at least two-fifths of the child population in 24 states. Therefore future public officials and political candidates at all levels of government, if they are not members of racial minorities themselves, will need to pay close attention to needs and concerns of minority voters, including issues affecting their economic well-being.

It is not just their larger size and increased political clout that will bring greater power to racial minorities. Their potential will be most clearly understood as members of the older white population begin to retire from the labor force, leaving far fewer whites to take their place. Between 2010 and 2030, the primary labor force–age population will experience a net loss of 15 million whites; at the same time, it will gain 27 million racial minorities. All of the latter will be needed, in private and public sector jobs in all parts of the country, since the number of workers that the economy is expected to require will far exceed the number needed to replace retiring workers. Furthermore, although openings will skew toward workers with higher education and more experience, openings will be available at all skill levels.[29]

Thus, as mentioned earlier, the growth of new minorities from the bottom of the age distribution upward is happening just in time to fill a substantial workforce void. This demographic transformation will also serve to enhance the prospects for minority workers themselves. In *Blurring the Color Line,* sociologist Richard Alba shows how the opening up of good jobs due to the retirement of baby boomers can provide opportunities for upward mobility for immigrant and second-generation Hispanics and Asians. Moreover, because the new minority workers are replacing and not competing with existing white workers, they will be more readily accepted by their co-workers and by society at large.[30]

There are many other areas in which racial minorities will make their presence felt as they become part of the country's mainstream—as leaders in industry and government, as celebrities in sports and entertainment, and as contributors to the broader popular culture (beyond just youth culture)—especially as the highly diverse millennial generation ages further into adulthood. There are several reasons why I foresee their eventual widespread acceptance and assimilation into a new American mainstream.

First, most Americans take pride in the national immigrant heritage, which has been passed down as part of U.S. history, and have learned firsthand the value of immigrants' contributions to the country. Older baby boomers, many descending from European ethnic stock, will, despite recent political divisions, eventually become inclined to accept new minorities from Latin American, Asian, and other national origins as they come to value their contributions to U.S. society. Second, by making racial discrimination unacceptable and the inclusion of racial groups a broadly held social value for most Americans, civil rights legislation itself has had a profound and lasting impact on American sensibilities that did not exist prior to its passage.[31] Third, the globalization of commerce and communications, expedited by the information technology revolution, will continue to broaden Americans' understanding and acceptance of people from different cultures and nations in ways that would have been impossible to imagine just a decade or two ago.

The foremost reason why I anticipate the integration of both new and old racial minorities into the nation's mainstream is the sheer force of the unprecedented change in the nation's racial demographics. As many more Americans experience day-to-day interactions with members of different racial groups, they will come to value their contributions as co-workers, neighbors and family members. They will become more willing than ever before to support community, private-sector, and government efforts to foster those groups' interests. The diversity explosion that the country is now experiencing will alter all aspects of society in ways that can help the nation prosper, make it more inclusive, and increase its global connectivity. The 2020 census will make even more apparent what this book had demonstrated: that the United States is on the cusp of great change—toward a new national demographic transformation in the twenty-first century.

# Acknowledgments

I owe much to people I have known in many different venues, only a few of whom I have space to acknowledge here. First, I am grateful to my colleagues at the Brookings Institution Metropolitan Policy Program, which supported my work on this book. I have been lucky in many ways in my career and one of them was in joining this program at Brookings. Program director Amy Liu and former director Bruce Katz have been hugely supportive of my demographic work and have provided me the latitude, encouragement, and wherewithal to expound on demographic trends that are an integral part of the evolution of the nation's cities, suburbs, and regions. I am fortunate to work with Alan Berube—scholar, administrator, adviser, and frequent editor of my writing—who did much to ease my transition from academia into the think tank world. My former colleague David Jackson, editor and communications advisor extraordinaire, was responsible for coordinating the editing of this book's first edition. Also contributing to an always stimulating intellectual environment are current and former Brookings colleagues, including Jennifer Bradley, Anthony Downs, Marek Gootman, Joseph Kane, Elizabeth Kneebone, Rob Lang, Chris Leinberger, Mark Muro, Joseph

Parilla, Andre Perry, Rob Puentes, Andrew Reamer, Alice Rivlin, Martha Ross, Jonathan Rothwell, Neil Ruiz, Richard Shearer, Jenny Schuetz, Audrey Singer, Adie Tomer, Jennifer Vey, Howard Wial, and Jill Wilson. In addition, I am grateful to several people who, over the years, have made my work available to a wide audience though their outreach and communications efforts: David Nassar, Julia Kraeger, David Lanham, Emily Rabadi, Carly P. Anderson, Fred Dews, Anthony Fiano, Alec Fried-hoff, Brennan Hoban, Christopher McKenna, Karen Slachetka, Luisa Zottis, Ellen Ochs, and Barbara Semedo.

My career had taken an earlier fortunate turn in 1981, when I joined my long-term academic home, the University of Michigan Population Studies Center. My association with the center contributed to this book both indirectly and directly: indirectly, because much of the material that I cover draws on years of research and interaction with students and colleagues at the center; directly, because much of the statistical material presented here comes from the center's extensive archive of U.S. Census Bureau data and other resources. I want to thank center directors Al Hermalin, Barbara Anderson, David Lam, Arland Thornton, Pamela Smock, and Jeffrey Morenoff for making it possible for me to use the center's resources over the years. I especially want to thank two people who devoted great effort to this book: Cathy Sun, an expert on U.S. census data and programming, who has assisted me on projects for over 35 years, and John P. DeWitt, a project manager who has worked with me on U.S. census–related projects for over a decade.

Preparing this book was a multilayered process. Working with me on the first edition was Nathan Einstein, a superb, multitalented research aide at Brookings who was truly indispensable to everyone involved. Equally impressive was the data preparation for both editions that underlies most of the book's 100+ maps, charts, and tables, which was orchestrated by John P. DeWitt with help from Cathy Sun. Preliminary advice on graphics was provided by Christopher Ingraham and additional research assistance was provided by Nathan Arnosti. References were found at lightning speed thanks to the efforts of Sarah Chilton of the Brookings Library and Yan Fu and Lee Ridley of the Population Studies Center. Administrative support to solve all problems, large and small, was provided at Brookings by Joe Rooney, Michelle Carter, Elizabeth

Dang, Katie Palmer Finn, Evan Fontana, and Reda Urmanaviciute. From the Population Studies Center, expert computer support was provided by Ricardo Rodriguiz, Mark Sandstrom, and David Sasaki; data archive support was provided by Lisa Neidert and Sherry Briske; and publications advice was provided by N. E. Barr.

I am grateful to Reynolds Farley and Haya El Nasser for reading and commenting on early drafts of the manuscript. I also want to acknowledge the U.S. Census Bureau for making publicly available a wide range of data, both historical and current, from decennial censuses, surveys, projections, and population estimates, which were the primary sources of the statistics presented here.

A team of people was responsible for the editing and preparation of the final product. Janet Walker, managing editor at Brookings Institution Press, oversaw editing of both editions of the book, in collaboration with production coordinator, Elliott Beard, and his predecessor, Larry Converse. Additional editing assistance for the first edition was provided by Barbara Ray and associates and by Eileen Hughes at Brookings. The designs for both editions of the book and cover as well as the graphics were produced with artistic flair by Debra Naylor of Naylor Design, Inc. Brookings Press did an excellent job of coordinating all aspects of the publication process. I am grateful to the Press's director, William Finan and his predecessor, Valentina Kalk, to assistant director, Yelba Quinn, and her staff as well as to former publicity manager, Carrie Engel, and former marketing manager, Rebecca Campany. I could not be more pleased with their enthusiastic efforts throughout.

Other people and organizations whose influence continues to impact my work also deserve mention here. The late Alden Speare Jr., my mentor and collaborator, broadened my horizons about what demographic studies can do in ways that have shaped how I think about the field. Sidney Goldstein, from whom I learned the fundamentals of demography, has been a continuing source of advice and support. My collaboration with geographer Kao-Lee Liaw helped me to better understand the nuances of recent racial migration dynamics within the United States. My collaboration and friendship with journalist Jonathan Tilove led me to appreciate the real-world consequences of rapid racial change in different parts of the country. My work with political experts Ruy Teixeira and Robert Griffin permitted me to explore in depth how demographic change has affected the electorate and the nation's politics. I am grateful to Peter Passell for enticing me to create short-form demographic "charticles," which he publishes in the Milken Institute Review. I benefitted greatly from my interactions with author and commentator, Joel Kotkin. I have also learned much from my past association with the Population Reference Bureau, for which I served as a visiting scholar and contributor to publications, and with the former American Demographics magazine, for which I was a contributing editor.

Although my work as a demographer has taken several forms, the part that I enjoy most is reaching out to broad audiences—through short articles, op-eds, speaking engagements, and interviews, among other formats—with clear and positive messages. I like to think that reflects the influence of my late father, Elwood H. Frey. As a boy, I came to appreciate my father's ability to inspire and entertain audiences in his roles as public official, part-time newspaper correspondent, drum major, amateur cartoonist, and sometimes night club comedian in the small town where I grew up. By example, he made me understand the value of reaching out to people in all walks of life and speaking out—both to them and for them. I hope that he would have liked this book, which is dedicated to his memory.

Last and certainly most, I owe more than I can articulate here to my wife, Olivia Golden. Olivia's distinguished career as a public servant, scholar, and advocate is well known to many. But to me, she is everything and anything that I could have imagined in a life partner. In addition to providing moral support and constant positive energy during my writing, she offered key suggestions, which I adopted, and kept me balanced when my steadiness started to slip. More than anyone else, she is responsible for my completing this book.

# Notes

## CHAPTER 1

1. Sabrina Tavernise, "Whites Account for Under Half of Births in U.S.," *New York Times,* May 17, 2012, p. A1 (www.nytimes.com/2012/05/17/us/whites-account-for-under-half-of-births-in-us.html?_r=0).
2. The white 18- to 29-year-old population is now experiencing a decline and the white 30- to 44-year-old population is projected to decline after the year 2024. Author's calculations of U.S. Census Bureau projection data released March 2018 (www.census.gov/data/tables/2017/demo/popproj/2017-summary-tables.html).
3. William H. Frey, "Immigrant and Native Migrant Magnets," *American Demographics* (November 1996), pp. 1–5 (www.frey-demographer.org/briefs/B-1996-2_Immigrant-NativeMigrantMagnets.pdf).
4. William H. Frey and Jonathan Tilove, "Immigrants In, Native Whites Out," *New York Times Magazine,* August 20, 1995, pp. 44–45 (www.frey-demographer.org/briefs/B-1995-1_ImmigrantsIn.pdf); William H. Frey and Kao-Lee Liaw, "The Impact of Recent Immigration on Population Redistribution within the United States," in *The Immigration Debate: Studies of Economic, Demographic and Fiscal Effects of Immigration,* edited by James P. Smith and Barry Edmonston (Washington: *National Academy Press, 1998*), pp. 388–448 (www.frey-demographer.org/reports/R-1998-2_ImpactImmigrationPopulationRedistribution.pdf).
5. William H. Frey, "Diversity Spreads Out: Metropolitan Shifts in Hispanic, Asian, and Black Populations since 2000," Living Cities Census Series (Metropolitan Policy

Program, Brookings, March 2006), pp. 1–26 (http://www.frey-demographer.org/reports/R-2006-1_DiversitySpreadsOut.pdf ); William H. Frey and Kao-Lee Liaw, "Interstate Migration of Hispanics, Asians, and Blacks: Cultural Constraints and Middle-Class Flight" (University of Michigan Population Studies Center, 2005) (www.psc.isr.umich.edu/pubs/pdf/rr05-575.pdf ).

6. Kenneth Prewitt, *What Is Your Race? The Census and Our Flawed Efforts to Classify Americans* (Princeton University Press, 2013).

7. Questions and tabulations from the 2010 census appear in Karen R. Humes and others, "Overview of Race and Hispanic Origin: 2010," 2010 Census Briefs C2010BR-02 (U.S. Census Bureau, 2011)(www.census.gov/prod/cen2010/briefs/c2010br-02.pdf ).

8. This classification pertains to the following mutually exclusive categories: Hispanics, non-Hispanic whites, non-Hispanic blacks, non-Hispanic Asians, non-Hispanic American Indians and Alaska Natives; non-Hispanic Native Hawaiians and other Pacific Islanders; non-Hispanic—some other race; and non-Hispanic—two or more races. For ease of exposition, the qualifier "non-Hispanic" is dropped on tables, figures, and discussions (for example, non-Hispanic whites is abbreviated as "whites"). Also, in many instances, categories with small populations are grouped together under the label "Other races."

9. These exceptions are noted in appropriate chapters. For example, analyses of blacks in chapter 6 include both Hispanic and non-Hispanic blacks because historical data do not permit focusing on just non-Hispanic blacks; analyses of Asians in chapter 5 include both Hispanic and non-Hispanic Asians because it was not possible to delineate non-Hispanic Asians for different Asian origin groups; analyses of "two or more races" in chapters 3 and 10 and of American Indians and Alaska natives in chapter 3 include both Hispanic and non-Hispanic members because of small sizes and to be consistent with other studies.

10. Joel Perlmann and Mary C. Waters, *The New Race Question: How the Census Counts Multiracial Individuals* (New York: Russell Sage Foundation, 2002).

## CHAPTER 2

1. U.S. Census Bureau estimates indicated that, for the first time, in 2011 white babies constituted less than one-half (49.6 percent) of all births. See Sabrina Tavernise, "Whites Account for Under Half of Births in U.S.," *New York Times,* May 17, 2012, p. A1 (www.nytimes.com/2012/05/17/us/whites-account-for-under-half-of-births-in-us.html?_r=0).

2. Replacement level fertility can be assessed using the total fertility rate (TFR), which measures the average number of children born to a woman in her lifetime given current age-specific fertility and survival rates. A TFR value of 2.1 or higher indicates replacement level fertility. The TFR for U.S. whites stood below replacement level, ranging from 1.7 to 1.9 in 2000–14. See National Center for Health Statistics, "Trends and Variations in Reproduction and Intrinsic Rates: United States, 1990-2014," *National Vital Statistics Reports,* vol. 66, no. 2 (2017) (www.cdc.gov/nchs/data/nvsr/nvsr66/nvsr66_02.pdf ).

3. The share of women in the prime fertility age range (15 to 34 years of age) for 2015 was 24 percent for whites, 32 percent for Hispanics, 30 percent for blacks, and 29 percent for Asians. These statistics are based on an analysis of U.S. Census Bureau population estimates (www.census.gov/programs-surveys/popest/data/tables.2015.html).

4. See U.S. Census Bureau, Population Projections released March 2018 (www.census. gov/data/tables/2017/demo/popproj/2017-summary-tables.html).

5. In alternative projections, minorities are projected to constitute more than 54 percent of the 2030 child population under both "high" and "low" immigration assumptions. See U.S. Census Bureau, "2012 National Population Projections," 2012 (www.census.gov/population/projections/data/national/2012.html).

6. The crude birth rate—which is distinct from the TFR, discussed in note 2—is affected by both a group's fertility level and its age structure. Thus, "younger" groups—those with larger percentages of women in their childbearing years—tend to have higher crude birth rates. Crude birth rates in 2015 were 10.7 births per thousand for whites, 16.3 for Hispanics, 14.3 for blacks, and 14.0 for Asians. See National Center for Health Statistics (www.cdc.gov/nchs/data/hus/2016/003.pdf).

7. See appendix table 2 in Karina Fortuny, Donald J. Hernandez, and Ajay Chaudry, "Young Children of Immigrants: The Leading Edge of America's Future," *Children of Immigrants Research,* Brief 3 (Washington: Urban Institute, August 31, 2010) (www.urban.org/sites/default/files/publication/29106/412203-Young-Children-of-Immigrants-The-Leading-Edge-of-America-s-Future.PDF).

8. These trends pertain to persons of the traditional labor force ages, 18–64 years, as reported in U.S. Census Bureau projections and in recent decennial censuses. This group differs from actual labor force members, who include labor force participants of these and other ages, such young people under age 18 and people over age 65. Projections of actual labor force numbers are driven largely by underlying demographic forces and show a similar slowdown in labor force growth. See Mitra Toossi, "Labor Force Projections to 2024: The Labor Force Is Growing, but Slowly," *Monthly Labor Review* (December 2015) (www.bls.gov/opub/mlr/2015/article/labor-force-projections-to-2024.htm).

9. See U.S. Census Bureau, Population Projections released March 2018 (www.census. gov/data/tables/2017/demo/popproj/2017-summary-tables.html).

10. Jeffrey S. Passel, "Demography of Immigrant Youth: Past, Present and Future," *Future of Children,* vol. 21 (Spring 2011), pp. 19–41 (https://ncfy.acf.hhs.gov/sites/default/files/docs/20060-Demography_of_Immigrant.pdf).

11. Lauren Musu-Gillette, Cristobal de Brey, Joel McFarland, William Hussar, William Sonnonberg, and Sidney Wilkinson-Flicker, "Status and Trends in the Education of Racial and Ethnic Groups," NCES 2017-051 (Department of Education, National Center for Education Statistics, 2017) (http://nces.ed.gov/pubs2010/ 2010015.pdf); Pew Research Center, "Facts on US Latinos, 2015: Statistical Portrait of Hispanics in the United States," 2017 (www.pewhispanic.org/2017/09/18/facts-on-u-s-latinos/).

12. Gary Orfield, John Kucsera, and Genevieve Siegel-Hawley, "E Pluribus . . . Separation: Deepening Double Segregation for More Students" (Los Angeles: UCLA Civil Rights Project, 2012) (www.civilrightsproject.ucla.edu/research/k-12-education/integration-and-diversity/mlk-national/e-pluribus...separation-deepening-double-segregation-for-more-students/orfield_epluribus_revised_omplete_2012.pdf); U.S. Government Accountability Office, "K-12 Education: Better Use of Information Could Help Agencies Identify Disparities and Address Racial Discrimination," April 2016 (www.gao.gov/assets/680/676745.pdf).

13. Marta Tienda and Ron Haskins, "Immigrant Children: Introducing the Issue," *Future of Children,* vol. 21 (Spring 2011), pp. 3–18 (http://futureofchildren.org/futureofchildren/publications/docs/21_01_01.pdf); Olivia Golden and Karina Fortuny, "Young Children of Immigrants and the Path to Education Success: Key Themes from an Urban Institute Roundtable" (Washington: Urban Institute, April 22, 2011) (www.urban.org/UploadedPDF/412330-young-children.pdf).

14. Lauren Musu-Gillette, Cristobal de Brey, Joel McFarland, William Hussar, William Sonnonberg, and Sidney Wilkinson-Flicker, "Status and Trends in the Education of Racial and Ethnic Groups"; Pew Research Center, "The Rise of Asian Americans," *Social and Demographic Trends Report* (Washington: Pew Research Center, July 12, 2012) (www.pewsocialtrends.org/files/2012/06/SDT-The-Rise-of-Asian-Americans-Full-Report.pdf).

15. See Nicholas Eberstadt, "The Demographic Future—What Population Growth—and Decline—Means for the Global Economy," *Foreign Affairs* (November/December 2010) (www.foreignaffairs.com/articles/2010-11-01/demographic-future); Nicholas Eberstadt, "Japan Shrinks," *Wilson Quarterly* (Spring 2012), pp. 30–37 (www.wilsonquarterly.com/sites/default/files/articles/Feat_Eberstadt.FNL.pdf).

16. The millennial generation can considered to be born between the years 1981 and 1997 and were ages 18 and 34 in 2015. See William H. Frey, "The Millennial Generation—A Demographic Bridge to America's Future," Metropolitan Policy Program, Brookings Institution, 2018 (www.brookings.edu/wp-content/uploads/2018/01/2018-jan_brookings-metro_millennials-a-demographic-bridge-to-americas-diverse-future.pdf).

17. "The Generation Gap and the 2012 Election" (Washington: Pew Research Center, November 3, 2011) (www.people-press.org/2011/11/03/the-generation-gap-and-the-2012-election-3/); Ronald Brownstein, "The Great Divide," *National Journal* (August 23, 2011).

18. Morley Winograd and Michael D. Hais, *Millennial Momentum: How a New Generation Is Remaking America* (Rutgers University Press, 2011); Frey, "The Millennial Generation—A Demographic Bridge to America's Future" (www.brookings.edu/wp-content/uploads/2018/01/2018-jan_brookings-metro_millennials-a-demographic-bridge-to-americas-diverse-future.pdf).

19. United Nations, "World Population Prospects: The 2017 Revision" (New York: Department of Economic and Social Affairs, United Nations, 2017) (www.un.org/development/desa/publications/world-population-prospects-the-2017-revision.html).

20. It should be noted that unlike in Japan and several countries in Europe where old-age dependency already is greater than child dependency, higher U.S. fertility and immigration keeps youth dependency high. Yet old-age dependency will increase sharply at the same time that child dependency remains virtually flat.

21. For blacks, 2010 youth and old-age dependency ratios are 43 and 14, respectively; for Asians, they are 33 and 14, respectively.

22. Ronald Brownstein, "The Gray and the Brown: The Generational Mismatch," *National Journal* (July 24, 2010), pp. 14–22.

23. Brownstein, "The Great Divide."

24. Adam Liptak, "Blocking Parts of Arizona Law, Justices Allow Its Centerpiece," *New York Times,* June 25, 2012, p. 1 (www.nytimes.com/2012/06/26/us/supreme-court-rejects-part-of-arizona-immigration-law.html?pagewanted=all).

25. Behavior Research Center, "Attitudes on Recent Immigration Law Divides Arizona on Partisan and Ethnic Grounds: Support Now Only 52 Percent," press release (Phoenix, Ariz.: Rocky Mountain Poll, Behavior Research Center, May 5, 2010) (www.brcpolls.com/10/RMP%202010-II-03.pdf).

26. Andrew Cohen, "How Voter ID Laws Are Being Used to Disenfranchise Minorities and the Poor," *The Atlantic* (March 16, 2012) (www.theatlantic.com/politics/archive/2012/03/how-voter-id-laws-are-being-used-to-disenfranchise-minorities-and-the-poor/254572/); Brownstein, "The Gray and the Brown." Tony Pugh, "Voter

Supression Laws Likely Tipped the Scales for Trump, Civil Rights Groups Say," *McClatchey News,* November 10, 2016 (www.mcclatchydc.com/news/politics-government/election/article113977353.html).

27. Margareta Calderon, Robert Slavin, and Marta Sanchez, "Effective Instruction for English Learners," *Future of Children,* vol. 21 (Spring 2011), pp. 103–19 (https://ncfy.acf.hhs.gov/sites/default/files/docs/20062-Effective_Instruction.pdf ).

## CHAPTER 3

1. Stanley Lieberson, *A Piece of the Pie: Blacks and White Immigrants since 1880* (University of California Press, 1981); Stanley Lieberson and Mary C. Waters, *From Many Strands: Ethnic and Racial Groups in Contemporary America* (New York: Russell Sage Foundation, 1988.

2. The underlying migration dynamics are discussed in William H. Frey, "Three Americas: The Rising Significance of Regions," *Journal of the American Planning Association,* vol. 68 (Autumn 2002), pp. 349–55.

3. The Immigration and Nationality Act of 1965, also known as the Hart-Celler Act, dismantled previous immigration quotas based on national origin, which favored immigrants from northern European countries and effectively barred Asian immigration. The act replaced previous quotas to encourage broader immigration from all countries, although a cap was placed on total immigrants from the Eastern Hemisphere. The act had the overall effect of increasing immigration from Asia and Latin America, although the increase in the latter was also a result of aspects of the law that gave preferences to family unification. The increase occurred despite the fact that Western Hemisphere immigration was capped for the first time in 1976. It has been argued that aside from the effect of family reunification on Latin American immigration, the cap on Latin American immigration led to the rise in undocumented workers from Latin America in response to continued labor demand. For an overview of the national origin and race effects of U.S. immigration policy, see Richard Alba and Victor Nee, "The Background to Contemporary Immigration," in *Remaking the American Mainstream: Assimilation and Contemporary Immigration* (Harvard University Press, 2003), pp. 167–84. For a broader examination of U.S. immigration policy, see Philip Martin and Elizabeth Midgley, "Immigration: Shaping and Reshaping America," *Population Bulletin,* vol. 61, no. 4 (2006) (Washington: Population Reference Bureau) (www.prb.org/pdf06/61.4USMigration.pdf ); Philip Martin and Elizabeth Midgley, "Immigration in America 2010," *Population Bulletin Update* (Washington: Population Reference Bureau, 2010) (www.prb.org/pdf10/immigration-update2010.pdf ).

4. William H. Frey, "Immigrant and Native Migrant Magnets," *American Demographics* (November 1996), pp. 1–5 (www.frey-demographer.org/briefs/B-1996-2_ImmigrantNativeMigrantMagnets.pdf ); William H. Frey, "Immigration, Domestic Migration, and Demographic Balkanization in America: New Evidence for the 1990s," *Population and Development Review,* vol. 22 (December 1996), pp. 741–63.

5. It should be noted that statewide boundaries, shown in map 3-1, sometimes understate the New Sun Belt's reach. For example, in the state of Florida, the metropolitan areas of Orlando and Tampa might be considered New Sun Belt areas because of their strong draw of domestic migrants (in contrast to Miami, which is a long-standing immigrant magnet). Moreover, the Texas metropolitan areas of Dallas and Houston have been strong draws for both immigrants and domestic migrants.

6. William H. Frey, "The New White Flight," *American Demographics* (April 1994), pp. 40–48 (www.frey-demographer.org/briefs/B-2002-5_NewWhiteflight.pdf); William H. Frey, "Immigration and Internal Migration Flight from U.S. Metropolitan Areas: Toward a New Demographic Balkanization," *Urban Studies*, vol. 32, nos. 4–5 (1995), pp. 733–57 (www.frey-demographer.org/reports/R-1995-2_ImmigrationBalkanization.pdf).

7. During the 1990s, the New Sun Belt states grew by 24 percent while the rate for the combined states of California, Florida, and Texas was only 18 percent. In the congressional reapportionment after the 2000 census, the New Sun Belt states gained seven new congressional seats while California, Texas, and Florida combined got just five. This contrasts with the reapportionment after the 1990 census, when the New Sun Belt states gained just five seats and California, Texas, and Florida combined gained 14 seats.

8. Between 1990 and 2000, nine of the ten states that gained white households headed by married couples who had children were located in the New Sun Belt, which thereby maintained the 1950s "suburbanite" image. Nationally, during the 1990s, the fastest-growing counties in the nation were largely white-dominated counties on the peripheries of New Sun Belt metropolitan areas.

9. For most of this period, family reunification represented the largest category of legal immigrants to the United States. Between 1993 and 2000, for example, immediate relatives of U.S. citizens and other family-sponsored immigrants constituted two-thirds of legal immigrants. See U.S. Department of Homeland Security, *Fiscal Year 2000 Statistical Yearbook: Immigrants,* table 4: "Immigrants Admitted by Type and Selected Class of Admission (1993–2000)" (www.dhs.gov/xlibrary/assets/statistics/yearbook/2000/Yearbook2000.pdf).

10. Frey, "Immigration, Domestic Migration, and Demographic Balkanization in America"; William H. Frey, "Immigration and Demographic Balkanization: Toward One America or Two?," in *America's Demographic Tapestry,* edited by James W. Hughes and Joseph J. Seneca (Rutgers University Press, 1999), pp. 78–100 (www.frey-demographer.org/reports/R-1999-1_ImmigrationDemographic.pdf).

11. William H. Frey and Jonathan Tilove, "Immigrants In, Native Whites Out," *New York Times Magazine,* August, 20 1995, pp. 44–45 (www.frey-demographer.org/briefs/B-1995-1_ImmigrantsIn.pdf).

12. William H. Frey and Kao-Lee Liaw, "The Impact of Recent Immigration on Population Redistribution within the United States," in *The Immigration Debate: Studies of Economic, Demographic, and Fiscal Effects of Immigration,* edited by James P. Smith and Barry Edmonston (Washington: National Academy Press, 1998), pp. 388–448 (www.frey-demographer.org/reports/R-1998-2_ImpactImmigrationPopulationRedistribution.pdf); Richard A. Wright, Mark Ellis, and Michael Reibel, "The Linkage between Immigration and Internal Migration in Large Metropolitan Areas of the United States," *Economic Geography,* vol. 73, no. 2 (April 1997), pp. 234–54.

13. George J. Borjas, *Heaven's Door: Immigration Policy and the American Economy* (Princeton University Press, 1999).

14. Samuel P. Huntington, "The Hispanic Challenge," *Foreign Policy* (March/April 2004), pp. 1–14 (www.foreignpolicy.com/articles/2004/03/01/the_hispanic_challenge).

15. William H. Frey, "Diversity Spreads Out: Metropolitan Shifts in Hispanic, Asian, and Black Populations since 2000," *Living Cities Census Series* (Brookings Metropolitan Policy Program, 2006) (www.frey-demographer.org/reports/R-2006-1_

DiversitySpreadsOut.pdf); Audrey Singer, Susan W. Hardwick, and Caroline B. Brettell, *Twenty-First Century Gateways: Immigrant Incorporation in Suburban America* (Brookings, 2008); Douglas S. Massey, *New Faces in New Places: The Changing Geography of American Immigration* (New York: Russell Sage Foundation, 2008).

16. William H. Frey, "Immigration and Domestic Migration in U.S. Metro Areas: 2000 and 1990 Census Findings by Education and Race" (University of Michigan Population Studies Center, 2005) (www.psc.isr.umich.edu/pubs/pdf/rr05-572.pdf); William H. Frey and Kao-Lee Liaw, "Interstate Migration of Hispanics, Asians, and Blacks: Cultural Constraints and Middle-Class Flight" (University of Michigan Population Studies Center, 2005) (www.psc.isr.umich.edu/pubs/pdf/rr05-575.pdf); Daniel T. Lichter and Kenneth M. Johnson, "Immigrant Gateways and the Hispanic Migration to New Destinations," *International Migration Review,* vol. 43 (2009), pp. 496–518; William H. Frey and Julie Park, "Migration and Dispersal of Hispanic and Asian Groups: An Analysis of the 2006–2008 Multiyear American Community Survey" (University of Michigan Population Studies Center, 2010) (www.psc.isr. umich.edu/pubs/pdf/rr10-722.pdf).

17. Emilio A. Parrado and William Kandel, "New Hispanic Migrant Destinations: A Tale of Two Industries," in *New Faces in New Places,* edited by Massey, pp. 99–123.

18. Frey and Park, "Migration and Dispersal of Hispanic and Asian Groups."

19. Frey and Liaw, "Interstate Migration of Hispanics, Asians, and Blacks."

20. Frey, "Immigration and Domestic Migration in U.S. Metro Areas."

21. Examples of such laws were passed by state legislatures in Arizona, Utah, Georgia, South Carolina, and Alabama. See National Conference of State Legislatures, "State Omnibus Immigration Legislation and Legal Challenges," August 27, 2012 (www.ncsl.org/issues-research/immig/omnibus-immigration-legislation.aspx). An inventory of state legislation is compiled by the National Conference of State Legislatures (www.ncsl.org/issues-research/immig/state-immigration-legislation-report-dec-2011.aspx).

22. Map 3-2 identifies counties where one or more minority groups are represented at the same or at a higher percentage than the national percentage for Hispanics (16.3 percent), blacks (12.2 percent), and Asians (4.7 percent). Counties classed under "Other minorities" include those in which the combined percentage of American Indians and Alaska Natives, multiracial persons, and "some other race" exceed 4 percent. Counties classed under "two or more minority groups" are those in which two or more of the above groups are each represented at a percentage that is the same or greater than their national percentage. An example would be a county where Hispanics equal or exceed 16.3 percent of the population and where blacks equal or exceed 12.2 percent of the population.

23. Tina Norris, Paula L. Vines, and Elizabeth M. Hoefel, *The American Indian and Alaska Native Population: 2010,* 2010 Census Briefs C2010BR-10 (Census Bureau, 2012) (www.census.gov/prod/cen2010/briefs/c2010br-10.pdf).

24. Calculations are based on U.S. Census Bureau estimates for 2000–09 with 2009–10 interpolated from 2008–09 and 2000–10 (data for 2009–10 are not available). U.S. Census Bureau, "Estimates of Components of Resident Change by Race and Hispanic Origin," April 1, 2000–July 1, 2009 and July 1, 2010–July 1, 2011 (www.census.gov/ popest/data/national/asrh/2009/tables/NC-EST2009-05.xls and www.census.gov/ popest/data/national/asrh/2011/tables/NC-EST2011-05.xls).

25. William Kandel and John Cromartie, "New Patterns of Hispanic Settlement in Rural America," Rural Development Research Report 99 (Department of Agriculture, Economic Research Service, 2004) (www.ers.usda.gov/media/561319/rdrr991.pdf).

26. Of the total 2010 Asian population, 67 percent were foreign born; in contrast, the figure was only 37 percent for the 2010 Hispanic population.

27. William H. Frey, "Immigration and Domestic Migration in U.S. Metro Areas: 2000 and 1990 Census Findings by Education and Race" (University of Michigan Population Studies Center, 2005) (www.psc.isr.umich.edu/pubs/pdf/rr05-572.pdf); Frey and Park, "Migration and Dispersal of Hispanic and Asian Groups."

28. C. Horace Hamilton, "The Negro Leaves the South," *Demography,* vol. 1 (1964), pp. 273–95; William H. Frey, "The New Great Migration: Black Americans' Return to the South, 1965–2000," Living Cities Census Series (Brookings  Metropolitan Policy Program, 2004) (www.brookings.edu/~/media/research/files/reports/2004/5/demographics%20frey/20040524_frey).

29. For discussions of changes in populations, including identification issues, see Jeffrey S. Passel, "The Growing American Indian Population, 1960–1990: Beyond Demography," in *Changing Numbers, Changing Needs: American Indian Demography and Public Health,* edited by Gary D. Sandefur, Ronald R. Rindfuss, and Barney Cohn (Washington: National Academy Press, 1996), pp. 72–92; C. Matthew Snipp, "American Indian and Alaska Native Children: Results from the 2000 Census" (Washington: Population Reference Bureau, 2005) (www.prb.org/pdf05/americanindianalaskachildren.pdf).

30. The present analysis focuses on persons who claim a single racial identity as American Indian or Alaska Native, including both Hispanics and non-Hispanics.

31. C. Matthew Snipp, "The Size and Distribution of the American Indian Population: Fertility, Mortality, Migration, and Residence," in *Changing Numbers, Changing Needs,* edited by Sandefur, Rindfuss, and Cohn, pp. 17–52; Tina Norris, Paula L. Vines, and Elizabeth M. Hoefel, "The American Indian and Alaska Native Population: 2010," 2010 Census Briefs C2010BR-10 (Census Bureau, 2012) (www.census.gov/prod/cen2010/briefs/c2010br-10.pdf).

32. Norris, Vines, and Hoefel, "The American Indian and Alaska Native Population: 2010."

33. These statistics for multiracial persons include both Hispanics and non-Hispanics.

34.  Karen R. Humes, Nicholas A. Jones, and Roberto R. Ramirez, "Overview of Race and Hispanic Origin: 2010," 2010 Census Briefs C2010BR-02 (Census Bureau, 2011) (www.census.gov/prod/cen2010/briefs/c2010br-02.pdf).

35. In 2010, 88 percent of the U.S. Asian population, 79 percent of the Hispanic population, and 74 percent of the black population resided in large metropolitan areas (those with a population of more than 500,000) while just 59 percent of the white population resided in these areas.

36. Note that among the 22 minority-majority metropolitan areas, 14 showed white population declines in 2000-10, including New York, Los Angeles, Miami, and San Francisco. Notable exceptions are Las Vegas, Washington, D.C., Houston, and San Antonio, which experienced both white and minority population gains, although in each, minority population gains exceeded those for whites. See William H. Frey, "The New Metro Minority Map: Regional Shifts in Hispanics, Asians, and Blacks from Census 2010" (Brookings Metropolitan Policy Program, 2011) (www.brookings.edu/~/media/research/files/papers/2011/8/31%20census%20race%20frey/0831_census_race_frey).

37. Frey, "Immigration and Domestic Migration in U.S. Metro Areas."

## CHAPTER 4

1. National Research Council, "Multiple Origins, Hispanic Portrait," in *Multiple Origins, Uncertain Destinies: Hispanics and the American Future*, edited by Marta Tienda and Faith Mitchell (Washington: National Academies Press, 2006), pp. 19–34 (www.ncbi. nlm.nih.gov/books/NBK19804/).

2. Hispanic immigration rose during this period in large measure because of the family unification provisions of U.S. immigration law, increased demand for labor (drawing both documented and undocumented workers), and immigrant refugee and asylum-seeker programs. See Philip Martin and Elizabeth Midgley, "Immigration: Shaping and Reshaping America," *Population Bulletin,* vol. 61, no. 4 (2006) (Washington: Population Reference Bureau) (www.prb.org/pdf06/61.4USMigration. pdf); and Douglas S. Massey and Karen A. Pren, "Unintended Consequences of U.S. Immigration Policy: Explaining the Post-1965 Surge from Latin America," *Population and Development Review,* vol. 38, no. 1 (2012), pp. 1–29. Declines in migration from Mexico and other countries began in the late 2000–10 decade. See Jeffrey S. Passel, D'Vera Cohn, and Anna Gonzalez Barrera, "Net Migration from Mexico Falls to Zero and Perhaps Less" (Washington: Pew Research Center, April 2012) (www.pewhispanic.org/files/2012/04/Mexican-migrants-report_ final.pdf).

3. U.S. Census Bureau, "Estimates of Components of Resident Change by Race and Hispanic Origin," April 1, 2000–July 1, 2009 (www.census.gov/popest/data/national/ asrh/2009/tables/NC-EST2009-05.xls); "Estimates of Components of Resident Change by Race and Hispanic Origin, April 1, 2010–July 1, 2016 (https://factfinder. census.gov). Also see Pew Hispanic Center, "The Mexican-American Boom: Births Overtake Immigration" (Washington: Pew Research Center, March 2011) (www. pewhispanic.org/2011/07/14/the-mexican-american-boom-brbirths-overtake- immigration/).

4. An alternative census bureau projection conducted in 2009, which assumes zero immigration, shows projected Hispanic population growth of 60 percent between 2010 and 2050. See U.S. Census Bureau, "2009 National Population Projections (Supplemental): Summary Tables: Zero Net Migration Series" (www.census.gov/ population/projections/data/national/2009/2009znmsSumTabs.html). Later projections assuming middle-level immigration show continued larger Hispanic population gains from natural increase than from immigration through 2060. See U.S. Census Bureau, "2014 National Population Projections" (www.census. gov/data/tables/2014/demo/popproj/2014-summary-tables.html).

5. In 2010, approximately 6.5 million of the 31 million residents of Mexican origin were undocumented immigrants. Among all 50 million Hispanic residents, approximately 9.1 million were undocumented immigrants. See Jeffrey S. Passel and D'Vera Cohn, "Unauthorized Immigrant Population: National and State Trends, 2010" (Washington: Pew Research Center, February 2011) (www.pewhispanic.org/files/reports/ 133.pdf).

6. Sharon R. Ennis, Merarys Rios-Vargas, and Nora G. Albert, "The Hispanic Popula- tion: 2010," 2010 Census Briefs C2010BR-04 (U.S. Census Bureau, 2011) (www. census.gov/prod/cen2010/briefs/c2010br-04.pdf).

7. Alejandro Portes and Ruben G. Rumbaut, *Immigrant America: A Portrait,* 3rd ed. (University of California Press, 2006).

8. Undocumented immigration from Mexico and other Latin American countries, such as El Salvador and Guatemala, rose after 1970 through the latter part of the first decade of the 2000s because of demand for labor, with large numbers of undocu-

mented workers in occupations such as farming, construction, grounds keeping, and food preparation and serving. See Massey and Pren, "Unintended Consequences of U.S. Immigration Policy"; Passel and Cohn, "Unauthorized Immigrant Population"; and Jeffrey S. Passel and D'Vera Cohn, "A Portrait of Unauthorized Immigrants in the United States" (Washington: Pew Research Center, April 2009) (http://pewhispanic. org/files/reports/107.pdf).

9. National Research Council, "Realms of Integration: Family, Education, Work, and Health," in *Multiple Origins, Uncertain Destinies,* edited by Tienda and Mitchell, pp. 77–114; Richard Fry and Mark Hugo Lopez, "Hispanic Student Enrollments Reach New Heights in 2011" (Washington: Pew Research Center, August 2012) (www.pewhispanic.org/files/2012/08/Hispanic-Student-Enrollments-Reach-New-Highs-in-2011_FINAL.pdf).

10. Shirin Hakimzadeh and D'Vera Cohn, "English Usage among Hispanics in the United States" (Washington: Pew Research Center, November 2007) (www.pewhispanic.org/files/reports/82.pdf).

11. Julie Park and Dowell Myers, "Intergenerational Mobility in the Post-1965 Immigration Era: Estimates by an Immigrant Generation Cohort Method," *Demography,* vol. 47, no. 2 (2010), pp. 369–92 (www.ncbi.nlm.nih.gov/pmc/articles/PMC3000029/); Dowell Myers and John Pitkin, "Assimilation Today: New Evidence Shows the Latest Immigrants to America Are Following in Our History's Footsteps" (Washington: Center for American Progress, September 2010) (www.americanprogress.org/ issues/2010/09/pdf/immigrant_assimilation.pdf).

12. Nancy S. Landale, R. Salvedor Oropesa, and Cristina Bradatan, "Hispanic Families in the United States: Family Structure and Process in an Era of Family Change," in National Research Council, *Hispanics and the Future of America* (Washington: National Academies Press, 2006), pp. 138–78 (www.ncbi.nlm.nih.gov/books/ NBK19902/).

13. Mary J. Fischer and Marta Tienda, "Redrawing Spatial Color Lines: Hispanic Metropolitan Dispersal, Segregation, and Economic Opportunity," in National Research Council, *Hispanics and the Future of America,* pp. 100–37.

14. See Mary E. Odom, "Unsettled in the Suburbs: Latino Immigration and Ethnic Diversity in Metro Atlanta," in *Twenty-First Century Gateways: Immigrant Incorporation in Suburban America,* edited by Audrey Singer, Susan W. Hardwick, and Caroline B. Brettell (Brookings, 2008), pp. 281–307; Heather J. Smith and Owen J. Furuseth, "The "Nuevo South": Latino Place Making and Community Building in the Middle-Ring Suburbs of Charlotte," in *Twenty-First Century Gateways,* edited by Singer, Hardwick, and Brettell, pp. 105–36.

15. These three types of metropolitan areas together account for 222 of the total 366 metropolitan areas.

16. See Matthew Hall and others, "The Geography of Immigrant Skills: Educational Profiles of Metropolitan Areas" (Brookings Metropolitan Policy Program, 2011) (www.brookings.edu/~/media/research/files/papers/2011/6/immigrants%20 singer/06_immigrants_singer.pdf).

17. National Research Council, "Multiple Origins, Hispanic Portrait," in *Multiple Origins, Uncertain Destinies,* edited by Tienda and Mitchell, pp. 19–34.

18. Antonio Flores, "How the US Hispanic Population is Changing," Pew Research Center, September 28, 2017 (www.pewhispanic.org/2017/09/18/facts-on-u-s-latinos-current-data/).

19. Brian Gratton and Myron P. Gutmann, "Hispanics in the United States, 1850–1990: Estimates of Population Size and Natural Origin," *Historical Methods,* vol. 33, no. 3

(2000), pp. 137–53 (www.latinamericanstudies.org/immigration/Hispanics-US-1850-1990.pdf); Rogelio Saenz, "Latinos and the Changing Face of America," in *The American People: Census 2000,* edited by Reynolds Farley and John Haaga (New York: Russell Sage Foundation, 2005), pp. 352–79.

20. Saenz, "Latinos and the Changing Face of America"; *Yearbook of Immigration Statistics: 2010* (Department of Homeland Security, Office of Immigration Statistics, 2011) (www.dhs.gov/xlibrary/assets/statistics/yearbook/2010/ois_yb_2010.pdf).

21. Silvia Pedraza, "Cuba's Refugees: Manifold Migrations," in *Origins and Destinies: Immigration, Race, and Ethnicity in America,* edited by Silvia Pedraza and Ruben G. Rumbaut (Belmont, Calif.: Wadsworth, 1996) (www.ascecuba.org/publications/proceedings/volume5/pdfs/FILE26.pdf).

22. Hector A. Carrasquillo and Virginia Sanchez-Korrol, "Migration, Community, and Culture: The United States Puerto Rican Experience," in *Origins and Destinies,* edited by Pedraza and Rumbaut.

23. Aaron Terrazas, "Salvadoran Immigrants in the United States" (Washington: Migration Policy Institute, April 2010) (www.migrationinformation.org/usfocus/display.cfm?ID=765).

24. James Smith, "Guatemala: Economic Migrants Replace Political Refugees" (Washington: Migration Policy Institute, April 2006) (www.migrationinformation.org/feature/display.cfm?ID=392).

25. William H. Frey and Julie Park, "Migration and Dispersal of Hispanic and Asian Groups: An Analysis of the 2006–2008 Multiyear American Community Survey" (University of Michigan Population Studies Center, 2010) (www.psc.isr.umich.edu/pubs/pdf/rr10-722.pdf).

## CHAPTER 5

1. The statistics in this chapter focus primarily on the Asian population (including Hispanic Asians) but not additional Asians who are multiracial. Multiracial populations are discussed in chapter 10. The 2010 census counted 14.7 million Asians and an additional 2.6 million persons who identified as Asian in combination with one or more races. See Elizabeth M. Hoefel and others, "The Asian Population, 2010," 2010 Census Briefs C2010BR-11 (U.S. Census Bureau, 2012) (www.census.gov/prod/cen2010/briefs/c2010br-11.pdf).

2. Congressional Budget Office, "Immigration Policy in the United States," February 2006 (www.cbo.gov/sites/default/files/cbofiles/ftpdocs/70xx/doc7051/02-28-immigration.pdf).

3. Mary M. Kritz and Douglas T. Gurak, "Immigration and a Changing America," in *The American People: Census 2000,* edited by Reynolds Farley and John Haaga (New York: Russell Sage Foundation, 2005), pp. 259–301; Nathan P. Walters and Edward N. Trevelyan, "The Newly Arrived Foreign-Born Population in the United States, 2010," American Community Survey Brief ACSBR/10-16 (2011) (www.census.gov/prod/2011pubs/acsbr10-16.pdf). Between 2010 and 2016, 58 percent of U.S. net foreign born gains came from Asian countries, per author's calculations from the 2010 and 2016 American Community Survey (www.census.gov/programs-surveys/acs/).

4. Processed from public use microdata from the 2015 "Current Population Survey, Annual Social and Economic Supplement" (U.S. Census Bureau).

5. This discussion draws from more extensive treatments of this history in Yu Xie and Kimberly A. Goyette, "A Demographic Portrait of Asian Americans," in *The American People,* edited by Farley and Haaga, pp. 415–46; Sharon M. Lee, "Asian Americans:

Diverse and Growing," *Population Bulletin,* vol. 53, no. 2 (1998) (www.prb.org/source/53.2asianamerican.pdf ); Ronald Takaki, *Strangers from a Different Shore: A History of Asian Americans* (New York: Penguin Books, 1990).

6. Campbell Gibson and Kay Jung, "Historical Statistics on Population Totals by Race, 1790 to 1990, and by Hispanic Origin 1970 to 1990, for Large Cities and Other Urban Places in the United States," Population Division Working Paper 76 (U.S. Census Bureau, 2005) (www.census.gov/population/www/documentation/twps0076/twps0076.html).

7. Hoefel and others,"The Asian Population, 2010."

8. Of the several preference categories under which immigrants may enter, large Asian groups—including Chinese, Asian Indians, Filipinos, and Koreans—enter more often under employment-based preferences than do immigrants in general. Nonetheless, as with most immigrant groups, more Asian immigrants enter because of the family reunification preference than the employment preference. See Pew Research Center, "The Rise of Asian Americans" (Washington: 2012) (www.pewsocialtrends.org/files/2012/06/SDT- The-Rise-of-Asian-Americans-Full-Report.pdf ); and Office of Immigration Statistics, *2011 Yearbook of Immigration Statistics* (Department of Homeland Security, 2011) (www.dhs.gov/sites/default/files/publications/immigration-statistics/yearbook/2011/ois_yb_2011.pdf ).

9. Xie and Goyette, "A Demographic Portrait of Asian Americans," in *The American People,* edited by Farley and Haaga.

10. These statistics are drawn from Pew Research Center, "The Rise of Asian Americans."

11. Nevertheless, Asian fertility is slightly lower than that of the total population. Between 2005 and 2014, the total fertility rate (representing the average number of births over a woman's lifetime) ranged between 1.7 and 1.85 for Asian Americans and between 1.9 and 2.1 for the total population. See National Center for Health Statistics, "Trends and Variations in Reproduction and Intrinsic Rates: United States, 1990–2014," National Vital Statistics Reports, vol. 66, no. 2 (2017) (www.cdc.gov/nchs/data/nvsr66/nvsr66_02.pdf ).

12. From 2009 to 2011, 9.4 percent of Asian families were multigenerational; the corresponding percentage was 5.6 percent for all families and 3.6 percent for white families. See Daphne A. Lofquist, "Multigenerational Households, 2009–2011," American Community Survey Briefs ACSBR/11-03 (Census Bureau, 2012) (www.census.gov/prod/2012pubs/acsbr11-03.pdf ).

13. Historical shifts in the geographic distribution of Asian Americans are discussed in Herbert Barringer, Robert W. Gardner, and Michael J. Levin, *Asians and Pacific Islanders in the United States* (New York: Russell Sage Foundation, 1993).

14. Alejandro Portes and Ruben G. Rumbaut, *Immigrant America: A Portrait,* 3rd ed (University of California Press, 2006).

15. See discussions in Barringer, Gardner, and Levin, *Asians and Pacific Islanders in the United States,* and chapter 2, "Who They Are and Why They Come," in Portes and Rumbaut, *Immigrant America: A Portrait.*

16. These are areas in which the Asian share of the population is 5 percent or greater (the Asian percentage of the national population is 4.7 percent) and the 2000-10 growth rate of that population is less than the national Asian growth rate of 43 percent.

17. These are areas in which the Asian share of the population is 5 percent or greater and the 2000-10 growth rate of that population equals or exceeds the national Asian growth rate of 43 percent.

18. These are areas in which the Asian share of the population is between 1 and 5 percent and the 2000–10 growth rate of that population equals or exceeds 70 percent.

19. Additional analysis shows that Asian Indians accounted for 33 percent of the gains among the Asian populations in the new Asian destinations during 2000–10; other Asian groups showed far smaller gains. Moreover, Asian Indians constituted 29 percent of the 2010 Asian populations in these areas, up from 24 percent in 2000, and their share was larger than that of other major groups.

20. Analyses of 2006–08 internal migration of major Asian groups indicate that metropolitan areas in close proximity to major settlements of specific Asian-origin groups are likely destinations for those groups. For example, Las Vegas and Riverside are primary destinations for Filipino migrants from Los Angeles and San Diego. See William H. Frey and Julie Park, "Migration and Dispersal of Hispanic and Asian Groups: An Analysis of the 2006–2008 Multiyear American Community Survey" (University of Michigan Population Studies Center, 2010) (http://papers.ssrn.com/sol3/papers.cfm?abstract_id=1946781).

21. 2011 statistics from Consular Affairs (U.S. Department of State) cited in Pew Research Center, "The Rise of Asian Americans," p. 27 (www.pewsocialtrends.org/2012/06/19/the-rise-of-asian-americans/). The H-1B visa program began as part of the Immigration Act of 1990 to permit employers to hire foreigners on a temporary basis for highly sought specialty occupations, usually requiring a bachelor's degree. Some occupants of this status can eventually apply for U.S. citizenship. For a full discussion of the H-1B visa program and its effects on different regions of the United States, see Neil G.Ruiz, Jill H. Wilson, and Shyamali Choudhury, "The Search for Skills: Demand for H-1B Immigrant Workers in U.S. Metropolitan Areas" (Brookings Metropolitan Policy Program, 2012) (www.brookings.edu/~/media/research/files/reports/2012/7/18%20h1b%20visas%20labor%20immigration/18%20h1b%20visas%20labor%20immigration.pdf).

## CHAPTER 6

1. Whereas the statistics for blacks in all other chapters in this book exclude Hispanic blacks, the statistics in this chapter, except where noted, pertain to the entire black population, including both non-Hispanic and Hispanic blacks. (In 2010, Hispanic blacks represented 3.2 percent of all blacks.) Census Bureau sources documenting the black population in this time period include Campbell Gibson and Kay Jung, "Historical Census Statistics and Population Totals by Race, 1790 to 1990, and by Hispanic Origin, 1970 to 1990, for the United States, Regions, Divisions, and States," Population Division Working Paper 56 (Census Bureau, 2002) (www.census.gov/population/www/documentation/twps0056/twps0056.pdf); Karen R. Humes, Nicholas A. Jones, and Roberto R. Ramirez, "Overview of Race and Hispanic Origin: 2010," 2010 Census Briefs C2010BR-02 (Census Bureau, 2011) (www.census.gov/prod/cen2010/briefs/c2010br-02.pdf); and Sonya Rastogi and others, "The Black Population: 2010," 2010 Census Briefs C2010BR-06 (Census Bureau, 2011) (www.census.gov/prod/cen2010/briefs/c2010br-06.pdf).

2. U.S. Census Bureau projections, released March 2018 (www.census.gov/data/tables/2017/demo/popproj/2017-summary-tables.html).

3. Gunnar Myrdal, *An American Dilemma: The Negro Problem and Modern Democracy* (New York: Harper and Brothers, 1944).

4. For a concise summary of events during this period, see chapter 1 in Reynolds Farley, *Blacks and Whites: Narrowing the Gap?* (Harvard University Press, 1984). See also

Taylor Branch, *Parting the Waters: America in the King Years, 1954–63* (New York: Simon and Schuster, 1988); Juan Williams, *Eyes on the Prize: America's Civil Rights Years, 1954–1965* (New York: Penguin Books, 1988).

5. Analyses of socioeconomic shifts among blacks and whites during the 1970s, 1980s, and 1990s can be found in Farley, *Blacks and Whites: Narrowing the Gap?;* Gerald D. Jaynes and Robin W. Williams Jr., *A Common Destiny: Blacks and American Society* (Washington: National Academy Press, 1989); Andrew Hacker, *Two Nations: Black and White, Separate, Hostile, Unequal* (New York: Scribner, 1992); Neil J. Smelser, William Julius Wilson, and Faith Mitchell, *America Becoming: Racial Trends and Their Consequences,* vols. 1 and 2 (Washington: National Academies Press, 2001); Michael A. Stoll, "African Americans and the Color Line," in *The American People: Census 2000,* edited by Reynolds Farley and John Haaga (New York: Russell Sage Foundation, 2005), pp. 380–414.

6. For example, the share of young adult black men in the broad "managerial and professional" category of workers rose from 12 percent in 1970 to 14.4 percent in 2015.

7. Gary Orfield, John Kucsera, and Genevieve Siegel-Hawley, "E Pluribus . . . Separation: Deepening Double Segregation for More Students" (Civil Rights Project, UCLA, 2012) (http://civilrightsproject.ucla.edu/research/k-12-education/integration-and-diversity/mlk-national/ e-pluribus...separation-deepening-double-segregation-for-more-students/orfield_epluribus_revised_omplete_2012.pdf).

8. U.S. Department of Labor, "The African American Labor Force in the Recovery" (Washington, 2012) (www.dol.gov/_sec/media/reports/BlackLaborForce/Black-LaborForce.pdf) and U.S. Bureau of Labor Statistics, Labor Force Statistics from the Current Population Survey Table A2 Employment status of the civilian population by race, sex and age (www.bls.gov/webapps/legacy/cpsatab2.htm).

9. See U.S. Bureau of Labor Statistics, Labor Force Statistics, from the Current Population Survey, Table A2, "Employment Status of the Civilian Population by Race, Sex and Age" (www.bls.gov/webapps/legacy/cpsatab2.htm).

10. Median wage and salary income for black males, in 2016 U.S. dollars, rose to an all-time high of $29,900 (69 percent of income for whites) in 2007, only to fall to $25,000 (61 percent of that for whites) in 2011—the lowest level since 1994. In 2015 it rose again to $ 27,700 (65 percent of that of whites). U.S. Bureau of the Census, Current Population Survey, Historical Income Tables: People, Table P-2, "Race and Hispanic Origin of People by Median Income and Sex" (www.census.gov/data/tables/time-series/demo/income-poverty/historical-income-people.html).

11. Female-headed families include households headed by a woman with no spouse present and with one or more children or relatives present. Females living alone ("single-person households") or with nonrelatives only, such as roommates, are nonfamily households and are not considered to be female-headed families. In 2015, 70 percent of all black female-headed families included a child of the household head; the remaining female-headed families included other relatives such as parents, siblings, or adult children of the household head.

12. Steven Ruggles, "The Origins of African American Family Structure," *American Sociological Review,* vol. 59 (February 1994), pp. 136–51 (www.hist.umn.edu/~ruggles/Articles/Af-Am-fam.pdf).

13. Daniel Patrick Moynihan, "The Negro Family: The Case for National Action" (Office of Policy Planning and Research, U.S. Department of Labor, 1965) (www.dol.gov/oasam/programs/history/webid-meynihan.htm).

14. See William Julius Wilson, *The Truly Disadvantaged: The Inner City, the Underclass, and Public Policy* (University of Chicago Press, 1987); Douglas S. Massey and Nancy

A. Denton, *American Apartheid: Segregation and the Making of the Underclass* (Harvard University Press, 1993).

15. Perhaps best known is the controversial "welfare reform" legislation of 1996, known as the Personal Responsibility and Work Opportunity Act, which included provisions to curtail what proponents thought of as "welfare dependency" among poor female-headed families, among other groups; critics, however, argued that the provisions removed a minimal social safety net for those groups. An assessment of this legislation's effect on mothers and children is found in Rachel Dunifon, "Welfare Reform and Intergenerational Mobility" (Washington: Pew Charitable Trusts, 2010) (www.pewtrusts.org/uploadedFiles/wwwpewtrustsorg/Reports/Economic_ Mobility/EMP_TANF%2015.pdf).

16. Isabel Sawhill, "Family Structure: The Growing Importance of Class" (Brookings, 2013) (www.brookings.edu/research/articles/2013/01/family-structure-class-sawhill); Frank F. Furstenberg, "If Moynihan Had Only Known: Race, Class, and Family Change in the Late Twentieth Century," *Annals of the American Academy of Political and Social Science,* vol. 621 (2009), pp. 94–110.

17. U.S. Census Bureau, Current Population Survey, Historical Poverty Tables: People and Families, Table 4, "Poverty Status of Families by Type of Family, Presence of Related Children, Race and Hispanic Origin" (www.census.gov/data/tables/ time-series/demo/income-poverty/historical-poverty-people.html).

18. Bart Landry, *The New Black Middle Class* (University of California Press, 1988).

19. Pew Research Center, "Fewer, Poorer, and Gloomier: The Lost Decade of the Middle Class" (Washington: 2012), p. 16 (www.pewsocialtrends.org/2012/08/22/the-lost-decade-of-the-middle-class); Pew Charitable Trusts, "Pursuing the American Dream: Economic Mobility across Generations" (Washington: 2012) (www.pewstates. org/uploadedFiles/PCS_Assets/2012/Pursuing_American_Dream.pdf); Emily Rosenbaum, "Home Ownership's Wild Ride, 2001–2011" (New York: Russell Sage Foundation, 2012) (www.s4.brown.edu/us2010/Data/Report/report03212012.pdf); Rakesh Kochhar, Richard Fry, and Paul Taylor, "Wealth Gaps Rise to Record Highs between Whites, Blacks, and Hispanics" (Washington: Pew Research Center, 2011) (www.pewsocialtrends.org/files/2011/07/SDT-Wealth-Report_7-26-11_FINAL.pdf).

20. Pew Research Center, "Collateral Costs: Incarceration's Effect on Economic Mobility" (Washington: Pew Charitable Trusts, 2010) (www.pewtrusts.org/~/media/ legacy/uploadedfiles/pcs_assets/2010/collateralcosts1pdf.pdf); U.S. Department of Justice, Civil Rights Division, "Investigation of the Ferguson Police Department," May 4, 2015 (www.justice.gov/sites/default/files/opa/press-releases/attachments/ 2015/03/04/ferguson_police_department_report.pdf); Elizabeth Day, "#Black Lives Matter: The Birth of a New Civil Rights Movement," *The Guardian,* July 19, 2015 (www.theguardian.com/world/2015/jul/19/blacklivesmatter-birth-civil-rights-movement).

21. Eugene Robinson, *Disintegration: The Splintering of Black America* (New York: Doubleday, 2010).

22. Mary Mederios Kent, "Immigration and America's Black Population," *Population Bulletin,* vol. 62, no. 4 (Washington: Population Reference Bureau, 2007) (www.prb. org/pdf07/62.4immigration.pdf); Donald J. Hernandez, "Changing Demography and Circumstances for Young Black Children in African and Caribbean Immigrant Families" (Washington: Migration Policy Institute, 2012) (www.migrationpolicy.org/ pubs/cbi-hernandez.pdf); Kevin J. A. Thomas, "A Demographic Profile of Black Caribbean Immigrants to the United States" (Washington: Migration Policy Institute, 2012) (www.migrationpolicy.org/pubs/cbi-caribbeanmigration.pdf); Randy Capps,

Kristen McCabe, and Michael Fix, "Diverse Streams: Black African Migration to the United States" (Washington: Migration Policy Institute, 2012) (www.migrationpolicy.org/pubs/CBI-AfricanMigration.pdf).

23. The analyses in this chapter pertain only to the black-race-only (or "black alone") population. Chapter 10 discusses the size of and the shifts among the population of persons identifying with two or more races and entering multiracial marriages.

24. Campbell Gibson and Kay Jung, "Historical Statistics on Population Totals by Race, 1790 to 1990, and by Hispanic Origin, 1970 to 1990, for Large Cities and Other Urban Places in the United States," Population Division Working Paper 76 (Census Bureau, 2005) (www.census.gov/population/www/documentation/twps0076/twps0076.html); U.S. Bureau of the Census, *Historical Statistics of the United States, Colonial Times to 1970, Bicentennial Edition,* part 1 (Government Printing Office, 1975), Series A 172–194, p. 22 (www2.census.gov/prod2/statcomp/documents/CT1970p1-01.pdf).

25. See chapter 2 in Karl E. Taeuber and Alma F. Taeuber, *Negroes in Cities: Residential Segregation and Neighborhood Change* (Chicago: Aldine, 1965); William J. Collins, "When the Tide Turned: Immigration and the Delay of the Great Black Migration," *Journal of Economic History,* vol. 57, no. 3 (1997), pp. 607–32.

26. Scholarly and journalistic accounts documenting this movement include Daniel N. Johnson and Rex R. Campbell, *Black Migration in America: A Social Demographic History* (Duke University Press, 1981); Carole Marks, *Farewell—We're Good and Gone: The Great Black Migration* (Indiana University Press, 1989); Stewart E. Tolnay, "The African American 'Great Migration' and Beyond," *Annual Review of Sociology,* vol. 29 (2003), pp. 209–32; James N. Gregory, *The Southern Diaspora: How the Great Migrations of Black and White Southerners Transformed America* (University of North Carolina Press, 2005); Nicholas Lemann, *The Promised Land: The Great Migration and How It Changed America* (New York: Knopf, 1991); Isabel Wilkerson, *The Warmth of Other Suns: The Epic Story of America's Great Migration* (New York: Random House, 2010).

27. See chapter 1 in Gregory, *The Southern Diaspora.*

28. Neil Fligstein, *Going North: Migration of Blacks and Whites from the South, 1900–1950* (New York: Academic Press, 1981); Tolnay, "African American 'Great Migration' and Beyond"; Stewart E. Tolnay and E. M. Beck, "Racial Violence and Black Migration in the South, 1910 to 1930," *American Sociological Review,* vol. 57 (1992), pp. 103–16.

29. Estimates in figure 1-2 of chapter 1 in Gregory, *The Southern Diaspora,* show that approximately 1.2 million blacks left the South between 1910 and 1930 and 3.4 million left between 1940 and 1970.

30. Gregory, *The Southern Diaspora.*

31. William H. Frey, "Metropolitan America: Beyond the Transition," *Population Bulletin,* vol. 45, no. 2 (Washington: Population Reference Bureau, 1992) (www.frey-demographer.org/reports/R-1990-1_BeyondTransition.pdf).

32. Taeuber and Taeuber, *Negroes in Cities;* William H. Frey, "Central City White Flight: Racial and Nonracial Causes," *American Sociological Review,* vol 44, no. 3 (1979), pp. 425–48.

33. Riots in Detroit, Chicago, Newark, Los Angeles, and other cities prompted an investigation by the presidentially appointed Kerner Commission, which produced the *Report of the National Advisory Commission on Civil Disorders* (New York: Bantam Books, 1968).

34. Larry Long, "Migration and Residential Mobility" (New York: Russell Sage Foundation, 1988), chapter 5.

35. For analyses and data on state and metropolitan black migration for the periods 1965–70 through 1995–2000, see William H. Frey, "The New Great Migration: Black Americans Return to the South, 1965–2000," Living Cities Census Series (Brookings, 2004) (www.brookings.edu/research/reports/2004/05/demographics-frey).

36. Ibid., appendix B.

37. William H. Frey, "The New Metro Minority Map: Regional Shifts in Hispanics, Asians, and Blacks from Census 2010" (Brookings Metropolitan Policy Program, 2011) (www.brookings.edu/~/media/research/files/papers/2011/8/31%20census%20 race%20frey/0831_census_race_frey.pdf).

38. Kyle D. Crowder, Stewart E. Tolnay, and Robert M. Adelman, "Intermetropolitan Migration and Locational Improvement for African American Males, 1970–1990," *Social Science Research,* vol. 30 (2001), pp. 449–72.

39. Frey, "The New Great Migration."

40. U.S. Census Bureau, 2006–2010 American Community Survey (2010).

41. Frey, "The New Great Migration."

42. Carol Stack, *Call To Home: African Americans Reclaim the Rural South* (New York: Basic Books, 1996).

43. U.S. Census Bureau, 2006–2010 American Community Survey.

44. Neighborhood segregation patterns are discussed in more detail in chapter 9. Studies documenting black segregation patterns in the South include Reynolds Farley and William H. Frey, "Changes
in Segregation of Whites from Blacks during the 1980s: Small Steps toward a More Integrated Society," *American Sociological Review,* no. 59 (1994), pp. 23–45 (www. frey-demographer.org/reports/R-1992-10_ChangesSegregation.pdf); John Iceland, Gregory Sharp, and Jeffrey M. Timberlake, "Sunbelt Rising: Regional Population Change and the Decline of Black Residential Segregation, 1970–2009," *Demography,* vol. 50 (2013), pp. 97–123.

45. Chapter 11 discusses how changing racial demographics affected the results of the 2008 and 2012 presidential elections. For a thorough assessment of how changing demographics are interrelated to political shifts in the South, see Earl Black and Merle Black, *The Rise of Southern Republicans* (Harvard University Press, 2002).

## CHAPTER 7

1. As elsewhere in this book, this analysis examines the white population that is not of Hispanic origin.

2. Early views of assimilation typically depicted mainstream Americans as whites of northern and western European heritage, not as those whites who arrived later from southern and eastern Europe. See Milton Gordon, *Assimilation in American Life: The Role of Race, Religion, and Natural Origins* (Oxford University Press, 1964). See also chapter 1 in Richard Alba and Victor Nee, *Remaking the American Mainstream: Assimilation and American Immigration* (Harvard University Press, 2003).

3. Campbell Gibson and Kay Jung, "Historical Statistics on Population Totals by Race, 1790 to 1990, and by Hispanic Origin, 1970 to 1990, for the United States, Regions, Divisions, and States," Population Division Working Paper 56 (Census Bureau, 2002) (www.census.gov/population/www/documentation/twps0056/twps0056.pdf).

4. Rebecca M. Blank, "An Overview of Trends in Social and Economic Well-Being by Race," in *America Becoming: Racial Trends and Their Consequences,* edited by Neil Smelser, William Julius Wilson, and Faith Mitchell (Washington: National Academies Press, 2001).

5. U.S. Census Bureau, released March 2018 (www.census.gov/data/tables/2017/demo/popproj/2017-summary-tables.html)

6. Recent trends in white inequality are discussed in Charles Murray's provocative book *Coming Apart: The State of White America, 1960–2010* (New York: Crown Forum, 2012).

7. Kenneth Johnson, "Natural Decrease in America: More Coffins than Cradles," Issue Brief 30 (Carsey Institute, University of New Hampshire, Spring 2011) (www.carseyinstitute.unh.edu/publications/IB-Johnson-Natural-Decrease.pdf).

8. William H. Frey, "Metropolitan Magnets for International and Domestic Migrants" (Brookings Metropolitan Policy Program, 2003) (www.brookings.edu/~/media/research/files/reports/2003/10/demographics%20frey/200310_frey); William H. Frey, "Metro America in the New Century: Metropolitan and Central City Demographic Shifts Since 2000" (Brookings Metropolitan Policy Program, 2005) (www.frey-demographer.org/reports/R-2005-5_MetroAmNewCentury.pdf).

9. William H. Frey, "Population Growth in Metro America since 1980: Putting the Volatile 2000s in Perspective" (Brookings Metropolitan Policy Program, 2012) (www.brookings.edu/~/media/research/files/papers/2012/3/20%20population%20frey/0320_population_frey.pdf).

10. Karl E. Taeuber and Alma F. Taeuber, *Negroes in Cities: Residential Segregation and Neighborhood Change* (Chicago: Aldine, 1965); William H. Frey, "Central City White Flight: Racial and Nonracial Causes," *American Sociological Review*, vol. 44, no. 3 (1979) pp. 425–48.

11. William H. Frey and Kao-Lee Liaw, "Interstate Migration of Hispanics, Asians, and Blacks: Cultural Constraints and Middle Class Flight" (University of Michigan Population Studies Center, 2005) (www.psc.isr.umich.edu/pubs/pdf/rr05-575.pdf).

12. William H. Frey, "The New White Flight," *American Demographics* (April 1994), pp. 40–48; William H. Frey, "Immigration and Internal Migration 'Flight': A California Case Study," *Population and Environment*, vol. 16, no. 4 (1995), pp. 353–75 (http://deepblue.lib.umich.edu/bitstream/handle/2027.42/43483/11111_2005_Article_BF02208119.pdf?sequence=1).

13. These statistics are based on a typology of counties within the 100 largest metropolitan areas with populations of 500,000 or more (shown in table 7.3). The typology is rooted in density criteria outlined in "The State of Metropolitan America: On the Frontlines of Demographic Transformation" (Brookings Metropolitan Policy Program), pp. 16–19 (www.brookings.edu/~/media/Research/Files/Reports/2010/5/09%20metro%20america/metro_america_report.pdf).

14. Elizabeth Kneebone and Alan Berube, *Confronting Suburban Poverty in America* (Brookings, 2013).

15. William H. Frey, "Immigration and Domestic Migration in U.S. Metro Areas: 2000 and 1990 Census Findings by Education and Race" (University of Michigan Population Studies Center, 2005) (www.psc.isr.umich.edu/pubs/pdf/rr05-572.pdf).

## CHAPTER 8

1. Reynolds Farley and others, "Chocolate City, Vanilla Suburbs: Will the Trend toward Racially Separate Communities Continue?," *Social Science Research*, vol. 7, no. 4 (1978), pp. 319–44 (http://deepblue.lib.umich.edu/bitstream/handle/2027.42/22472/0000013.pdf?sequence=1); William H. Frey and Alden Speare Jr., *Regional and Metropolitan Growth and Decline in the United States* (New York: Russell Sage Foundation, 1988); William H. Frey and Elaine L. Fielding, "Changing Urban

Populations: Regional Restructuring, Racial Polarization, and Poverty Concentration," *CityScape: A Journal of Policy Development and Research*, vol. 1, no. 2 (1995), pp. 1–38 (www.huduser.org/Periodicals/CITYSCPE/VOL1NUM2/ch1.pdf).

2. The cities and suburbs discussed in this chapter are those within the nation's 100 largest metropolitan areas. Cities pertain to the major city or cities within each metropolitan area and the suburbs pertain to the territory in the rest of the metropolitan areas. These definitions vary slightly from census definitions and are discussed in the following report, on which some of the material in this chapter is based: William H. Frey, "Melting Pot Cities and Suburbs: Racial and Ethnic Change in Metro America in the 2000s" (Brookings Metropolitan Policy Program, 2011) (www.brookings.edu/~/media/research/files/papers/2011/5/04%20census%20 ethnicity%20frey/0504_census_ethnicity_frey.pdf).

3. Audrey Singer, Susan W. Hardwick, and Caroline B. Brettell, *Twenty-First Century Gateways: Immigrant Incorporation in Suburban America* (Brookings, 2008).

4. William H. Frey and Alden Speare Jr., *Regional and Metropolitan Growth and Decline in the United States* (New York: Russell Sage Foundation, 1988), appendix table E8B; Campbell Gibson and Kay Jung, "Historical Statistics on Population Totals by Race, 1790 to 1990, and by Hispanic Origin, 1970 to 1990, for Large Cities and Other Urban Places in the United States," Population Division Working Paper 76 (U.S. Census Bureau, 2005) (www.census.gov/population/www/documentation/twps0076/ twps0076.html).

5. Frey and Speare, *Regional and Metropolitan Growth and Decline in the United States,* appendix table E8A; William H. Frey, "Minority Suburbanization and Continued 'White Flight' in U.S. Metropolitan Areas: Assessing Findings from the 1990 Census," Research Report 92-247 (University of Michigan Population Studies Center, 1992) (www.frey-demographer.org/reports/R-1992-7_MinoritySuburbanization WhiteFlight.pdf).

6. For example, suburban shifts in age structure and household type are discussed in William H. Frey, "The Uneven Aging and 'Younging' of America" (Brookings Metropolitan Policy Program, 2011) (www.brookings.edu/~/media/research/files/ papers/2011/6/28%20census%20age%20frey/0628_census_aging_frey.pdf); William H. Frey, "Households and Families," in "State of Metropolitan America: On the Front Lines of Demographic Transformation" (Brookings Metropolitan Policy Program, 2010), pp. 90–107 (www.brookings.edu/~/media/Research/Files/Reports/2010/5/ 09%20metro%20america/metro_america_report.pdf).

7. Frey and Speare, *Regional and Metropolitan Growth and Decline in the United States,* appendix table E8C.

8. These statistics are based on a typology of metropolitan counties based on density and developed by the Brookings Metropolitan Policy Program. The "inner and middle suburbs" discussed in the text refer to the typology types "high-density counties" and "mature suburban counties." For definitions, see "State of Metropolitan America: On the Frontlines of Demographic Transformation," pp. 16–19.

9. Myron Orfield and Thomas Luce, "America's Racially Diverse Suburbs: Opportunities and Challenges" (University of Minnesota Law School, Institute on Metropolitan Opportunity, 2012) (www.law.umn.edu/uploads/e0/65/ e065d82a1c1da0bfef7d86172ec5391e/Diverse_Suburbs_FINAL.pdf).

10. R. J. Johnston, *Urban Residential Patterns* (New York: Praeger, 1971).

11. Frey and Speare, *Regional and Metropolitan Growth and Decline in the United States,* chapters 7–11.

12. Frey, "Minority Suburbanization and Continued 'White Flight' in U.S. Metropolitan Areas.

13. Richard D. Alba and John R. Logan, "Variations on Two Themes: Racial and Ethnic Patterns in the Attainment of Suburban Residence," *Demography*, vol. 28 (1991), pp. 431–53.

14. Frey and Speare, *Regional and Metropolitan Growth and Decline in the United States*, chapters 8–10 and appendix tables E9B, E9D, and E10D.

15. Of all Asian-origin groups, Asian Indians, the group with the highest education attainment, have the highest share of suburban residents, at 70 percent.

16. Mark Schneider and Thomas Phelan, "Black Suburbanization in the 1980s," *Demography*, vol. 30 (1993), pp. 269–79; John R. Logan, Richard D. Alba, and Wenquan Zhang, "Immigrant Enclaves and Ethnic Communities in New York and Los Angeles," *American Sociological Review*, vol. 67 (2002), pp. 299–322 (http://isites.harvard.edu/fs/docs/icb.topic868440.files/Logan%20Immigrant%20 enclavbes%20and%20thnic%20communities.pdf).

17. Orfield and Luce, "America's Racially Diverse Suburbs: Opportunities and Challenges."

## CHAPTER 9

1. Gunnar Myrdal, *An American Dilemma: The Negro Problem and Modern Democracy* (New York: Harper and Brothers, 1944); Douglas S. Massey and Nancy Denton, *American Apartheid: Segregation and the Making of the Underclass* (Harvard University Press, 1993); David M. Cutler and Edward L. Glaeser, "Are Ghettos Good or Bad?," *Quarterly Journal of Economics*, vol. 112 (1997), pp. 827–72 (www.jstor.org/ stable/2951257). Richard Rothstein, *The Color of Law: A Forgotten History of How Our Government Segregated America* (Liverlight, 2017).

2. Stanley Lieberson, *Ethnic Patterns in American Cities* (New York: Free Press of Glencoe, 1963); Stanley Lieberson, *A Piece of the Pie: Blacks and White Immigrants since 1880* (University of California Press, 1980).

3. Figure 9-1 measures for 1990–2010 are calculated from census tract data in the 1990–2010 U.S. censuses. Those for 1930–80 are drawn from appendix A1 of David M. Cutler, Edward L. Glaeser, and Jacob L. Vigdor, "The Rise and Decline of the American Ghetto," *Journal of Political Economy*, vol. 107 (1999), pp. 455–506 (www.jstor.org/stable/10.1086/250069).

4. The index of dissimilarity used here to measure segregation levels is calculated from the racial composition of each neighborhood in the metropolitan area, with census tracts used as proxies for neighborhoods. The measure compares the distribution across census tracts of one group (in this case, blacks) with another group (whites) using the following formula,

$$D = \frac{1}{2} \sum_{i=1}^{n} \left| \frac{P_{1i}}{P_1} - \frac{P_{2i}}{P_2} \right| \times 100$$

, where

$P_1$ = metropolitan-wide population of group 1 (blacks)
$P_2$ = metropolitan-wide population of group 2 (whites)
$P_{1i}$ = neighborhood $i$ population of group 1 (blacks)
$P_{2i}$ = neighborhood $i$ population of group 2 (whites)
$n$ = number of neighborhoods in metropolitan area.

For further information see Michael J. White, "Segregation and Diversity: Measures in Population Distribution," *Population Index,* vol. 52, no. 2 (1986), pp. 198–221 (www. jstor.org/stable/3644339).

5. Karl E. Taeuber and Alma F. Taeuber, *Negroes in Cities: Residential Segregation and Neighborhood Change* (Chicago: Aldine, 1965); Massey and Denton, *American Apartheid;* Reynolds Farley and William H. Frey, "Changes in the Segregation of Whites from Blacks during the 1980s: Small Steps toward a More Integrated Society," *American Sociological Review,* no. 59 (1994), pp. 23–45 (www.jstor.org/stable/ 2096131); Camille Zubrinsky Charles, "The Dynamics of Racial Residential Segregation," *American Review of Sociology,* vol. 29 (2003), pp. 167–207 (www.jstor. org/stable/30036965).

6. Farley and Frey, "Changes in the Segregation of Whites from Blacks during the 1980s."

7. Massey and Denton, *American Apartheid,* pp. 36–38; Taeuber and Taeuber, *Negroes in Cities.*

8. Cutler and Glaeser, "Are Ghettos Good or Bad?"

9. National Opinion Research Center, *White Attitudes toward Negroes* (University of Denver, 1942).

10. Kenneth Jackson, *Crabgrass Frontier: The Suburbanization of the United States* (Oxford University Press, 1985), pp. 185–203.

11. Arnold R. Hirsch, *Making the Second Ghetto: Race and Housing in Chicago 1940–1960* (University of Chicago Press, 1984); Massey and Denton, *American Apartheid,* pp. 200–05.

12. National Advisory Commission on Civil Disorders, *Report of the National Advisory Commission on Civil Disorders* (New York: Bantam Books, 1968).

13. Farley and Frey, "Changes in the Segregation of Whites from Blacks during the 1980s"; Allen J. Fishbein, "The Ongoing Experiment with 'Regulation from Below': Expanded Reporting Requirements for HMDA and CRA," *Housing Policy Debate,* vol. 3 (1992), pp. 601–39.

14. Massey and Denton, *American Apartheid,* pp. 61–67, 85–88.

15. Ibid.

16. Ronald E. Wienk and others, *Measuring Racial Discrimination in American Housing Markets: The Housing Market Practices Survey* (U.S. Department of Housing and Urban Development, 1979); Margery Austin Turner, Raymond L. Stryk, and John Yinger, *Housing Discrimination Study: Synthesis* (U.S. Department of Housing and Urban Development, 1991).

17. Farley and Frey, "Changes in the Segregation of Whites from Blacks During the 1980s."

18. Reynolds Farley and others, "Chocolate City, Vanilla Suburbs: Will the Trend toward Racially Separate Communities Continue?," *Social Science Research,* vol. 7, no. 4 (1978), pp. 319–44 (http://deepblue.lib.umich.edu/bitstream/handle/2027.42/22472/ 0000013.pdf?sequence=1).

19. Glaeser and Vigdor report that only 424 of more than 72,000 census tracts have no black residents. See Edward Glaeser and Jacob Vigdor, "The End of the Segregated Century: Racial Separation in America's Neighborhoods, 1890 to 2010," Civic Report 66 (New York: Manhattan Institute, Center for State and Local Leadership, 2012), p. 7 (www.manhattan-institute.org/html/cr_66.htm).

20. John R. Logan, Brian J. Stults, and Reynolds Farley, "Segregation of Minorities in the Metropolis: Two Decades of Change?," *Demography,* vol. 41, no. 1 (2004), pp. 1–22.

21. John Iceland, Gregory Sharp, and Jeffrey M. Timberlake, "Sun Belt Rising: Regional Population Change and the Decline in Black Residential Segregation, 1970–2009," *Demography,* vol. 50, no. 1 (2013), pp. 97–123.

22. Evidence shows that while all racial groups accept some degree of spatial integration with other groups, they express a strong preference for certain "out groups" over others, with blacks being the least favored out group. See Camille Zubrinsky Charles, "Processes of Residential Segregation," in *Urban Inequality: Evidence from Four Cities,* edited by Alice O'Connor, Chris Tilley, and Lawrence Bobo (New York: Russell Sage Foundation, 2001), pp. 271–89.

23. William H. Frey and Reynolds Farley, "Latino, Asian, and Black Segregation in U.S. Metropolitan Areas: Are Multiethnic Metros Different?," *Demography,* vol. 33, no. 1 (1996), pp. 35–50; William H. Frey and Dowell Myers, "Racial Segregation in U.S. Metropolitan Areas and Cities, 1990–2000: Patterns, Trends and Explanations," Research Report 05-573 (University of Michigan Population Studies Center, 2005) (http://www.psc.isr.umich.edu/pubs/pdf/rr05-573.pdf); Mary J. Fischer and Marta Tienda, "Redrawing Spatial Color Lines: Hispanic Metropolitan Dispersal, Segregation, and Economic Opportunity," in National Research Council, *Hispanics and the Future of America* (Washington: National Academies Press, 2006), pp 100–37.

24. Richard D. Alba, John R. Logan, and Brian J. Stults, "How Segregated Are Middle-Class African Americans?," Social Problems, vol. 47, no. 4 (2000), pp. 543–58 (www.jstor.org/stable/3097134); John Iceland, *Where We Live Now: Immigration and Race in the United States* (University of California Press, 2009), pp. 46–48.

25. Frey and Myers, "Racial Segregation in U.S. Metropolitan Areas and Cities, 1990–2000."

26. Map 9-1 depicts 87 of the 100 largest metropolitan areas where blacks represent at least 3 percent of the population. These and other segregation values for these metropolitan areas for 1990–2010 are available in appendix E of William H Frey, "The New Metro Minority Map: Regional Shifts in Hispanics, Asians and Blacks from Census 2010" (Brookings Metropolitan Policy Program, 2011) (www.brookings. edu/~/media/research/files/papers/2011/8/31%20census%20race%20frey/0831_census_race_frey). Segregation measures are affected by the definitions of neighborhoods, metropolitan areas, and racial groups. As a consequence, the measures shown here may differ from those reported elsewhere.

27. Research has shown a decline in the more blatant discriminatory practices among real estate agents, although more informal discrimination continues to exist. See Stephen L. Ross and Margery Austin Turner, "Housing Discrimination in Metropolitan America: Explaining Changes between 1989 and 2000," *Social Problems,* vol. 52, no. 2 (2005), pp. 152–80 (www.jstor.org/stable/10.1525/sp.2005.52.2.152); Margery Austin Turner and others, *Housing Discrimination against Racial and Ethnic Minorities 2012* (U.S. Department of Housing and Urban Development, Office of Policy Development and Research, 2013) (www.huduser.org/Publications/pdf/HUD-514_HDS2012.pdf).

28. See Patrick Sharkey, *Stuck in Place: Urban Neighborhoods and the End of Progress toward Racial Inequality* (University of Chicago Press, 2013); John R. Logan, "Separate and Unequal: The Neighborhood Gap for Blacks, Hispanics and Asians in Metropolitan America," Project US2010 Census Brief (Brown University and Russell Sage Foundation, 2011) (www.s4.brown.edu/us2010/Data/Report/report0727.pdf).

29. Iceland, *Where We Live Now.* The term "spatial assimilation" was coined in Douglas S. Massey and Nancy A. Denton, "Spatial Assimilation as a Socioeconomic Outcome," *American Sociological Review,* vol. 50 (1985), pp. 94–105.

30. Ninety-three of the largest 100 metropolitan areas where Hispanics represent at least 3 percent of the population.

31. Daniel T. Lichter and others, "Residential Segregation in New Hispanic Destinations: Cities, Suburbs, and Rural Communities Compared," *Social Science Research,* vol. 39, no. 2 (2010), pp. 215–30 (www.sciencedirect.com/science/article/pii/ S0049089X09000908).

32. Map 9-3 shows the 45 metropolitan areas (of the 100 largest metropolitan areas) where Asians constitute at least 3 percent of the population.

33. The neighborhood racial makeup for an average member of a specific racial group is the weighted average of the neighborhood composition, among all neighborhoods, for that group. For example, the neighborhood racial makeup of the average black resident in a metropolitan area is the weighted average of the racial compositions of all neighborhoods in that metropolitan area, wherein each neighborhood's racial composition is weighted by the proportion of the metropolitan area's blacks who reside in that neighborhood. (In the case of Los Angeles, shown in figure 9-4, the average black resident resides in a neighborhood that is 17 percent white, 28 percent black, 8 percent Asian, 44 percent Hispanic, and 3 percent all other races.) This measure is sometimes referred to as an exposure measure, indicating the racial makeup of the neighborhood to which an average resident of a specific group is exposed.

34. See Wenquan Zhang and John R. Logan, "Global Neighborhoods: Beyond the Multiethnic Metropolis," *Demography,* vol. 53 (2016), pp. 1933–53.

35. The minority composition in neighborhoods of average white residents has increased measurably since 1980, as white segregation from minorities has declined. See John Iceland and Gregory Sharp, "White Residential Segregation in U.S. Metropolitan Areas: Conceptual Issues, Patterns and Trends from the U.S. Census, 1980 to 2010," *Population Research and Policy Review,* vol. 32 (2013), pp. 663–86.

36. The percent of *racially integrated* metropolitan neighborhoods increased from less than 20 percent in 1990 to more than 30 percent in 2010. See Ingrid Gould Ellen, Keren Horn, and Katherine O'Regan, "Pathways to Integration: Examining Changes in the Prevalence of Racially Integrated Neighborhoods," *Cityscape: A Journal of Policy Development and Research,* vol. 14 (2012), pp. 33–53 (www.huduser.org/portal/ periodicals/cityscpe/vol14num3/Cityscape_Nov2012_pathways_int.pdf). See also Jonathan Spader and Shannon Rieger, "Patterns and Trends of Residential Integration in the United States since 2000," Research Brief (Cambridge, Mass.: Joint Center for Housing Studies of Harvard University, September 2017) (www.jchs.harvard.edu/ research/publications/patterns-and-trends-residential-integration-united-states-2000).

37. Gary Orfield and Chungmei Lee, *Historic Reversals, Accelerating Resegregation, and the Need for New Integration Strategies* (UCLA Civil Rights Project, 2007) (http://civilrightsproject.ucla.edu/research/k-12-education/integration-and-diversity/historic-reversals-accelerating-resegregation-and-the-need-for-new-integration-strategies-1/orfield-historic-reversals-accelerating.pdf); Gary Orfield, John Kucsera, and Genevieve Siegel-Hawley, "E Pluribus . . . Separation: Deepening Double Segregation for More Students" (UCLA Civil Rights Project, 2013) (http://civilrightsproject.ucla.edu/research/k-12-education/integration-and-diversity/mlk-national/e-pluribus...separation-deepening-double-segregation-for-more-students/orfield_epluribus_revised_omplete_2012.pdf).

## CHAPTER 10

1. As in the other chapters in this book, Hispanics are treated as a racial category. The categories for this multiracial analysis, though all are not displayed, include whites, blacks, Asians, American Indians and Alaska Natives, "some other race," multiracial persons, and Hispanics. All but the last category pertain to non-Hispanic members of these groups. This method differs from census practices, as discussed later in this chapter.

2. Stanley Lieberson and Mary C. Waters, *From Many Strands: Ethnic and Racial Groups in Contemporary America* (New York: Russell Sage Foundation, 1988).

3. Dianna L. Pagnini and S. Philip Morgan, "Intermarriage and Social Distance among U.S. Immigrants at the Turn of the Century," *American Journal of Sociology,* vol. 96, no. 2 (1990), pp. 405–32 (www.jstor.org/stable/2781107).

4. Mary C. Waters, *Ethnic Options: Choosing Identities in America* (University of California Press, 1990).

5. Milton M. Gordon, *Assimilation in American Life: The Role of Race, Religion, and National Origins* (Oxford University Press, 1964).

6. Richard Alba and Victor Nee, *Remaking the American Mainstream: Assimilation and Contemporary Immigration* (Harvard University Press, 2003).

7. Gary D. Sandefur and Carolyn A. Liebler, "The Demography of American Indian Families," in *Changing Numbers, Changing Needs: American Indian Demography and Public Health,* edited by Gary D. Sandefur, Ronald L. Rindfuss, and Barney Cohen (Washington: National Academies Press, 1996); Tina Norris, Paula L. Vines, and Elizabeth M. Hoeffel, "The American Indian and Alaska Native Population: 2010," Census Briefs C2010BR-10 (U.S. Census Bureau, 2010) (www.census.gov/prod/cen2010/briefs/c2010br-10.pdf).

8. Zhenchao Qian and Daniel T. Lichter, "Social Boundaries and Marital Assimilation: Interpreting Trends in Racial and Ethnic Intermarriage," *American Sociological Review,* vol. 72 (2007), pp. 68–94 (www.jstor.org/stable/25472448).

9. Daniel T. Lichter, "Integration or Fragmentation: Racial Diversity and the American Future," *Demography,* vol. 50, no. 2 (2013), pp. 359–91.

10. *Loving* v. *Virginia,* 388 U.S. 1 (1967).

11. Aaron Gullickson, "Black/White Multiracial Marriage Trends, 1850–2000," *Journal of Family History,* vol. 31, no. 3 (2006), pp. 289–312 (http://paa2006.princeton.edu/papers/60719).

12. Jennifer Lee and Frank D. Bean, *The Diversity Paradox: Immigration and the Color Line in Twenty-First Century America* (New York: Russell Sage Foundation, 2010), chapter 5.

13. Pew Research Center, "Marrying Out" (Washington, June 15, 2010), p. 29 (www.pewsocialtrends.org/files/2010/10/755-marrying-out.pdf).

14. On average, black men who marry white women are of higher economic status than their wives. An early explanation of this trend, which sociologists have termed "status exchange theory," presumed that black men in such an arrangement exchanged their higher economic status for the higher social status of white women. However, as gender roles and race relations have changed over time, there is less consensus about the explanation. See Gullickson, "Black/White Multiracial Marriage Trends, 1850–2000."

15. In a series of studies, demographers Zhenchao Qian and Daniel T. Lichter and their colleagues showed that this occurred in the 1990s and early 2000s, with significant increases in the rate of multiracial marriages occurring between first- and second-

generation Hispanics and Asians. Moreover, they also examined three generations of Hispanics and found that "third plus" generations are more likely to out-marry than the first two generations. See Qian and Lichter, "Social Boundaries and Marital Assimilation"; Zhenchao Qian and Daniel T. Lichter, "Changing Patterns of Multiracial Marriage in a Multiracial Society," *Journal of Marriage and Family,* vol. 73 (2011), pp. 1065–84; Daniel T. Lichter, Julie H. Carmalt, and Zhenchao Qian, "Immigration and Intermarriage among Hispanics: Crossing Racial and Generational Boundaries," *Sociological Forum,* vol. 26, no. 2 (2011), pp. 241–64.

16. Projections indicate that within the Hispanic and Asian populations, the share of those who are foreign born will decrease and the share of individuals in the third generation or higher will increase through at least 2050. See Jeffrey S. Passel and D'Vera Cohn, "U.S. Population Projections: 2005–2050" (Washington: Pew Research Center, February 11, 2008) (www.pewhispanic.org/files/reports/85.pdf).

17. Qian and Lichter, "Social Boundaries and Marital Assimilation."

18. Pew Research Center, "The Generation Gap and the 2012 Election" (Washington, November 3, 2011), p. 48 (www.people-press.org/files/legacy-pdf/11-3-11%20Generations%20Release.pdf).

19. An overview of the history of race and ethnic group statistics in censuses appears in Joel Perlmann and Mary C. Waters, "Introduction," in *The New Race Question: How the Census Counts Multiracial Individuals,* edited by Joel Perlmann and Mary C. Waters (New York: Russell Sage Foundation, 2002), pp. 1–30.

20. Margo J. Anderson, "Counting by Race: The Antebellum Legacy," in *The New Race Question,* edited by Perlmann and Waters, pp. 269–87.

21. C. Matthew Snipp, "American Indians: Clues to the Futures of Other Racial Groups," in *The New Race Question,* edited by Perlmann and Waters, pp. 189–214.

22. Perlmann and Waters, "Introduction," pp. 7–11.

23. Reynolds Farley, "Racial Identities in 2000: The Response to the Multiple-Race Response Option," in *The New Race Question,* edited by Perlmann and Waters, pp. 33–61.

24. The original 1977 standards set by the Office of Management and Budget in Statistical Policy Directive No. 15 provided instructions to all federal agencies on how to collect racial data and mandated the inclusion of mutually exclusive categories. The 1997 revision required that individuals be allowed to select more than one race; the revision also came with a recommendation that Hispanic status be recorded under a question of ethnicity, distinct from racial identification. See Office of Management and Budget, Executive Office of the President, "Revisions to the Standards for the Classification of Federal Data on Race and Ethnicity," *Federal Register,* vol. 62, no. 10 (1997), pp. 58782–90 (www.whitehouse.gov/omb/fedreg_1997standards).

25. Because the Census Bureau classifies Hispanic status as separate from race status, the multiracial categories, shown in table 10-4 of this book, disregard a person's Hispanic or non-Hispanic heritage. For example, a woman with a mother who is white and Hispanic and a father who is white and non-Hispanic would not be counted as multiracial, since the Hispanic status of her parents is not taken into account.

26. This likely practice of Hispanic respondents erroneously identifying their Hispanic status on the race question, thus increasing the size of the "some other race" category, is suggested in the following studies: Charles Hirschman, Richard Alba, and Reynolds Farley, "The Meaning and Measurement of Race in the U.S. Census: Glimpses into the Future," *Demography,* vol. 37 (2000), pp. 381–93 (www.jstor.org/stable/2648049); and Elizabeth Compton and others, "2010 Census Race and

Hispanic Origin Alternative Questionnaire Experiment" (Census Bureau, 2013) (www.census.gov/2010census/pdf/2010_Census_Race_HO_AQE.pdf ).

27. Jeffrey S. Passel, "The Growing American Indian Population, 1960–1990: Beyond Demography," in *Changing Numbers, Changing Needs,* edited by Sandefur, Rindfuss, and Cohn, pp. 72–92; C. Matthew Snipp, "America Indian and Alaska Native Children: Results from the 2000 Census" (Washington: Population Reference Bureau, 2005) (www.prb.org/pdf05/americanindianalaskachildren.pdf ).

28. Office of Management and Budget, "Guidance on Aggregation and Allocation of Data on Race for Use in Civil Rights Monitoring and Enforcement," Bulletin 00-02 (Washington, March 9, 2000) (www.whitehouse.gov/omb/bulletins_b00-02).

29. Nicholas A. Jones, "The Two or More Races Population: 2010," 2010 Census Briefs C2010BR-13 (Census Bureau, 2012)(www.census.gov/prod/cen2010/briefs/ c2010br-13.pdf ).

30. See table 8 in Compton and others, "2010 Census Race and Hispanic Origin Alternative Questionnaire Experiment," p. 42.

31. See table 9-8 in Barry Edmonston, Sharon M. Lee, and Jeffrey S. Passel, "Recent Trends in Intermarriage and Immigration and the Effects on the Future Racial Composition of the U.S. Population," in *The New Race Question,* edited by Perlmann and Waters, pp. 227–58.

32. An analysis by Jennifer Lee and Frank Bean showed that among multiracial couples with children, only about half or less selected "two or more races" to identify their children: 49 percent for white-black couples, 52 percent for white-Asian couples, and 25 percent for white-Hispanic couples. Of the couples who did not select "two or more races," white-Asian and white-Hispanic parents were more likely to select "white" and white-black parents were more likely to select "black." See Lee and Bean, *The Diversity Paradox,* p. 103.

33. Sam Roberts and Peter Baker, "Asked to Declare His Race, Obama Checks 'Black,'" *New York Times,* April 2, 2010 (www.nytimes.com/2010/04/03/us/politics/ 03census.html?_r=0).

## CHAPTER 11

1. Michael Barone, *Shaping Our Nation: How Surges in Migration Have Transformed America and Its Politics* (New York: Crown Forum, 2013).

2. According to the Pew Research Center, by 2015 only about 52 percent of Latino lawful immigrants who were eligible to become citizens had been naturalized, a rate that is higher for other groups.  See Pew Research Center, "Mexican Lawful Immigrants among the Least Likely to Become U.S. Citizens" (Washington: Pew Hispanic Center, June 29, 2017), p. 5 (http://assets.pewresearch.org/wp-content/ uploads/sites/7/2017/06/28172853/PH_2017.06.29_Among-Lawful-Immigrants-to-US-Mexicans-Least-Likely-to-Apply-for-Citizenship_Full-Report.pdf ).

3. In the 2016 election, only 57 percent of Hispanic eligible voters and 56 percent of Asian eligible voters registered to vote, while 69 percent of black eligible voters and 74 percent of white eligible voters registered to vote. See U.S. Census Bureau, "Voting and Registration," Historical Reported Voting Rates, Table A-6 (www.census.gov/ data/tables/time-series/demo/voting-and-registration/voting-historical-time-series. html). As discussed below and shown in figure 11-4, the turnout rate (percentage of eligible voters who voted) also was lower for Hispanics and Asians than for blacks and whites.

4. These voting percentages and those in figure 11-2 were calculated using the U.S. Census Bureau's Current Population Survey, "Voting and Registration," November Supplements for election years 2004, 2008, 2012, and 2016 (www.census.gov/topics/public-sector/voting.html).

5. Robert Griffin, William H. Frey, and Ruy Teixeira, "States of Change: Demographic Change, Representation Gaps and Challenges to Democracy, 1980–2060," Center for American Progress, Brookings Institution, and Bipartisan Policy Center, February 2017 (www.brookings.edu/wp-content/uploads/2017/02/states-of-change-report-2017.pdf).

6. Pew Research Center, "Millennials Make Up Almost Half of Latino Eligible Voters in 2016" (Washington: Pew Research Center, January 19, 2016) (www.pewhispanic.org/2016/01/19/millennials-make-up-almost-half-of-latino-eligible-voters-in-2016/); Pew Research Center, "An Awakened Giant: The Hispanic Electorate Is Likely to Double by 2030" (Washington: Pew Hispanic Center, November 14, 2012), p. 7 (www.pewhispanic.org/2012/11/14/an-awakened-giant-the-hispanic-electorate-is-likely-to-double-by-2030/).

7. Pew Research Center, "Mexican Lawful Immigrants among the Least Likely to Become U.S. Citizens" p. 5 (www.pewhispanic.org/2017/06/29/mexican-lawful-immigrants-among-least-likely-to-become-u-s-citizens/).

8. Rosa Ramirez, "Fights over Voter ID Grows Fierce," *The Atlantic,* July 20, 2012 (www.theatlantic.com/politics/archive/2012/07/fights-over-voter-id-grow-fierce/428235/); Jeff Zeleny, "Election Opponents Team Up on Panel to Fix Voting System," *New York Times,* February 14, 2013 (www.nytimes.com/2013/02/15/us/politics/opposing-election-lawyers-to-lead-obama-voting-panel.html); Patricia Mazzei, "Presidential Commission Probes Florida Voting Lines, Which Study Shows Were Longest for Hispanics," *Tampa Bay Times,* June 28, 2013 (www.miamiherald.com/2013/06/28/3475051/study-finds-hispanic-voters-waited.html); Tony Pugh, "Voter Suppression Laws Likely Tipped the Scales for Trump, Civil Rights Groups Say," McClatchey News, November 10, 2016 (www.mcclatchydc.com/news/politics-government/election/article113977353.html).

9. See table 1 in David A. Bositis, "Blacks and the 2004 Democratic National Convention" (Washington: Joint Center for Political and Economic Studies, 2004), p. 9 (http://jointcenter.org/sites/default/files/Blacks%20and%20the%202012%20Democratic%20National%20Convention.pdf).

10. See figure 1 in Pew Research Center, "Latino Voters in the 2012 Election" (Washington: November 7, 2012), p. 4 (www.pewhispanic.org/files/2012/11/2012_Latino_vote_exit_poll_analysis_final_11-07-12.pdf); and CNN Election Center, 2016 exit polls (www.cnn.com/election/results/exit-polls).

11. Latino Decisions 2016 National Election Eve Poll, November 2016 (www.latinodecisions.com/files/8614/7866/3919/National_2016__Xtabs.pdf).

12. Karthik Ramakrishnan, Janelle Wong, Jennifer Lee, and Tokee Lee, *2016 Post-Election National Asian American Survey,* May 16, 2016 (http://naasurvey.com/wp-content/uploads/2017/05/NAAS16-post-election-report.pdf).

13. See John B. Judis and Ruy Teixeira, *The Emerging Democratic Majority* (New York: Scribner, 2002), chapter 2.

14. Ronald Brownstein, "The Hidden History of the American Electorate (II)," *National Journal* (September 1, 2012), pp. 38–44 (www.nationaljournal.com/2012-election/the-hidden-history-of-the-american-electorate-ii--20120822); CNN Election Center, 2012 and 2016 exit polls (www.cnn.com/election/2012/results/race/president/#exit-polls) (www.cnn.com/election/results/exit-polls).

15. Thom File, "The Diversifying Electorate—Voting Rates by Race and Hispanic Origin in 2012 (and Other Recent Elections): Population Characteristics: Current Population Survey" (Census Bureau, May 2013) (www.census.gov/prod/2013pubs/p20-568.pdf).

16. William H. Frey, Ruy Teixeira, and Robert Griffin, "America's Electoral Future: How Changing Demographics Could Impact Presidential Elections from 2016 to 2032," Center for American Progress, Brookings Institution, and American Enterprise Institute, February 2016 (www.brookings.edu/wp-content/uploads/2016/02/SOC2016report-1.pdf).

17. Karl Rove, "More White Votes Alone Won't Save the GOP," *Wall Street Journal,* June 26, 2013 (http://online.wsj.com/article/SB10001424127887323873904578569480696 746650.html).

18. Republican National Committee, "Growth and Opportunity Project" (Washington: Republican National Committee, 2013) (https://gop.com/growth-and-opportunity-project/).

19. Pew Research Center, "2016 Party Identification Tables" (Washington: Pew Research Center, September 15, 2016) (www.people-press.org/2016/09/13/2016-party-identi-fication-detailed-tables/).

20. Judis and Teixeira, *The Emerging Democratic Majority;* Ruy Teixeira and John Halpin, "The Obama Coalition in the 2012 Election and Beyond" (Washington: Center for American Progress, December 2012) (www.americanprogress.org/wp-content/uploads/2012/12/ObamaCoalition-5.pdf).

21. Ronald Brownstein, "The Coalition of Transformation vs the Coalition of Restoration," *The Atlantic,* November 21, 2012 (www.theatlantic.com/politics/archive/2012/11/the-coalition-of-transformation-vs-the-coalition-of-restoration/265512/); and Ronald Brownstein, "State: America, a Year Later," CNN, November 2017 (www.cnn.com/interactive/2017/politics/state/2016-election-anniversary/).

22. Pew Research Center, "The Generation Gap and the 2012 Election" (Washington: November 3, 2011), pp. 5–6 (www.people-press.org/files/legacy-pdf/11-3-11%20 Generations%20Release.pdf); and Pew Research Center, "Millennials in Adulthood: Detached from Institutions, Networked with Friends" (Washington: March 2014) (www.pewsocialtrends.org/files/2014/03/2014-03-07_generations-report-version-for-web.pdf).

23. Morley Winograd and Michael D. Hais, *Millennial Momentum: How a New Generation Is Remaking America* (Rutgers University Press, 2011), p. 27.

24. Pew Research Center, "The Generation Gap and the 2012 Election," pp. 6–9.

25. Ibid., pp.19–21.

26. Earl Black and Merle Black, *The Rise of Southern Republicans* (Belknap Press, 2002).

27. For a detailed account of these shifts prior to the 2012 elections, see William H. Frey and Ruy Teixeira, "America's New Swing Region: The Political Demography and Geography of the Mountain West," in *America's New Swing Region: Changing Politics and Demographics in the Mountain West,* edited by Ruy Teixeira (Brookings, 2012), pp. 11–68; and William H. Frey, "Hispanics, Race, and the Changing Political Landscape of the United States and the Mountain West," in *America's New Swing Region,* edited by Teixeira, pp. 82–106.

28. This was not the case for Colorado in 2008 because both whites and blacks voted for Obama.

29. According to Edison Research, margins in 2008 and 2012 for white Republicans were 6 and 16, respectively, in Ohio, and 3 and 15, respectively, in Pennsylvania.

30. Further discussion of the 2016 election can be found in Michael Barone, "The President and Vice President," pp. 10–16, in Richard E. Cohen and James A. Barnes,

*The Almanac of American Politics, 2018* (Bethesda, Md.: Columbia Books and Information Services and *National Journal,* 2017); Ronald Brownstein, "Are Demographics Really Destiny for the GOP?" *The Atlantic,* May 31, 2017 (www. theatlantic.com/politics/archive/2017/05/trump-2016-election/528519/); William H. Frey, "The Demographic Blowback That Elected Donald Trump," Brookings Institution, November 10, 2016 (www.brookings.edu/blog/the-avenue/2016/11/10/ the-demographic-blowback-that-elected-donald-trump/); and Robert Griffin, Ruy Teixeira, and John Halpin, "Voter Trends in 2016: A Final Examination," Center for American Progress, November 2017 (www.americanprogress.org/issues/democracy/ reports/2017/11/01/441926/voter-trends-in-2016/).

31.  David Jackson and Doug Staglin, "Trump Is Now President: The Forgotten . . . Will Be Forgotten No Longer," *USA TODAY,* January 20, 2017 (www.usatoday.com/story/ news/politics/2017/01/20/donald-trump-inauguration-day-president-white-house/ 96782700/).

32.  More than half of 2016 voters in the five states of Iowa, Michigan, Ohio, Pennsylvania, and Wisconsin were whites without college educations, compared with 42 percent nationally, and in each of these states, the Republican voter margin for these voters was greater than in 2016. See U.S. Census Bureau, Current Population Survey, November 2016 Supplement (www.census.gov/data/tables/time-series/demo/ voting-and-registration/p20-580.html); and Griffin, Teixeira, and Halpin, "Voter Trends in 2016: A Final Examination."

33.  Lois Becket, "Trump Digital Director Says Facebook Helped Win the Whitehouse," *The Guardian* October 7, 2017 (www.theguardian.com/technology/2017/oct/08/ trump-digital-director-brad-parscale-facebook-advertising).

34.  William H. Frey, "Census Shows Pervasive Decline in 2016 Minority Voter Turnout," Brookings Institution, May 18, 2017 (www.brookings.edu/blog/the-avenue/2017/ 05/18/census-shows-pervasive-decline-in-2016-minority-voter-turnout/); also CNN Election Center, 2012 (www.cnn.com/election/2012/results/race/president/ #exit-polls) and 2016 (www.cnn.com/election/results/exit-polls) exit polls.

35.  In 2016 Clinton carried voters within metropolitan areas of over one million in the Midwest and Pennsylvania by a similar voting margin (54 percent to 40 percent) as did Obama in 2012 (57 percent to 42 percent); but she lost smaller areas in those states by a much larger margin (37 percent to 57 percent) than did Obama (46 percent to 53 percent). See Barone, "The President and Vice President," p. 13.

36.  William H. Frey, "A Substantial Majority of Americans Live outside of Trump Counties, Census Shows," Brookings Institution, March 23, 2017 (www.brookings. edu/blog/the-avenue/2017/03/23/a-substantial-majority-of-americans-live- outside-trump-counties-census-shows/).

37.  This was demonstrated in a demographic simulation that assumed that 2012 turnout and voting rates among whites without college degrees held for the 2016 election among each state's eligible voter population, while all other aspects of 2016 voting stayed the same. This would have resulted in Democratic victories in the states of Michigan, Pennsylvania, Wisconsin, and Florida leading to a simulated Electoral College win for Hillary Clinton over Barack Obama. See Griffin, Teixeira, and Halpin, "Voter Trends in 2016: A Final Examination."

38.  Brownstein, "Are Demographics Really Destiny for the GOP?" Also, William H. Frey, "Census Shows Nonmetropolitan America Is Whiter, Getting Older, and Losing Population: Will It Retain Political Clout?," Brookings Institution, June 27, 2017 (www.brookings.edu/blog/the-avenue/2017/06/27/census-shows-nonmetropolitan- america-is-whiter-getting-older-and-losing-population/).

**CHAPTER 12**

1. Jeffrey M. Humphreys, "The Multicultural Economy, 2016," (Selig Center for Economic Growth, Terry College of Business, University of Georgia, 2017).

2. Fernando Peinado, "Spanish or English? The Dilemma of the Booming Hispanic TV Market," *Miami Herald,* July 22, 2013 (www.miamiherald.com/2013/07/21/3512427/spanish-or-english-the-dilemma.html). David Adams, "A New Latino Frontier: Univision Launches News in English," Univision News, June 23, 2016 (www.univision.com/univision-news/united-states/a-new-latino-frontier-univision-launches-news-in-english).

3. For assessments of immigrant contributions to the skill levels and economies of metropolitan areas, see Matthew Hall and others, "The Geography of Immigrant Skills: Educational Profiles of Metropolitan Areas" (Brookings Metropolitan Policy Program, 2011) (www.brookings.edu/~/media/research/files/papers/2011/6/immigrants%20singer/06_immigrants_singer.pdf); and Jacob Vigdor, "Immigration and the Revival of American Cities: From Preserving Manufacturing Jobs to Strengthening the Housing Market" (New York: Americas Society/Council of the Americas and Partnership for a New American Economy, 2013) (www.as-coa.org/sites/default/files/ImmigrationUSRevivalReport.pdf).

4. Humphreys, "The Multicultural Economy, 2016."

5. In addition to the main projections, used in this book, the Census Bureau produced alternative projections based on assumptions of "high" and "low" immigration. Under both assumptions, during the 2012–30 period the projected growth in the minority child (under age 18) population occurs with a projected decline in the white child population. Projections based on the high immigration assumption show minority growth of 29 percent and a white decline of 7 percent; those based on the low immigration assumption show minority growth of 23 percent and a white decline of 8 percent. In each, minorities are projected to constitute more than 54 percent of the child population in 2030. The higher minority child growth in each case reflects the higher fertility and younger initial age structure for minorities than for whites, in addition to the assumed immigration levels. Further information on the U.S. Census Bureau 2012 projections is available at www.census.gov/population/projections/data/national/2012.html

6. Jeffrey S. Passel, "Demography of Immigrant Youth: Past, Present and Future," *Future of Children,* vol. 21, no. 1 (Spring 2011), pp. 19–41 (futureofchildren.org/futureofchildren/publications/docs/21_01_02.pdf); "Parental Education: Indicators of Child and Youth Well-Being," Child Trends Data Bank, December 2015 (www.childtrends.org/wp-content/uploads/2015/12/67-Parental_Education.pdf); Tabulations of U.S. Census Current Population Annual Social and Economic Survey, March 2017.

7. John Gramlich, "Hispanic Dropout Rate Hits New Low, College Enrollment at New High" (Washington: Pew Research Center, September 2017)(http://www.pewresearch.org/fact-tank/2017/09/29/hispanic-dropout-rate-hits-new-low-college-enrollment-at-new-high/). Richard Fry and Paul Taylor, "Hispanic High School Graduates Pass Whites in Rate of College Enrollment" (Washington: Pew Research Center, May 2013) (www.pewhispanic.org/files/2013/05/PHC_college_enrollment_2013-05.pdf); Dowell Myers and John Pitkin, "Assimilation Today: New Evidence Shows the Latest Immigrants to America Are Following in Our History's Footsteps" (Washington: Center for American Progress, September 2010) (www.americanprogress.org/issues/2010/09/pdf/immigrant_assimilation.pdf); Julie Park and Dowell Myers, "Intergenerational Mobility in the Post-1965 Immigration Era:

Estimates by an Immigrant Generation Cohort Method," *Demography*, vol. 47, no. 2 (May 2010), pp. 369–92 (www.ncbi.nlm.nih.gov/pmc/articles/PMC3000029/).

8. Gary Orfield, John Kucsera, and Genevieve Siegel-Hawley, "E Pluribus . . . Separation: Deepening Double Segregation for More Students" (UCLA Civil Rights Project, September 2012) (civilrightsproject.ucla.edu/research/k-12-education/integration-and-diversity/mlk-national/e-pluribus...separation-deepening-double-segregation-for-more-students/orfield_epluribus_revised_omplete_2012.pdf); Gary Orfield, Jongyeon Ee, Erica Frankenberg, and Genevieve Siegel-Hawley, "Brown at 62: School Segregation by Race, Poverty and State" (UCLA Civil Rights Project, May 2016) (www.civilrightsproject.ucla.edu/research/k-12-education/integration-and-diversity/brown-at-62-school-segregation-by-race-poverty-and-state/Brown-at-62-final-corrected-2.pdf). See also Grover J. Whitehurst, Richard Reeves, and Edward Rodrigue, "Segregation, Race, and Charter Schools: What We Know," Brookings Institution Center on Children and Families, October 2016 (www.brookings.edu/wp-content/uploads/2016/10/ccf_20161021segregation_version-10_211.pdf).

9. Jonathan Rothwell, "Housing Costs, Zoning, and Access to High-Scoring Schools" (Brookings Metropolitan Policy Program, April 2012) (www.brookings.edu/~/media/research/files/papers/2012/4/19%20school%20inequality%20rothwell/0419_school_inequality_rothwell.pdf).

10. Orfield, Kucsera, and Siegel-Hawley, "E Pluribus . . . Separation"; Orfield, Ee, Frankenberg, and Siegel-Hawley, "Brown at 62."

11. Anthony P. Carnevale and Nicole Smith, "The Economic Value of Diversity," in Earl Lewis and Nancy Cantor, eds., *Our Compelling Interests: The Value of Diversity for Democracy and a Prosperous Society*, pp. 106–60 (Princeton University Press, 2016).

12. Pew Research Center, "Between Two Worlds: How Young Latinos Come of Age in America" (Washington: Pew Research Center, December 2009), p. 52 (www.pewhispanic.org/files/reports/117.pdf).

13. An overview of barriers is provided in Daniel T. Lichter, "Integration or Fragmentation? Racial Diversity and the American Future," *Demography*, vol. 50 (2013), pp. 359–91.

14. While sanctuary city status is not a legal designation, it reflects cities and other jurisdictions that have given instructions to local law enforcement to limit cooperation in various ways with federal immigration authorities in the transfer of information about, or detainment of, persons regarding their immigration status. States as well as localities have proposed or enacted laws about this policy. According to the National Conference of State Legislatures, as of July 2017, thirty-three states have considered legislation that would prohibit sanctuary policies; fifteen states and the District of Columbia would support such policies; and twelve would introduce legislation on both sides of the issue. Various lists of sanctuary cities, counties, and states have been compiled, although not using consistent definitions. They tend to be clustered in areas with large foreign-born populations (www.ncsl.org/research/immigration/immigration-laws-database.aspx). See National Conference of State Legislators, "Sanctuary Policy: FAQ," July 27, 2017 (www.ncsl.org/research/immigration/sanctuary-policy-faq635991795.aspx).

15. One study classified state immigration legislation over several years through 2008 on a scale from "integrative" to "punitive." Seven of the eight Melting Pot states were classified as "integrative" or "somewhat integrative" while all of the 14 states classified as "punitive" or "somewhat punitive" were located in New Sun Belt or Heartland states. See Progressive States Network, "The Anti-Immigrant Movement That Failed" (New York: September 2008) (www.progressivestates.org/files/reports/

immigrationSept08.pdf). A 2007 analysis of local housing ordinances that target immigrants found that ordinances were not correlated with the size of a locality's foreign-born or Hispanic population but with a recent rapid increase in the foreign-born or Hispanic share of the population since 2000. See Jill Esbenshade, "Division and Dislocation: Regulating Immigration through Local Housing Ordinances" (Washington: Immigration Policy Center, Summer 2007) (www. immigrationpolicy.org/sites/default/files/docs/IPC%20Special%20Report%20PR. pdf). Another analysis of local municipalities emphasizes the pace of immigrant population growth as a predictor of exclusionary policies. See Kyle E. Walker and Helga Leitner, "The Variegated Landscape of Local Immigration Policies in the United States," *Urban Geography*, vol. 32 (2011), pp. 156–78 (www.sscnet.ucla.edu/ geog/downloads/7235/494.pdf).

16. Ricardo Gambetta and Zivile Gedrimaite, "Municipal Innovations in Immigrant Integration: 20 Cities, 20 Good Practices," American Cities Series (Washington: National League of Cities, 2010) (www.nlc.org/Documents/Find%20City%20 Solutions/Research%20Innovation/Immigrant%20Integration/municipal-innovations-immigrant-integration-20-cities-sep10.pdf); Hall and others, "The Geography of Immigrant Skills," pp. 20–21.

17. Pew Research Center, "October 2011 Generations Survey" (Washington: Pew Research Center for the People and the Press, 2011) (www.people-press. org/2011/10/04/october-2011-generations-survey/).

18. Pew Research Center, "The Generation Gap in American Politics" (Washington: Pew Research Center, 2018) (file:///C:/Users/billf.SSDAN12/Downloads/03-01-18-Generations-release%20(5).pdf).

19. Pew Research Center, "October 2011 Generations Survey" and "The Generation Gap in American Politics."

20. This is demonstrated in a study that shows support for school financing to be negatively related to the portion of elderly individuals who age in place within the community, a relationship that is heightened when  the school-aged population is heavily nonwhite. See David N. Figlio and Deborah Fletcher, "Suburbanization, Demographic Change, and the Consequences for School Finance," *Journal of Public Economics,* no. 96 (2012), pp. 1144–53.

21. Ronald Brownstein, "The Gray and the Brown: The Generational Mismatch," *National Journal* (July 24, 2010), pp. 14–22.

22. A similar case is made about the relationship between immigrants and the baby boom generation in Dowell Myers, *Immigrants and Boomers: Forging a New Social Contract for the Future of America* (New York: Russell Sage Foundation, 2007).

23. See Generations United, "Out of Many, One: Uniting the Changing Faces of America" (Washington: Generations United and Generations Initiative, 2013) (www.gu.org/ LinkClick.aspx?fileticket=_Te_mh9OznI%3d&tabid=475&mid=1049); and Vanessa Cardenas and Sarah Treuhaft, "All-In Nation: An America that Works for All" (Washington: Center for American Progress and PolicyLink, 2013) (http://images2. americanprogress.org/CAP/2013/12/AllInNation.pdf).

24. William H. Frey, "The Millennial Generation: A Demographic Bridge to America's Diverse Future," Metropolitan Policy Program, Brookings Institution, January 2018 (www.brookings.edu/wp-content/uploads/2018/01/2018-jan_brookings-metro_millennials-a-demographic-bridge-to-americas-diverse-future.pdf).

25. William H. Frey, "The Millennial Generation"; PRRI 2015 American Values Survey, October 2015 (www.prri.org/data-vault/?topic%5B%5D=&meta_year%5B%5D=2015).

26. Cathy J. Cohen, Matthew D. Luttig, and Jon C. Rogowski, "A Report on the Lived Economic Lives of Millennials," GenForward Survey, June 2017 (https://genforward-survey.com/assets/uploads/2017/06/Millennials-Economic-Lives.pdf ).

27. Ronald Brownstein, "Millennials to Pass Baby Boomers as Largest Voter-Eligible Age Group, and What It Means," *Fault Lines,* CNN Politics, July 25, 2017 (www.cnn.com/2017/07/25/politics/brownstein-millennials-largest-voter-group-baby-boomers/index.html).

28. U.S. Bureau of Labor Statistics, "Labor Force Characteristics by Race and Ethnicity, 2016," BLS Reports (Department of Labor, 2017) (www.bls.gov/opub/reports/race-and-ethnicity/2016/pdf/home.pdf ); Christian E. Weller and Farah Ahmad, "The State of Communities of Color in the U.S. Economy" (Washington: Center for American Progress, 2013) (www.americanprogress.org/wp-content/uploads/2013/10/CommunitiesOfColor-4.pdf ); Pew Research Center, "How Wealth Inequality Has Changed in the US Since the Great Recession, by Race, Ethnicity, and Income" (Washington: Pew Research Center, November 2017) (www.pewresearch.org/fact-tank/2017/11/01/how-wealth-inequality-has-changed-in-the-u-s-since-the-great-recession-by-race-ethnicity-and-income/).

29. Mitra Toosi, "Labor Force Projections to 2024: The Labor Force Is Growing but Slowly," Monthly Labor Review (December 2015) (www.bls.gov/opub/mlr/2015/article/labor-force-projections-to-2024.htm); Dowell Myers, Stephen Levy, and John Pitkin, "The Contributions of Immigrants and Their Children to the American Workforce and Jobs of the Future" (Washington: Center for American Progress, June 2013) (www.americanprogress.org/wp-content/uploads/2013/06/OurFuture Together.pdf ); Anthony P. Carnavale, Jeff Strohl, and Neil Ridley, "Good Jobs That Pay without a BA: A State-by-State Analysis" (Washington: Center on Education and the Workforce, Georgetown University, 2017) (https://goodjobsdata.org/wp-content/uploads/Good-Jobs-States.pdf ).

30. Richard Alba, *Blurring the Color Line: The New Chance for a More Integrated America* (Harvard University Press, 2009).

31. This point is made in Richard Alba and Victor Nee, *Remaking the American Mainstream: Assimilation and Contemporary Immigration* (Harvard University Press, 2003), chapter 7.

# Index

*Figures, maps, and tables are indicated by "f," "m," and "t" following page numbers.*

New Sun Belt region: Asian migration to, 8, 50, 55; battleground states of, 231–34; black migration to, 46, 47, 107, 122, 128; black-white segregation and integration in, 177; demographic change in, 8–10, 13, 46–47, 46*f*, 50*f*, 128, 248, 252–53; as "emerging melting pot," 49–53, 50*f*, 188; future voting trends of, 242; Hispanic migration to, 8, 14, 50, 55, 151; Hispanic segregation in, 180; map of, 45*m*; minority share of population in, 9*f*, 52*t*; minority voters in, 231–34; multiracial marriages in, 18, 201, 202, 202*t*, 203; multira-cial population in, 59, 174; and Obama election, 213, 230–31; size of, 47; suburbs of, 166; voting trends in, 234, 242; white migration to, 8, 16, 46–47, 60, 136–38, 136*m*, 148, 154, 248; white population share, decline of, 50, 50*f*

New "white flight," 8–10, 16, 131, 138–44, 153; demographic attributes by geographic area, 144, 145*t*; to exurbs, 140–42, 141*m*, 145*t*, 146; motivation for, 49, 60, 139; to smaller metropolitan areas, 139–40, 140*f*; "soft separation" between whites and other groups, 142–44, 143*f*

New York (state): black and white college graduates migrating from, 122; black population in, 117, 119; child population decline in, 25; Dominican Americans in, 80; Hispanic vote in, 231; Puerto Ricans in, 81; Salvadorans in, 82; voting trends in, 234; white population decline in, 137

New York City: Asian population in, 8, 55, 96, 97, 151; Asian segregation in, 182; black population in, 56, 115, 116, 125, 154, 170; Dominican Americans in, 80; exurbs gaining white population, 141–42, 141*m*; Guatemalans in, 82; Hispanic population in, 8, 54, 70, 72, 83, 84*f*, 85, 94, 151, 178–79; history as traditional gateway city, 43, 44; middle-class flight from, 148; multiracial population in, 59; white population decline in, 16, 60, 131, 152, 153, 154; white population education in, 147

Nicaragua as country of origin, 77
Nixon, Richard, 219
"No majority" communities, 4–5
North Carolina: as battleground state, 238–39, 242; black population in, 119, 122; child population in, 26; minority voters in, 233*f*, 234; multiracial marriages in, 203; in New Sun Belt region, 46; Obama voters in, 234; white-black multiracial population in, 210
Northeast: Asian segregation in, 182; black migration from, 124*f*; black migration to, 118*f*; Hispanic segregation in, 179; voting trends in, 234; white population decline in, 137, 138, 139;

youth population, slow growth or decline in, 37. *See also* New England; *specific states*

## O

Obama, Barack: and battleground states, 242–43; choice of race by, 209; election and reelection of, 7, 18, 213, 221–24; and minority voters, 225, 230–31, 234–39; socioeconomic status of, 113; and young voters, 228. *See also* Presidential elections
Ogden, Utah, languages other than English in, 40
Ohio: as battleground state, 233, 236*t*, 238–40, 243; black and white college graduates migrating from, 122; black voters in, 231; child population decline in, 25; white population decline in, 137
Oklahoma: American Indian and Alaska Native population in, 57; multiracial marriage in, 201; multiracial population in, 207
Oklahoma City: Asian population in, 104; Hispanic population in, 72, 83
Omaha: Asian population in, 104; Hispanic population in, 72, 75, 84; white population in, 154
"Open housing" movement, 171
Oregon, multiracial marriages in, 202
Orfield, Gary, 250
Orlando: Asian segregation in, 182, 183; black population in, 57; Hispanic population in, 70, 72, 75, 84*f*, 85; Puerto Ricans in, 81, 85
Oxnard, California: Asian population in, 101; Asian segregation in, 182

## P

Pacific Coast. *See* West coast
Palm Coast, Florida, white population in, 140
Pennsylvania: as battleground state, 236*t*, 238–40, 243; black population in, 119; black voters in, 231; child population decline in, 25; Dominican Americans in, 80; Hispanic segregation in, 179; multiracial marriages in, 202; Puerto Ricans in, 81; white population decline in, 137
Peruvian Americans, 24, 79, 82. *See also* Hispanic population
Pew Research Center polls: on baby boomers' voting trends, 228–29; on immigration as positive or negative for U.S., 31–32, 253–54, 254*t*; on millennials' voting trends, 227; on minorities' voting trends, 226; on multiracial marriage acceptance, 203; on naturalization of Hispanics, 217; on size of government, 35
Philadelphia: Asian population in, 96, 98; Asian segregation in, 182; black population in, 115,